DATE DUE

JA 2 6 06			
FE 9 06			

DEMCO 38-296

CURRENT ISSUES IN CRIMINAL JUSTICE
(VOL. 3)

UNDERSTANDING CORPORATE CRIMINALITY

GARLAND REFERENCE LIBRARY
OF SOCIAL SCIENCE
(VOL. 845)

CURRENT ISSUES IN CRIMINAL JUSTICE

GENERAL EDITORS: FRANK P. WILLIAMS III AND MARILYN D. MCSHANE

UNDERSTANDING CORPORATE CRIMINALITY

Edited by
Michael B. Blankenship
East Tennessee State University

GARLAND PUBLISHING, Inc.
New York & London / 1993

Library of Congress Cataloging-in-Publication Data

Understanding corporate criminality / [edited by Michael
B. Blankenship]
    p. cm. — (Garland reference library of social science ; v.
845. Current issues in criminal justice ; v. 3)
  Includes bibliographic references.
  ISBN 0-8153-0883-3
    1. White collar crime—United States. I. Blankenship, Michael
B., 1955– . II. Series: Garland reference library of social
science ; v. 845. III. Series: Garland reference library of social
science. Current issues in criminal justice ; v. 3.
HV8079.W47U53 1993
364.1'68—dc20   93-18139

Printed on acid-free, 250-year-life paper
Manufactured in the United States of America

This work is dedicated to Sheila, my partner in life who has taught me so much, especially about the importance of family and friends, and to my parents, Ed and Pal, who instilled within me an appreciation for right and wrong.

Contents

Foreword

As we note the twentieth anniversary of Watergate, it is apparent how much knowledge has since developed on the topic of political, white-collar, occupational, and corporate crime. We have also seen that the creation of regulatory agencies and citizen-watchdog groups does not appear to have eliminated or even substantially reduced corporate misbehavior. With the many bank scandals, suspicions about big business, and awareness of the tremendous cost of white-collar crime, we find this text to be particularly relevant and meaningful.

Today we have greater scrutiny of the legislative process, greater access to information on special-interest groups, and closer coverage of lobbying and political campaign contributions than ever before. One of the benefits of the Freedom of Information Act is the ability to study closely the complex workings of businesses and their varied relationships with government, including the criminal justice system. It is not surprising that many of the thought-provoking pieces on corporate crime and the role of regulatory agencies have evolved from a critical perspective. As evidenced by some of the writings here, the political/legal framework of our current system of government not only inspires, but also nurtures and protects corporate crime schemes. Indeed, the concept of a corporate body that is accountable to criminal law is itself a legal fiction that serves to protect the officers of the corporation.

The articles in this volume cover the full historical spectrum of the study of corporate crime, from Sutherland's original writings through conflict and containment theories to the more recent theoretical approaches of routine activities and rational choice. One of the major themes of this work is the parallel between the relatively recent development of a study of corporate crime and traditional crime theories. Concepts such as "career criminals" and small numbers of offenders being responsible for disproportionate amounts of crime provide arguments for integrating this area into mainstream criminology. The authors also discuss difficulties in the conduct of theoretical development and empirical research in this area (including problems of definition, data gathering, measurement, analysis, and interpretation).

As with the other books in this series, the Blankenship work broadens the boundaries of traditional criminal justice theory, pushing our exploration into less familiar but challenging and exciting, frontiers.

Frank P. Williams III and Marilyn D. McShane

Understanding Corporate Criminality: Challenges and Issues

Michael B. Blankenship

> Great is truth, but still greater, from a practical point of
> view, is silence about truth.
>
> Aldous Huxley
> *Brave New World*

> Better to reign in hell than serve in heaven.
>
> John Milton
> *Paradise Lost*

Crime is a topic that enthralls the populace like few others. Our society is both fearful of and fascinated with crime. Each year, Americans spend millions of dollars trying to protect themselves from human predators and *more* millions being entertained by the very subject that makes them so fearful in the first place. What is it about crime, especially violent crime, that captivates so many?

Could it be the sheer violence that many of us find so addictive? After all, television renditions of mass murders are often sold as nightly entertainment! Or is it the mystery that attracts many of us to the "who-done-it" variety of crime. Perhaps it is the thirst for justice (or more appropriately revenge) that makes crime such an alluring topic.

If any or all of these reasons explain our fascination with crime, then why is so-called *street* crime the preeminent focus of our interest? It cannot possibly be that crimes committed by the upper class are not sufficiently violent to entertain us. Many corporate crimes that masquerade as disasters or accidents are the stuff of television "docudramas." Nor do corporate crimes lack for suspicion and intrigue that would rival the most bizarre conspiracies. And what appetite for retribution cannot be temporarily satiated when the likes of Charles Keating, the new breed of robber baron, is seen on the nightly news being pummelled by one of his elderly victims during his recent trial for fraud?

Perhaps the reason that corporate crime does not receive the attention afforded street crime is that the phrase *corporate crime* is an oxymoron. How can a corporation, a nonliving entity, commit any act, let alone a criminal deed? Even if we overlook the anthropomorphism, is it likely that the people who form the corporation *intend* to commit crimes? Is it really a crime to succeed in business? Aren't the people who run corporations well-heeled pillars of the community, while "real" criminals are usually young, black, and male? If corporations do sometimes err, isn't it because of overregulation by the government?

This text is dedicated to addressing these and other questions about the illegal behavior of corporations in our society. Compared to conventional crime, we know relatively little about the frequency, duration, causation, or cessation of illegal corporate behavior. Not only do we lack adequate measures of corporate crime, but intersubjective definitions of *crime, criminal,* and *victim* that could lead to improved measurements have yet to be formulated.

For example, in Chapter Five, Simpson, Harris, and Mattson demonstrate the inadequacy of using officially reported offenses, victimization surveys, and self-reported studies to measure corporate crime. Aside from the issues of construct validity (Kitsuse & Cicourel, 1963) and bias (Sutherland, 1983), a fundamental limitation of each of these reporting methods is in accurately counting all crimes. The problem of counting corporate crimes is compounded because of the structure of corporations.

The dumping of Kepone (a pesticide) into the James River in Virginia illustrates the problem. In 1976, Life Science Products, two of its managers, and Allied Chemical were indicted for polluting the James River (Fisse & Braithwaite, 1983). Life Science Products had been formed by two former Allied employees to produce Kepone for Allied. While Allied Chemical was sanctioned for its part in polluting the river, it was acquitted on some of the charges because the state failed to prove that Allied was vicariously liable for the actions of Life Sciences Products and its employees.

Thus the issue of culpability complicates the counting of corporate crimes. Assuming that Allied Chemical was factually guilty (as opposed to establishing legal guilt) of polluting the environment in conjunction with Life Sciences Products, how many violations occurred? Did the decision to dump the carcinogen count as one offense, while the actual dumping, each time it occurred, count as another crime? Or should the decision to dump the chemical illegally be considered part of the traditional principles of defining acts as criminal (Hall, 1947), even though one principal conceived the act while the other actually carried it out?

Simpson, Harris, and Mattson propose a method of counting corporate crime that considers the opportunity to commit an illegal act, the serial production (interconnectivity between principals) of such acts, and the number of transactions among principals. While their scheme perhaps offers a more valid method for counting corporate crime, uncovering the frequency with which corporate crime occurs still remains problematic.

Just as perplexing is the issue of causality. As Sutherland (1983) notes, prevailing criminological theories are biased in that the data on which they are based largely measures crimes of the lower class. In the quest for a grand unifying theory that explains all criminal behavior, conventional biological and psychological theories must yield to sociological theories because the former cannot explain white-collar criminality in terms of issues such as heredity, hormonal imbalance, or mental deficiency.

Progress toward such a unifying criminological theory has been glacially slow (the assumption is that such an accomplishment is possible, Hirschi & Gottfredson, 1987). Some headway has been made in terms of combining various theories in order to increase explanatory power. For example, Elliot,

Huizinga, and Ageton (1985) combined strain, control, and learning theories to create a model that predicted delinquency and drug use among juveniles.

In Chapter Six, Shover and Bryant use this approach to create a more powerful analytical framework to better understand the etiology of corporate crime. They approach the problem from a different perspective in that previous attempts to combine theories have been confined to microlevel theories. Shover and Bryant incorporate both macro- and microlevel theories in their analytical framework. For example, they consider how legal, structural, and economic factors affect the opportunity to commit corporate crime, as well as how a crime-facilitative culture evolves and how it operates to mitigate resistance to legal and ethical compliance. Their analytical framework assumes a crime-as-choice perspective of offending. This framework appears better suited to understanding organizational crime than conventional crime, for corporate crime is rational by definition (we might excuse ignorance of the applicable laws if not deliberate, such as the case of "vice-presidents who go to jail" in the pharmaceutical industry; Braithwaite, 1984).

Yet any attempt to measure accurately or to explain the etiology of corporate crime begs the question of definition. Many researchers seem content to use the standard imposed by Clinard and Yeager (1980) that includes any act committed on behalf of the corporation that is punishable by civil, criminal, or administrative sanctions. But does this definition accurately demarcate criminal from noncriminal acts? Any comprehensive study of corporate crime reveals a host of dastardly acts perpetrated by corporations that result in death, injury, and financial loss, but these are not treated as crimes (Simon & Eitzen, 1993).

In Chapter Two, Brown and Chiang address the limits of current definitions of corporate crime. In perhaps the most controversial chapter in the text, they criticize prevailing definitions of corporate crime as being too legalistic. Brown and Chiang recognize how the power of the upper class influences the social construction of reality, which involves creating the false perception that law—and its concomitant parts—reflects the legitimate interests of society and is administered in a neutral fashion. Instead of defining corporate crime as acts that *are punishable*, their thesis is that social scientists should be free to study acts that *should be punishable* but fail to do so because of the prevailing conservative ideology.

While their position will probably attract a great deal of criticism, the most flattering of which would be the charge of utopian thinking, their purpose was not to establish policy, but rather to challenge the status quo. Perhaps their apostasy will strike a responsive note for those awaiting the revolution as foretold by Kuhn (Blankenship & Brown, 1993). At the very least, Brown and Chiang have clearly demonstrated the inadequacy of prevailing definitions of corporate crime.

Their struggle to broaden the definition of crime is also emblematic of the larger problem facing criminologists. As Geis notes in Chapter One, there are disciplinary pressures on the discourse community to approach the topic of crime from a value-free perspective. The danger in studying corporate crime is that such inquiry may go beyond description of the phenomenon and venture into ideological agendas. Criminologists who look to institutions and/or the social structure for explanations of corporate criminality run the risk of being criticized as ideological (or worse), while those who seek to control individuals, particularly from the lower class, tend to label themselves as "mainstream" or "scientific" criminologists (Tappan, 1947).

Despite the controversy over defining corporate crime, Geis reminds us that it is impossible totally to divorce the study of crime from legal definitions. The application of the criminal label distinguishes between acts that are merely deviant and those that define the scope of criminological inquiry. We have an opportunity to better understand the social and political forces that shape the labeling process by examining the basis for the criminal label. For example, it was only recently that the common law tradition allowed a corporation to be treated as a person, thus permitting these "juristic persons" to make contracts, to hold and dispose of property, and to be sued and/or prosecuted for criminal and civil offenses. Because corporations cannot form intent, a traditional requirement under the common law, new legal strategies have developed to deal with the unique problems presented by illegal corporate behavior.

In Chapter Eight, Belbot traces the evolution of the corporation and the laws that were enacted to control harmful organizational behavior, both in England and in the United States. In pre-industrial communities, informal social control of illegal behavior was much more feasible. The baker or shoemaker, or any other merchant, who cheated customers was easily identified and sanctioned by the community. Word would spread quickly of the chicanery, resulting in a loss of business. With the rise of corporations, both harm and identity of the miscreant became more obscure, thus giving rise to the phrase *caveat emptor* (Geis, 1988). Many people never realize that they are victims of corporate crime, and even when they do, it is difficult to fix blame because of the size and structure of many modern corporations.

Geis and Belbot both discuss the South Sea Bubble case as an example of the lack of the failure of strict liability doctrine to protect investors. As the need for new and larger amounts of capital increased, and the corporate form of business evolved to meet this demand, a new legal doctrine was needed to protect investors. Without their trust, the wheels of capitalism grind slowly (Shapiro, 1984). In order to protect this trust, the concept of vicarious liability emerged, whereby the actions of employees are imputed to the corporation. This doctrine is not without its problems and limitations, as was revealed in the Allied Chemical case. However, current research suggests that there is a new level of awareness of the harms from corporate crimes and, concomitantly, an increased demand for accountability for these harms.

Such attentiveness to corporate and white-collar illegality has resulted in new conceptions of victimization. In Chapter Three, Stitt and Giacopassi explore this issue. They remind us of the relative unimportance of victims in the criminal justice process. Corporate crime victims are even more "invisible" than those individuals harmed by conventional criminals. Many victims of corporate crime fail to recognize their victimization because of factors such as the time and the distance between the harmful act and the realization of harm or because of the hegemonic influence that blinds many of us to the realization of the ubiquity of corporate crime.

Stitt and Giacopassi maintain we could increase our understanding of corporate criminality by studying the *consequences* of corporate behavior. Not only would this approach avoid the many pitfalls of determining which acts constitute crimes, but also might enhance theoretical understanding of disparate acts (e.g., toxic dumping and insider trading) according to the magnitude of harm that results from each corporate act. Just as we know more about conventional crime based on the information provided by victims, similar benefits could be gained by widening the current scope of victimology to include victims of corporate crime.

There is one obvious difference between corporate crime and conventional crime that renders Stitt and Giacopassi's recommendation problematic. Most victims of street crime realize their victimization, while the victims of corporate crime may never perceive the harm done to them. Thus the problem of uncovering the frequency of corporate crime, regardless of the method of counting (victimization surveys or official reports), remains a formidable task.

Yet surveys suggest that the public is cognizant of the problem of corporate crime, but there remains obvious disparity between citizens' fear of street crime and their concern with corporate crime. Many scholars have laid the blame for lax prosection of white-collar criminals on public apathy. Sutherland (1940:11), for example, opined that white-collar crime largely went unpunished "because the community is not organized solidly against that behavior."

More recently, James Q. Wilson (1975: xx) purposely omits any discussion of white-collar crime because

> predatory crime is a far more serious matter than consumer fraud, antitrust violation . . . because predatory crime makes difficult or impossible the maintenance of meaningful human communities.

Moreover, Wilson is tolerant of political corruption and illegal bribery if the end justifies the means, or, as he illustrates in his example, "if a mayor can stay in office or govern effectively only by making a few deals with highway contractors and insurance agents. . . ."

Evans, Cullen, and Dubeck (Chapter Four) suggest that the previously held notion of public apathy toward white-collar crime must give way because of a growing demand for protection from unscrupulous individuals and dangerous products. Television programs such as "60 Minutes," "20/20," and "Dateline" presently provide a weekly litany of corporate abuses. The most recent exposé alleged that General Motors' dual gas-tank, light-duty trucks were prone to explode in the event of side collisions. Despite the fiasco that resulted from a rigged crash demonstration, such media interest is indicative of the increasing awareness of the harmful behaviors of corporations.

Evans et al. argue that the various surveys of perceptions of white-collar crime reveal a growing lack of public confidence in the legitimacy of the legal system because the system has failed to respond adequately to corporate crime. Yet there is a need for caution in interpreting these results. Most of the surveys employed closed-ended or forced choice questions. One limitation of this particular methodology is that when respondents are "reminded" of corporate crime, then the form of the question can influence the response. It remains to be seen if the results would be the same if open-ended questions about the seriousness of corporate crime were utilized.

The fact that there is a need to explore public perceptions about who is a criminal and what constitutes a serious crime *at all* testifies to the virtual omnipotence of the social and political forces that delimit the construction of reality. While the evidence does suggest that public apathy is not as rampant as previously thought, the same cannot be said for the attitudes of criminal justice practitioners. Benson, Cullen, and Maakestad (1990:360–361) found that, from a national survey of prosecutors, "only 3.6% of urban prosecutors rated corporate crime as a 'very serious' problem. About one third saw it as 'somewhat serious' and about half regarded it as 'not at all serious.' Almost no rural prosecutors (0.4%) regarded corporate crime as a very serious problem."

Given this attitude of prosecutors, it is little wonder that corporations are frequently able to evade punishment for the harm that results from the relentless pursuit of profits. The notion of a criminal master status (Becker, 1963) does not seem to apply to corporations. As will be pointed out in this text and elsewhere (Sutherland, 1983), corporations redistribute wealth, influence public opinion, and manipulate social and political actors (Clinard & Yeager, 1980; Cullen, Maakestad, & Cavender, 1987). This ability to influence the political process also includes the administration of justice and extends from avoiding the stigma associated with the criminal label to negating the imposition of criminal and civil sanctions. The intervention by the so-called "Keating Five" (U.S. Senators Cranston, Glenn, DeConcini, McCain, and Riegle) in the investigation and federal takeover of Lincoln Savings and Loan is the quintessential exemplar (Calavita & Pontell, 1990). The study of corporations thus provides an opportunity to understand *power in action*. In order to better appreciate the structure and functions of society, we need to examine more closely how powerful people manipulate a society and its institutions.

Take, for example, one of the most egregious thefts of this century, which occurred in the savings and loan industry. Calavita and Pontell (1990:309) report that the cost to prop up failed savings and loans institutions is estimated to be "$200 billion over the next decade, and range from $300 billion to $473 billion by the year 2021." Yet in a recent news article, more than 100 convicted savings and loan executives who agreed to pay fines and restitution in lieu of prison sentences have "repaid less than a half-penny per dollar of the $133.8 million they owe" (S&L Defendants, 1993:1). For example, Morris John McCleary embezzled $2 million from the institution he once managed. He pays $30 per month for restitution. At that rate, he will be 5,139 years old before repaying what he stole!

That members of the upper class continue to evade punishment proportionate to the harm they inflict is well documented and bears no reiteration here. That such outcomes of the criminal justice process are fairly predictable is also not surprising to adherents of the conflict perspective. Simply stated, this perspective anticipates the creation and administration of law to favor the interests of the dominant group.

In Chapters Seven and Nine, Snider and Goff (respectively) examine the process of regulating and sanctioning corporations, which is indeed an opportunity to explore power in action and the conflict perspective. For example, Snider discusses the two dominant regulatory models—criminalization and cooperation. The criminalization model is characterized by a legalistic approach to the resolution of problems presented by the regulatory process. Regulatory agencies that follow this model frequently invoke the legal process as a means of controlling illegal corporate behavior. On the other hand, regulatory agencies that adhere to the cooperative model tend to implore corporations to comply with applicable laws. Agencies that follow this model utilize criminal sanctions only as a last resort, preferring instead to educate corporations and to mediate resolutions. It should not be surprising that most regulatory agencies follow the cooperative model. In order to ensure that most regulatory agencies maintain a pro-business attitude, corporations frequently employ a carrot-and-stick approach by offering regulatory personnel well-paying employment positions and by conjuring up legislative and executive wrath against overly aggressive regulatory personnel.

The ramifications of this lackadaisical approach on the part of regulatory agencies are manifested in the number of people killed or injured and the vast sums of money lost to corporate criminality. Goff notes that this regulatory indifference to harm also results in sentencing disparity. Voluntary recalls and letters of reprimand are the most frequent sanctions imposed against wayward corporations. Even when a criminal sanction is imposed, the results are dissimilar from those imposed against individuals convicted of similar conventional crimes (Snider, 1982). The above example of the savings and loan executive is but one case in point. And, as Evans, Cullen, and Dubeck point out, the public may be growing weary of such regulatory and judicial apathy toward corporate criminality.

One of the motivations behind the creation of this text was to examine systematically the problem of corporate criminality, specifically addressing the evolution and limitations involved in understanding this genre of crime. The study of corporate criminality also provides us with the opportunity to explore larger issues, such as social justice. The weight of the evidence strongly suggests that the notion of the *rule of law* as a prevailing principle of justice is a cruel euphemism for hegemony. As George Orwell so aptly put it, "All animals are created equal, but some are more equal than others." What conclusions can we draw about a society that is willing to impose the death penalty on the poor and the powerless but permits members of the upper class literally to get away with murder?

That we are able to pose such questions suggests the theoretical and empirical progress that has occurred in the quest for knowledge about corporate criminality. Sutherland lacked a theoretical basis for analyzing the etiology and epidemiology of corporate crime. As Shover and Bryant point out, participation in corporate crime is influenced by the opportunities afforded by the law; that is, the law defines minimum standards of behavior. Thus we frequently learn of corporate behaviors that are outrageous violations of moral codes of conduct, but they are not violations of law. Even when criminal and civil violations occur, it is clear that corporate offenders are processed more leniently than conventional criminals. The conflict perspective offers a viable framework for analyzing the social reaction to the breaking of law.

One the other hand, there are serious impediments to the study of corporate criminality. In the pages that follow, the authors enumerate many of the problems and pitfalls that await researchers interested in this area. In essence, this text summarizes our current state of knowledge (and conversely, ignorance) about corporate criminality. It also represents a plan for future research. Researchers will have to overcome these limitations, as well as the metaphysical bickering (Hirschi & Gottfredson, 1989) and the permanent ideological agendas (Blankenship & Wachholz, 1989) endemic to criminology if progress toward understanding corporate criminality is to continue.

REFERENCES

Becker, H.S. (1963). *Outsiders: Studies in the sociology of deviance.* New York: Free Press.

Benson, M.L., Cullen, F.T., & Maakestad, W.J. (1990). Local prosecutors and corporate crime. *Crime & Delinquency, 36,* 356–372.

Blankenship, M.B., & Brown, S.E. (1993). Paradigm or perspective?: A note to the discourse community. *Journal of Crime & Justice, 16,* 167–175.

Blankenship, M.B., & Wachholz, S. (1989). Confronting ideology: The hidden agenda of criminological theory. *Quarterly Journal of Ideology, 13,* 1–9.

Braithwaite, J. (1984). *Corporate crime in the pharmaceutical industry.* London: Routledge and Kegan Paul.

Calavita, K., & Pontell, H.N. (1990). "Heads I win, tails you lose": Deregulation, crime, and the crisis in the savings and loan industry. *Crime & Delinquency, 36,* 309–341.

Clinard, M.B., & Yeager, P.C. (1980). *Corporate crime.* New York: Free Press.

Cullen, F.T., Maakestad, W.J., & Cavender, G. (1987). *Corporate crime under attack: The Ford Pinto case and beyond.* Cincinnati: Anderson.

Elliot, D.S., Huizinga, D., & Ageton, S.S. (1985). *Explaining delinquency and drug use.* Beverly Hills, CA: Sage.

Fisse, B., & Braithwaite, J. (1984). *The impact of publicity on corporate offenders.* Albany: State University of New York Press.

Geis, G. (1988). From Deuteronomy to deniability: A historical perlustration on white-collar crime. *Justice Quarterly, 5,* 7–32.

Hall, J. (1947). *General principles of criminal law* (2nd ed.). Indianapolis: Bobbs-Merrill.

Hirschi, T., & Gottfredson, M. (1987). Causes of white-collar crime. *Criminology, 25,* 949–974.

———. (1989). The significance of white-collar crime for a general theory of crime. *Criminology, 27,* 359–372.

Kitsuse, J.I., & Cicourel, A.V. (1963). A note on the uses of official statistics. *Social Problems, 11,* 131–139.

S&L defendants slow in paying debts (1993, February). *Asheville Citizen-Times,* p. 1, 2A.

Shapiro, S.P. (1984). *Wayward capitalists: Target of the Securities and Exchange Commission.* New Haven, CT: Yale University Press.

Simon, D.R., & Eitzen, D.S. (1993). *Elite deviance* (2nd ed.). Boston: Allyn and Bacon.

Snider, L. (1982). Traditional and corporate theft: A comparison of sanctions. In P. Wickman, & T. Dailey (Eds.), *White-collar and economic crime* (pp. 235–257). Lexington, MA: Lexington.

Sutherland, E.H. (1940). White-collar criminality. *American Sociological Review,* 5, 1–12.

————. (1983). *White collar crime: The uncut version.* New Haven: Yale University Press.

Tappan, P.W. (1947). Who is the criminal? *American Sociological Review,* 12, 96–102.

Wilson, J.Q. (1975). *Thinking about crime.* New York: Basic Books.

UNDERSTANDING
CORPORATE
CRIMINALITY

CHAPTER ONE

The Evolution of the Study of Corporate Crime

Gilbert Geis

Few kind words have been used over the centuries to characterize corporations and their executives, at least by those on the outside looking in. The corporate emphasis on making money, in large amounts, traditionally has offended a Christian ethic that in theory, if not in practice, has trouble coming to terms with filthy lucre, particularly when such wealth is not yours and when it can detour that final biblical trip to heaven that is said to be as difficult for a rich man to make as for a camel to pass through the eye of a needle.

Thomas Hobbes, the seventeenth-century English philosopher, stands out in the crowd that has been scornful of corporations. Hobbes' unsavory comparison was between corporations and ascarides, worms that eat at the entrails of what Hobbes called "natural man" (Hobbes, 1651:174). Centuries later, Robert Heilbroner (1973:223) would further castigate "the corporation with its wealth-seeking, its dehumanizing calculus of plus and minus, its careful inculcation of impulses and goals that should at most be tolerated."

Corporations and their officers also are often the object of deprecatory humor. As far back as 1635, a satirist had a businessman proclaiming: "I love churches. I mean to turn pirate, rob my countrymen and build one" (Hill, 1964:267). In more recent times, a U.S. senator told the story of a corporation officer who, when asked if he were not ashamed of double-dealing persons who trusted him, was puzzled: "Who else can

3

you cheat?" he wanted to know (Noonan, 1984:660). These putdowns of the business world are part of a common wisdom, reflected in the belief that the expression "legitimate business" is an oxymoron.

Such derogatory jabs at corporations indicate strong public doubts regarding their commitment to honest dealings, a matter confirmed in opinion polls (Walton, 1977). In 1991, hostility to corporations was confirmed in a survey that found that 70 percent of a sample of people who were eligible for jury duty favored an individual plaintiff over a corporate defendant before they knew anything whatever about the dispute (Adler, 1991). A significant number of Americans would undoubtedly agree with the view of Ralph Nader (Heilbroner, 1973:221) that "[c]orporations, yielding when they were forced to, have, in the end, overwhelmed populism, organized labor, the New Deal, the regulatory state, and they will so overwhelm the consumer movement."

It is arguable whether traditional distrust of corporations arises from an accurate assessment of their unsavory behavior or is rooted in some subconscious Freudian fear of impersonal monsters that might at any moment overwhelm us. Whatever the source of antagonism, Irwin Ross (1980:57) insists that today "crime in the executive suites has come to command media attention of a sort formerly reserved for ax murders." That statement contains much hyperbole, but it, nonetheless, reflects the growing attention now being paid to the criminal offenses of corporations.

Part of the problem for corporations inheres in the fact that, unlike private individuals, their executives are confronted with strong pressures from those who hold shares in the endeavor and whose overriding interest is their own profit, and the quicker the better. Nadine Gordimer (1973:207) describes the situation in one of her novels, telling of a mining director's assessment of the demands of English stockholders in a South African company: "[O]ur shareholders overseas want big dividends from mines that are in production, not expansion that will create employment but take five or six years before it begins to pay off."

What often makes the offenses of the corporations more disturbing than those of street offenders, such as robbers and murderers, is that business organizations have at their command extraordinary resources that allow them to inflict widespread and deep harm and also afford them an opportunity to eviscerate penalties for wrongdoing. Corporate lawbreaking also can undermine the faith of citizens in the integrity of all social institutions. When corporate executives are discovered to be crooks, these idols of achievement let us down and, perhaps, shatter our morale and ideals.

On the other hand, much more so than individuals, corporations have been surrounded by thousands of regulations, many carrying criminal penalties. You and I and he or she, for instance, might combine to restrain trade, say, by providing similar allowances to our children, but corporations are barred by antitrust regulations from such price-fixing conspiracies. This, among many other considerations—and most particularly the inanimate nature of the corporate form—renders corporate crime a particularly complicated area of criminological concern.

When the corporation first was accorded legal standing, derelictions tended to elicit responses from moralists, often based on theological imperatives. Then legislative forums and courts began to attend to such wrongdoing. Later, concern with corporate wrongdoing was placed into the theoretical and research agenda of the academic community, most notably that of sociological criminologists. Enunciation of the concept of white-collar crime by Edwin H. Sutherland in 1939 provided the first formal structure to embrace this academic study of corporate crimes and of offenses committed by high-status persons in the course of their business, professional, and political activities. Later, such work grew more ecumenical, embracing not only sociology and criminology, but also jurisprudence and political science (especially that branch concerned with regulatory actions), as well as, though to a much lesser extent, organizational and management studies, economics, and psychology.

This chapter examines some of the strengths and weaknesses of the various methods that, over time, have been brought to bear upon the scrutiny of corporate crime. Attention will be paid initially to the eighteenth-century South Sea Bubble case, England's first major corporate offense. The wild shenanigans that marked this case came under legislative scrutiny, with Parliament acting in both an investigative and judicial capacity. The muckraking years in the nineteenth century, the second topic to be addressed, were marked most notably by the involvement of what today would be known as investigative reporters, journalists who dug out scandalous facts about corporations and emblazoned them in the pages of high-circulation magazines. Academic concern with corporate wrongdoing, the next area to be discussed, began with the appearance of sociology as a university research discipline in the late nineteenth century, and became more focused with Sutherland's 1939 presidential address on white-collar crime (Sutherland, 1940). The path that this academic interest has taken, combined with the continuing concern of legislatures, regulatory bodies, public interest groups, journalists, and citizens in general, will be examined in the final chapter segment.

The South Sea Bubble Case

The South Sea Company was chartered in London in 1711 to accomplish two goals: first, the company promised to ease the backbreaking burden of a £10 million national debt by absorbing as stockholders those owed money by the government; second, it proposed to reward its shareholders with anticipated heady profits from the importation of slaves (Donnan, 1930) and, more importantly, profits from trade in what was called the "South Seas," by which was meant South America from the Orinoco River to the south of Terra del Fuego. The Scheme (as it was called) was magnificently improbable from the outset. "It was wholly impossible it should have issued in anything but disaster," Lecky (1907:I,372) points out. The company prospered at first, primarily because huge bribes, totaling more than £1.25 million, were slipped to members of Parliament to support it. It also flourished because English citizens with means enough to invest had virtually no previous experience regarding the brokering of stock from which to draw warnings. The Bank of England and the East India Company were the major stock companies of the time (Boyden, 1948). As late as 1693, the latter had only 499 shareholders, with eighty-eight men owning three-quarters of the total stock. One of three East India shareholders in that year had held his stock for the past sixteen years or more. A brisk market in shares only really began, though it increased with remarkable speed, after the incorporation of the South Sea Company (Carswell, 1960:10).

The South Sea Company scandal also arose because stockholders were misled throughout the life of the Scheme about the company's true financial condition. The price of South Sea stock surged wildly because of a snowball effect created by clever manipulation of the atmosphere surrounding the company and because of the great greed of a public scenting huge profits. The managers of the stock made it easy to invest, allowing purchases for amounts as low as 10 percent of the total value, contingent upon supplementary and higher charges over the later years. On the basis of what had been happening, purchasers presumed that they would be able to raise the money due later merely by selling at a magnificent profit just a small portion of the stock they were then purchasing.

A fierce "speculative mania" (Heckscher, 1930–1931:321) sent the price of South Sea stock on a ride that lasted almost a decade. At the beginning, when the stock first came onto the market in October 1711, it was quoted between 73 and 76 (Scott, 1912:III,297). Near the end, on July 16, 1720, South Sea stock, selling at nearly 2,000, reached its highest level (Mottran, 1929:133); by August 17, 1720, however, it had dropped to 900, and forty days later had plummeted to 190 (Cowles, 1960:141).

Ironically, part of the company's difficulty was created by passage of the Bubble Act (6 George I, c. 18), which was sponsored by South Sea directors. The success being enjoyed by South Sea investors had prompted the incorporation of myriad other enterprises, some of them wildly improbable, such as one that solicited funds to construct a perpetual motion wheel (Erleigh, 1933:95). In addition, some companies set up for one purpose had begun to seek and use funds for quite different kinds of enterprises. The money the other corporations were attracting reduced significantly the funds available for investment in the South Sea enterprise; its directors therefore sought to dry up such diversionary founts by severely controlling the formation and activities of other enterprises competing for investment monies. The unexpected upshot was that when the other corporations went downhill because of the new limitations placed upon them, they had to call for further money from those who had speculated on margin, leading to withdrawals by investors from their South Sea holdings, and thereby endangering that company's financial position.

Over the long run, the Bubble Act, until its repeal in 1825 (4 George IV, c.94), inhibited the development of corporate forms in England and, concomitantly, the emergence of a sophisticated body of law to dictate the boundaries within which such organizations could operate. Until 1825, for instance, an unauthorized joint stock company was regarded in law as a common nuisance, and its promoters were subject to the penalties of *praemunire*—a fine with no ceiling and perpetual imprisonment (Carswell, 1960:157).

The falling apart of the South Sea Company, as Viscount Erleigh (1933:10) has noted, was "not merely one of a long process of financial crises, but the first great crisis in the modern manner." King George I sounded a particularly loud blast against the company when things began going sour, referring to its "unwarrantable practices" and berating the speculative fever that he insisted was diverting people from more practical pursuits. The stock swindle, the King declared, had involved "ensnaring and defrauding unwary persons to their utter impoverishment and ruin" and "taking off the minds of many of our subjects from attending [to] their lawful employments and by introducing a general neglect of trade and commerce" (Cowles, 1960:138).

Ultimately, the near moribund condition of the South Sea Company led to a searching inquiry by parliamentary committees, whose members served both as investigators and judges. Many of those who had lost money sought revenge—122 members of the House of Lords and 462 members of the House of Commons had invested in the Scheme. Those who had been bribed, on the other hand, were looking for secrecy and/or mercy. The first surprise was that there was no statute allowing criminal proceedings to be launched against the malefactors. Robert Molesworth, who had lost £2,000 of borrowed money on South Sea stock (Sedgwick, 1970:II, 262) plunged into this gap by insisting that the company directors should be declared guilty of parricide by parliamentary fiat—they had, he argued, slaughtered their country—and subjected to the ancient Roman punishment for that crime by being sewn up in sacks with a monkey and a snake and cast headlong into the river (Carswell, 1960:210; Erleigh, 1933:128). Though that proposal withered, the House of Commons held what accurately had been labeled "a drum-head court martial" of those implicated in the scandal. Edward Gibbon, that most perspicacious of English historians, whose grandfather was sanctioned as one of the directors of the South Sea Company, accurately noted that "the equity of modern times must condemn the violent and arbitrary proceedings which . . . disgraced the cause of justice" (Gibbon, 1966:151).

The parliamentary hearings ran for three weeks from nine in the morning until eleven at night (Carswell, 1960:223–237), but charges and rumors proved difficult to substantiate because the official who had recorded the bribes to members of Parliament— as well as to two of the king's mistresses—had absconded with his books across the Channel to Brabant territory: "Self-preservation has compelled me to withdraw myself," he sensibly explained in the note he left behind (Cowles, 1960:160). The culprit had avoided extradition back to England, probably with the connivance of culpable members of the king's court, by invoking an obscure medieval treaty.

In the end the parliamentary committee was able to account for only about one-eleventh of the stock that had been employed to pay the bribes (Scott, 1912:III, 343). There were demands for capital punishment and imprisonment, but in the end those deemed to be guilty, despite the absence of specific prohibitions against what they had done, were required to submit statements indicating their net worth. Then, after wrangling and maneuvering, they were allowed to keep a portion of their estate, based upon what they were alleged to have done and what support they could muster in Parliament.

For some, the penalty was confiscatory: Francis Haws received the smallest allowance, on the ground that he had encouraged speculation with public funds by some clerks in the Navy Office. Of his estate of £400,031, he was permitted to retain only the £31. Edward Gibbon was permitted to keep only £10,000 of a total of £106,543, though in due time, his grandson tells us (Gibbon, 1966:16), he replenished his fortune. For others, the assessment was much lighter. In terms of the immediate consequences of the failure of the South Sea Company, Cowles (1960:175) undoubtedly is correct: "The blow to the national credit had been largely psychological. Many people had lost, but an equal number had gained. The money was still there, but in strange pockets." In a larger sense, though, as has been noted earlier, the South Sea Company fiasco handicapped for years the movement toward incorporation and, most particularly, the development of satisfactory mechanisms to control corporate enterprise.

The kind of legislative oversight and inquiry that constituted the response in the case of the South Sea Company scandals continues today as a major tactic for the study of corporate crime. It has the advantage of being able to discover information that ordinarily is not accessible to courts because of procedural restraints or not accessible to academic researchers because of their lack of standing and access and, typically, their limited resources. Nobody, for instance, had to respond to questions from academic scholars: legislators and courts, however, can employ the power of oaths and subpoenas and contempt citations.

From a policy standpoint, legislative inquiry into corporate crime offers the possibility of direct linkage between what had been learned and the ability to translate that knowledge into statutes to deal with the discovered difficulties. Of particular importance is the fact that legislative committees have an imprimatur: their conclusions, if the matter is relatively important, come from a source and wrapped in a form that virtually insists that attention be accorded to them. For scholars, it usually is a matter of chance whether what they believe, learn, and write about corporate crime circulates beyond their discipline and compeers.

On the other hand, the fact that only the most awful or most flamboyant corporate outrages usually engage the attention of legislatures inevitably produces an incomplete, distorted, and sensationalized portrait of the full range of corporate wrongdoing. The political agendas that typically prevail in legislative inquiries also distort the process and bias conclusions. While the voluminous hearing records of the peculations involved in the South Sea Company case provide very useful material for historians and economists, they fail to be particularly responsive to behavioral scientists who would prefer more pointed inquiry on issues that could lead to broader theoretical statements and supportable generalizations. Such assets and demerits of legislative study of corporate crime, first highlighted by the English Parliament in its pursuit of details of the South Sea Company scandal, by and large hold true today as well.

The Muckrakers

The muckraking period in the United States, which ran from about 1903 to 1912, illustrates some of the advantages and disadvantages of journalistic, as contrasted to legislative, monitoring of corporate crime. The work of the muckrakers captured the public imagination because of its verve. "Pallid conservative writing," Louis Filler (1976:330) has observed, "could not compete with it for attention."

During the muckraking period, crusading writers published some 90 books and more than 2,000 articles in mass-circulation magazines that had been made inexpensive by new techniques of printing and distribution. About a third of this writing was by a dozen leading figures, persons such as Ida Tarbell, David Graham Phillips, Upton Sinclair, and Lincoln Steffens (Chalmers, 1964).

The term "muckrake" had been coined by Arthur Dent, a Puritan clergyman, in his devotional guide, *The Plain Mans Pathway to Heaven* (1601), which by 1704 had gone through twenty-five editions (Law, 1942; Sharrock, 1954:26). Dent wrote of "gripple muck-rakers who had as leeve part with their blood, as their goods" (1601/1664:71). His book was one of the pitifully few possessions brought to her marriage by John Bunyan's first wife. Subsequently imprisoned for his feisty unwillingness to abandon his nonconformist preaching, Bunyan, while he was confined in the Bedford prison, wrote *The Pilgrim's Progress* (1678), an allegorical treatise that would become one of the two or three most widely read prose works in the world. In it Bunyan told of the man who was so preoccupied with his muckrake, gathering up the world's filth, that he failed to look upward at celestial glories.

Centuries later, President Theodore Roosevelt, generally friendly to the reformers, appropriated from Bunyan the term "muckrakers" to label the reformist writers pejoratively. Roosevelt, speaking at the dedication of a new building for the House of Representatives, was reacting angrily to a series of bitter articles by David Graham Phillips attacking the Senate, five of whose members were under indictment and a number of others under suspicion of illegal behavior (Marcosson, 1932:238–241). Roosevelt (1926:416) castigated "the man who never does anything else, who never thinks or speaks or writes, save of his feats with the muckrake." Such a person speedily becomes, Roosevelt insisted, "not a help to society, not an incitement to good, but one of the most potent forces for evil."

Five years later, Roosevelt sought to make amends for his fierce attack, noting in a speech at the Pacific Theological Seminary that "[m]uck-rakers who rake up much that ought to be raked up deserve well of the community, and the magazines who publish their writings do a public service." Nonetheless, Roosevelt retained some reservations: "But they must write the truth," he added, "and the service they do must be real" (Hart & Ferlager, 1989:357).

The muckrakers, though on occasion initiating exposures of graft and corruption, most usually brought before the public mountainous details gleaned from official records (Chalmers, 1964:14). They particularly focused on close alliances between business and politics, including both the legislatures and the judiciary, which involved bribes of "public servants" so that they would cast their votes for measures favoring corporations. The muckrakers often wrote in tones of scorn and indignation. Note, for instance, Thomas W. Lawson's diatribe:

> The public accustomed to invest its money in the legitimate securities of the country, had time and again lost hundreds of millions without dreaming that they had been as ruthlessly robbed as though held up at a pistol-point by a highwayman. The public imagined that the great capitalists ... were noble and public-spirited gentlemen of the highest moral principles and of absolute integrity. They know today that many of them are reckless and greedy stock gamblers, incessantly dickering with the machinery of finance for their own private enrichment. I have stripped the veil from these hypocrites and exposed to all the world their soulless rapacity. I have let the light of heaven into the dim recesses of Wall Street in which these buccaneers of commerce concocted their plots. (Lawson, 1905:173–174)

Some muckraking writers devoted years to meticulous research into the holdings and operations of the largest corporations in the country. A particularly good illustration is the work of Ida Tarbell, who discovered that the Standard Oil Company produced one-third and controlled all but 10 percent of the nation's supply of petroleum. Standard Oil would undersell rivals, cut off their supplies, or otherwise make it virtually impossible for them to conduct business. Central to Standard's power was its control of the railroads. Its surge to power appeared relentless, as it deployed part of its huge profits into continuing absorption of competitors and purchase of whatever resources were deemed necessary for its sensational level of prosperity (Tarbell, 1904).

The emasculation of political bodies as effective monitors of the corporate world helped to open up a gap in which the muckrakers could mount an effective crusade. S.S. McClure, editor of *McClure's*, for a time the leading muckraking magazine, with half a million monthly circulation, put the matter clearly: "[C]apitalists, workingmen, politicians, citizens—all breaking the law, or letting it be broke." "Who is left to uphold it?" McClure asked rhetorically. Lawyers were said to advise corporations on how to get around the law, judges to rely on quibbles to free the wealthy faced with evidence that was "overwhelmingly convincing to common sense," and churches to own unsanitary tenements that they rented to the poor. McClure then dismissively dealt with academia. "The colleges?" he asked. "They do not understand" (McClure, 1903:344–345).

The concept of "process" was central to the interpretation of the muckrakers' material. The muckrakers emphasized that what was happening in the United States could not be dismissed as the product of misbehavior by "bad" men but had to be understood as the result of identifiable economic and political forces now at work in the United States (McCormick, 1981:265). This is not to say that individual villains at whom readers might hiss were not portrayed. Ida Tarbell, with her mixture of "cold disdain and white-hot moral indignation controlled by excellent documentation and a facade of objectivity," painted a picture of "a reptilian" John D. Rockefeller, who "slithers" through the pages of her story of Standard Oil (Tomkins, 1974:55).

Fundamentally, though the solutions each offered varied considerably, most of the muckraking writers believed that if unfettered competition were allowed to operate, things would straighten out. Another part of the muckraking message was that responsibility for what was wrong lay in the indifference of citizens; everybody was cheating in a society based on cheating (Geiger, 1966). There was considerable support for the view that incorruptible government regulation ought to be established to make certain that the rules were adhered to, and some support for the idea that corporate leaders ought to be held personally responsible for wrongdoing on the part of the organizations they oversaw. But his last demand gave way before the typically insurmountable problems involved in bringing individuals from within the corporate world to justice, problems posed by their ability to obtain especially able counsel and by the inability of the prosecutors to prove criminal intent beyond a reasonable doubt (McCormick, 1981:270–271).

The demise of the muckraking effort not long after the beginning of the second decade of the twentieth century carries instructive lessons. Part, but only a very minor part, of the problem resulted from effective pressures exercised against the muckraking magazines by the objects of their attacks (Marcaccio,

1985). Wounded corporations curtailed advertising and, more effectively, bought out and buried some of the muckraking publications. Much more significant, however, was a growing tendency toward sensationalism and shrillness as the magazines, having mined the most promising fields, became more frantic about outdoing competitors and capturing public attention. The public, for its part, apparently became bored with what seemed an endless diet of social criticism (Regier, 1932).

Muckraking had virtually disappeared when the advent of the first world war conclusively turned citizens' attention to international concerns. The rather harsh summary judgment by Cornelius Regier (1932:212) does not seem unreasonable: "[M]uckraking, however necessary and however valuable it might have been for the time being, was essentially a superficial attack upon a problem which demanded—and demands—fundamental analysis and treatment."

In today's society, the role of muckraking has been institutionalized by investigative journalism and is practiced most effectively by a cadre of reporters working for the largest American daily newspapers. It reached its zenith when Carl Bernstein and Robert Woodward (1974) uncovered details of the Watergate break-in and coverup. Television on occasion, particularly in widely viewed network programs such as "60 Minutes" and "20/20," carries muckraking material and stories of corporate crime. The advantage of such work remains television's access to huge audiences and its consequent ability to influence public policy. The considerable resources at its disposal can be used to uncover information that might be analyzed by academics in a more leisurely and scientific manner than is possible under the deadline and attention-getting demands that bear upon media reporting.

The linkage of muckraking and investigative reporting later would be made explicit in a pair of federal court cases dealing with media liability. In 1967, the U.S. Supreme Court decreed that the *Saturday Evening Post,* intent upon what it called "sophisticated muckraking," was liable to a football coach when it incorrectly accused him of having conspired to fix a game (*Curtis Publishing Co. v. Butts,* 1967). Subsequently, the District of Columbia federal court held the *Washington Post* liable for falsely stating that the president of Mobil Oil Corporation had set up his son in a shipping business and diverted Mobil business to him. The court noted that editor Robert Woodward's demand for what he called "holy shit" stories—that is, hard-hitting investigative reports that would arouse readers to so exclaim— could be used as part of the evidence to determine whether the article was published with actual malice (*Tavoulareas v. Piro*, 1985).

Public-interest groups constitute another prominent post-muckraker force devoted to oversight of corporate crime. Particularly prominent in this genre had been the work of Ralph Nader and his associates. Two decades ago Nader supervised the publication of a series of volumes that represented penetrating inquiries into the operation of corporations and regulatory agencies (see, e.g., Fellmeth, 1970; Green, Moore, & Wasserstein, 1972; Turner, 1970). "Scratch the image of any industry and unsavory practices become visible" has been the watchword of the Nader teams (Nader, 1969:140). Nader's efforts have commanded considerable public attention, but, like the fate of the muckrakers, they now appear to suffer from an inability of public concern to remain focused overlong on particular social ills or individual prophets. Most citizens after a time apparently come to define persistent social critics as nags and tune them out.

The Academic Criminologists

Academic scholars have not, of course, replaced legislative bodies, courts, or journalists in the study of corporate crime; they merely have joined in the pursuit of the game. In doing so, they have infused a bit of extra respectability into the enterprise. The consequences of their work, however, at least in intuitive terms (the matter seems virtually beyond determinative measure), do not seem to have penetrated very deeply into public or political consciousness beyond the near universal adaptation of Sutherland's term "white-collar crime" to embrace derelictions such as corporate offenses. Unlike today, when criminologists generally are far removed from national debate, prominent early sociologists were among the contributors to the mass-circulation muckraking periodicals during their heyday. Despite his Stanford University and University of Wisconsin affiliations, however, the prose of Edward A. Ross, the academic who most often wrote about upper-class criminal behavior, was no less purple and polemical than that of the most flamboyant muckraker, though Ross (1907) favored tonier outlets, such as *The Atlantic Monthly*, instead of the muckraking dime and quarter magazines. Like the muckrakers, the earlier academic chroniclers of corporate crime often maintained close connections with the powerful: Ross, for example, corresponded frequently with President Theodore Roosevelt (Geis, 1962).

The virtual disappearance today of close relationships between criminological scholars and persons in positions of political power probably can be traced to the enormous growth in the number of highly educated persons and of the government bureaucracy, so that talented men and women who in earlier days might have chosen university positions now take up jobs in the government and in advisory agencies such as the Brookings Institute. Without teaching and other pedagogical and administrative obligations, and with the benefit of being located geographically at or near sites where power is exercised, these intellectuals are more likely then, say, a scholar in Lawrence, Kansas, or Madison, Wisconsin, to develop ties with prominent government officials seeking insights about corporate crime.

By the late 1930s, an academic scholar interested in corporate crime, such as Sutherland, was being pressed by the norms of his trade to move away from advocacy and to bring to his work an attitude that sought, with more or less success— usually less—to view corporate lawbreaking in a "neutral" and "objective" manner. The endorsed scientific approach aimed neither to condemn nor to defend corporate offenses, but only to document correlates of the behavior and to reach an understanding of the forces that underlay it. Sutherland's ground-breaking monograph *White Collar Crime* (1949) exemplifies its author's struggle between scorn and dispassionate analysis. Despite his disclaimers, Sutherland's distaste and impatience regarding corporate malfeasance and malversation lie only slightly, if at all, below the surface.

It was Sutherland's *White Collar Crime* (1949) that first, albeit almost inadvertently, drew a sharp distinction between high-status individuals in the business world who violated statutes pertaining to their work and the organizations that often bore the criminal responsibility for what these persons had done. The legislative committee examining the South Sea Company scandal and the muckrakers, though to a much lesser extent, had no problem pinpointing individual malefactors: these often were prominent persons in the commercial world whose identity overshadowed that of their companies. By Sutherland's time, however, corporations had grown enormously, and leadership had moved from the vivid personal style of an earlier period to a bureaucratic form, with faceless and seemingly interchangeable cogs carrying out actions in the name of the organization for which they worked.

Sutherland's monograph on white-collar crime presented case studies and some relatively crude analyses of corporate offenses. In addition, Sutherland often dealt with petty misdeeds by low-level employees, such as shoe and insurance salesmen, materials that seem to serve no purpose beyond extending what would remain a short book to a point where it had at least adequate bulk. Most of his data on corporate crime came from combing newspapers, the trade press, and the records of regulatory agencies. Sutherland never came to appreciate that he was treating huge corporations as a single entity, comparable to a person, though they had tens of thousands of employees and were governed by innumerable laws not applicable to individuals. His most notable descent into this kind of analytical carelessness came when he equated corporations adjudicated to have committed four or more offenses (be they regulatory or criminal) to habitual offenders (Sutherland, 1949:218).

Criminological scholarship following Sutherland at first tended to deal with issues of considerable public concern, such as wartime black markets (Clinard, 1952) and violations of price controls (Hartung, 1950). Compared to that of the muckrakers, this work reduced by a number of decibels the level of shrillness and sought to tie findings to ingredients in the social structure or to traits of the perpetrators. But research on corporate crime virtually ceased from the land during the time when

McCarthyism prevailed in the United States. In 1962, in one of the few articles on the subject published in this period, I argued that Sutherland had anthropomorphized corporations, treating them unthinkingly as if they were human beings, and in the same article suggested that studies of white-collar crime focus exclusively on corporate derelictions, an idea that deservedly met with monumental indifference (Geis, 1962).

My research on the 1961 antitrust violations in the heavy electrical industry, with General Electric and Westinghouse among the conspirators, provided some worthwhile ideas about the relationship between the offenses and the corporate conditions under which they arose, but most fundamentally it sought to locate the roots of the violations in the experiences of the individual wrongdoers (Geis, 1967). This quest would not have been possible, however, without the hearings by the Senate Subcommittee on Antitrust and Monopoly, headed by Estes Kefauver, which provided a superb array of statements by corporate officials in response to intense questioning.

Thereafter, one facet of the scholarship on corporate crime within academic circles became notably more ingrown and self-absorbed as scholars came to quarrel about such matters as the proper definition of their subject matter, value neutrality, and satisfactory theoretical interpretation of their findings, as well as the relationship of white-collar and corporate crime to general theories of lawbreaking that might embrace such a variety of crimes as arson, rape, and antitrust violations (see, e.g., Gottfredson & Hirschi, 1990).

At the same time, academics began to distinguish sharply between violations by individual white-collar offenders both within and outside the corporate world and behavior that they believed might better be understood by examining closely the dynamics of corporate life. Several conditions probably played into the development of the focus on corporations as criminal perpetrators. Certainly, the stage had been set by the Anglo-American legal provision that a corporation could be prosecuted and punished for the violation of criminal laws, a position absent in most of the world's legal systems (Bernard, 1984; Mueller, 1957). In addition, as business became less swashbuckling, individual leaders, except for instances where they chose to personify the organization (in the manner of Robert Maxwell, Donald Trump, and Lee Iococca) became faceless: the days had passed when John D. Rockefeller, Andrew Carnegie, E.F. Harrison, and J. Pierpont Morgan collectively could be embraced by a label such as "the robber barons" (Josephson, 1934).

The growing size, complexity, and sophistication of the corporate form also further protected individuals from the consequences of lawbreaking. The increasing use of strict liability statutes to hold corporations responsible for harms they had committed also moved attention away from individual perpetrators. In addition, from the viewpoint of ease and efficacy of prosecution, it often proved more expeditious to move against an organization and, particularly, much more profitable to obtain recovery from a deep-pocket firm than any individual within it. The records and correlates of the criminal behavior of corporations also proved to be more accessible to the criminologist seeking grist for a scholarly mill. Corporate crime records could be analyzed in terms of the numbers and kinds of offenses and correlated to items such as corporate size, profitability (particularly the direction in which the balance sheet was moving), method of management, ethical climate, style of leadership, political ethos (as indicated by PAC campaign contributions), and attitudes toward various elements of regulation. In short, data were readily available for academics willing to peruse government documents, follow the headlines, and steep themselves in other sources that offered information about the corporate world.

Attempts to study individual corporate offenders, on the other hand, risked the considerable likelihood that their personalities and demographic profiles would be little different from those of their nonviolating colleagues. Besides, such people, guarded by secretaries, public relations specialists, and law firms, were not readily accessible to the academic investigator. Neither were they as likely as the street offender to be impressed by and responsive to the credentials of the university-based criminology researcher.

In addition, the domination of academic criminology by sociologists virtually insisted upon a focus on units larger than individuals who, after all, are the basic stuff of psychological inquiry. The major theories of criminology almost invariably have been derived from inquiries into group behavior, especially that of gangs, and not from the study of criminal offenders such as arsonists and prostitutes.

This intellectual predilection of the field, however, created difficulty in the realm of public policy, often shutting out sociological findings from a political agenda that is geared toward changing individuals and disinterested (and perhaps by and large incapable) in doing very much to alter broad social themes. It is relatively easy to make a murderer undergo group therapy but much more difficult to change a subculture of violence. In the corporate world, however, the converse usually is true: it is likely to be more feasible to change the atmosphere by changing the internal rules under which business is conducted than to change the people who carry out the business (Braithwaite, 1985). For such reasons, the offenses of corporations became a particularly feasible topic for criminological inquiry.

The study of corporate crime had received its imprimatur from the specific bifurcation in 1973 by Clinard and Quinney of white-collar offenses into those committed by individuals and those by corporations. In 1979, Needleman and Needleman called attention to what they called "crime-facilitative" corporate environments that produced lawbreaking, and three years later, in a landmark effort, Ermann and Lundman published *Corporate Deviance*, a volume that developed "an organizationally sensitive analysis of deviance in those instances where large corporations are the appropriate units of analysis, while typically no one person is labelled deviant" (Ermann & Lundman, 1982:v). Later monographs include an organizationally sensitive study of Revco's offenses against the Medicaid program (Vaughan, 1983) and Clinard and Yeager's (1980) updating of Sutherland's work on corporate lawbreaking. Clinard and Yeager (1978:257) pointed out that Sutherland's methodological procedures were weak and that he had not made a systematic attempt to analyze his data in terms of independent variables. Shapiro (1984) added to this body of work by producing a participant-observation examination of the efforts of the Securities and Exchange Commission, and there were a host of inquiries into the operation of regulatory laws, including Shover, Clelland, and Lynxwiler's (1986) study of the enforcement of mining regulations.

The growing focus on corporate crime ultimately impelled Cressey to crusade for a return to the study of the individual offenders within the corporation rather than the corporate entity as malefactor; otherwise, Cressey argued, it becomes impossible to develop a satisfactory social psychological theory of wrongdoing. To study the corporation as criminal, Cressey (1988:32) argued, "is self-defeating because it is based on the erroneous assumption that organizations think and act, thus saddling theoretical criminologists with the impossible task of finding the cause of crimes committed by fictitious persons." Braithwaite and Fisse, responding to Cressey, argued for the focus on corporate wrongdoing, insisting that corporate decisions, much like those of individuals, have a diffuse grounding and that "[t]he products of organization are more than the sum of the products of individual actions" (Braithwaite & Fisse, 1990:20,22).

While the discussion over proper parameters goes on apace, only occasionally have particularly venturesome academic researchers adopted the traditional journalistic role and attempted at firsthand to acquire information from corporate officials about their experiences and those of their organizations in regard to lawbreaking. Among the most notable endeavors in this genre has been the series of interviews in corporate headquarters throughout the world conducted by Fisse and Braithwaite (1984) and discussions with former middle managers carried out in sunbelt retirement communities by Clinard (1983).

Conclusion

With only occasional dissent (Schwendinger & Schwendinger, 1970), criminologists have concluded that behaviors that violate the law constitute the proper fare for their study. This resolution has permitted them to place very specific limits on the matters that will occupy their attention. The price has been that they tend to ignore various kinds of harmful behavior that for any number of reasons have not been proscribed by the criminal law. It is common for criminologists with consciences troubled by this dilemma to insist that nothing precludes them, or anyone else, from examining awful acts or situations beyond the bounds of criminal law, though, in truth, probably because of the dictates of their business (i.e., what is publishable in criminological journals) they rarely do so.

Corporate crime became a legitimate topic for criminological study because of the Anglo-American code provisions that allow organizations to be prosecuted for offenses deemed to be commissions or omissions of the denominated group rather than derelictions of individuals within them. This juridical viewpoint arose, legal historians tell us (Holdsworth, 1925), primarily because officers and stockholders desired the advantages of equity, size, and resources as well as protection from personal liability. In time, corporations were deemed "persons" under the law, and, with some exceptions, they now are allowed to enjoy most privileges applicable to individuals.

Violations of law by corporations have come under the particular scrutiny of legislative bodies, regulatory agencies, journalists, public-interest groups, the courts, and academic criminologists. Each monitoring group, as this chapter has indicated, possesses strengths and shortcomings as an analytical and control mechanism. Academic criminologists appear most notably to lack the influence and the ability to translate their findings into action, presuming, of course, that reasonable action can be predicated on what they report. On the other hand, in their work they can be (or at least can usually claim that they are) more dispassionate and more scientific than groups that have a preset agenda and an inclination to seek only information that supports their bias.

The academic study of corporate crime at this moment seems to be drawing particular strength from the demise of the sociological stranglehold on criminological inquiry and from the infusion of interdisciplinary efforts—particularly those involving social scientists and legal scholars—into an examination of corporate offenses. The virtual absence of concern with the subject, either disciplinary or interdisciplinary, among business organization scholars and, particularly, among persons with an expertise in economics (a body of knowledge often not adequately understood by criminologists) continues to impede a fully satisfactory array of work on corporate crime. The inability, or unwillingness, of academic criminologists to become deeply involved on site with the corporate world and with corporate offenders appears to represent a major barrier for the moment against advancing our understanding of the dynamics of corporate crime.

On the upside of the ledger, a criminologist might note with pride the definition of their work by a prominent social scientist. In a 1986 speech, then President Ronald Reagan had proclaimed that "we don't need a bunch of sociology majors on the bench." The response of Herbert Gans of Columbia University, in a letter to the *New York Times*, was that "our anticrime [sic] policies have to be based on understanding why America creates so many criminals, on the streets and on Wall Street" and not on "tough talk" from politicians and judges (Gans, 1986).

REFERENCES

Adler, S.J. (1991, November 12). Companies face uphill fight in jury trials. *Wall Street Journal* (West Coast ed.), p. A12.

Bernard, T.J. (1984). The historical development of corporate criminal liability. *Criminology, 22,* 3–17.

Bernstein, C., & Woodward, B. (1974). *All the president's men.* New York: Simon & Schuster.

Boyden, R.W. (1948). *The English business corporation, 1660–1720.* Unpublished doctoral dissertation, Harvard University. Cambridge.

Braithwaite, J. (1985). *To punish or persuade: Enforcement of coal mine safety.* Albany: State University of New York Press.

Braithwaite, J., & Fisse, B. (1990). On the plausibility of corporate crime theory. In W.S. Laufer & F. Adler (Eds.), *Advances in criminological theory* (Vol. 2, pp. 15–38). New Brunswick, NJ: Transaction.

Bunyan, J. (1678). *The pilgrim's progress.* London: Nath. Ponder.

Carswell, J. (1960). *The South Sea bubble.* Stanford: Stanford University Press.

Chalmers, D.M. (1964). *The social and political ideas of the muckrakers.* New York: Citadel.

Clinard, M.B. (1952). *The black market: A study of white-collar crime.* New York: Holt.

———. (1983). *Corporate ethics and crime: The role of middle management.* Beverly Hills, CA: Sage.

Clinard, M.B., & Quinney, R. (1973). *Criminal behavior systems: A typology* (2nd ed.). New York: Holt, Rinehart and Winston.

Clinard, M.B., & Quinney, R. (1978). Corporate crime: Issues in research. *Criminology, 16,* 255–272.

Clinard, M.B., & Yeager, P.C. (1980). *Corporate crime.* New York: Free Press.

Cowles, V. (1960). *The great swindle: The story of the South Sea bubble.* New York: Harper.

Cressey, D.R. (1988). The poverty of theory in corporate crime research. In W.S. Laufer and F. Adler (Ed.), *Advances in criminological theory* (Vol. 1, pp. 31–56). New Brunswick, NJ: Transaction.

Curtis Publishing Corp. v. Butts. 1967. 388 U.S. 130.

Dent, A. (1601/1664). *The plain mans pathway to heaven, wherein every man may clearly see whether he shall be saved or damned.* London: John Wright.

Donnan, E. (1930). The early days of the South Sea Company, 1711–1781. *Journal of Economic and Business History, 2,* 419–450.

Erleigh, G.R. (1933). *The South Sea bubble.* New York: Putman's.

Ermann, M.D., & Lundman, R.J. (1982). *Corporate deviance.* New York: Holt, Rinehart, and Winston.

Fellmeth, R.C. (1970). *The interstate commerce omission.* New York: Grossman.

Filler, L. (1976). *The muckrakers.* University Park: The Pennsylvania State University Press.

Fisse, B.,& Braithwaite, J. (1984). *The impact of publicity on corporate offenders.* Albany: State University of New York Press.

Gans, H.J. (1986, October 12). Letter to the Editor. *New York Times*, p. A4.

Geiger, L.G. (1966). Muckrakers—then and now. *Journalism Quarterly*, 43, 469–476.

Geis, G. (1962). Toward a delineation of white-collar offenses. *Sociological Inquiry*, 32, 160–171.

———. (1964). Sociology and sociological jurisprudence: A mixture of lore and law. *Kentucky Law Journal*, 52, 267–293.

———. (1967). The heavy electric equipment antitrust case of 1961. In M.B. Clinard and R. Quinney (Ed.), *Criminal behavior systems: A typology* (pp. 139–150). New York: Holt, Rinehart, and Winston.

Gibbon, E. (1966). *Memoirs of my life* (G.A. Bonnard, Ed.). London: Thomas Nelson.

Gordimer, N. (1973). *A guest of honour*. London: Penguin.

Gottfredson, M.G., & Hirschi, T. (1990). *A general theory of crime*. Stanford: Stanford University Press.

Green, M.J., Moore, B.C., Jr., & Wasserstein, B. (1972). *The Closed Enterprise System*. New York: Grossman.

Hart, A.B., & Ferlager, H.F. (1989). *Theodore Roosevelt cyclopedia* (rev. ed.). Oyster Bay, NY: Theodore Roosevelt Association.

Hartung, F.E. (1950). White-collar offenses in the wholesale meat industry in Detroit. *American Journal of Sociology*, 56, 25–34.

Heckscher, E.F. (1930–1931). A note on South Sea finance. *Journal of Economics and Business*, 3, 321–328.

Heilbroner, R., & others. (1973). *In the name of profit*. New York: Doubleday.

Hill, C. (1964). *Society and puritanism in pre-revolutionary England*. London: Secker & Warburg.

Hobbes, T. (1651). *Leviathan*. London: Andrew Crooke.

Holdsworth, S. (1925). *A history of English law*. London: Methuen.

Josephson, M. (1934). *The robber barons: The great American capitalist, 1861–1901*. New York: Harcourt, Brace.

Law, R.A. (1942). 'Muck-rakers' before Bunyon. *Modern Language Notes*, 57, 455–457.

Lawson, T.W. (1905). Frenzied finance. *Everybody's Magazine*, 12, 173–180.

Lecky, W.E.H. (1907). *A history of England in the eighteenth century*. London: Longmans, Green.

McClure, S.S. (1903). Editorial. *McClure's Magazine*, 22, 336.

McCormick, R.L. (1981). The discovery that business corrupts politics: A reappraisal of the origins of progressivism. *American Historial Review, 86,* 247–274.

Marcaccio, M.D. (1985). Did a business conspiracy end muckraking? *Historian, 47,* 58–71.

Marcosson, I.F. (1932). *David Graham Phillips and his times.* New York: Dodd, Mead.

Mottran, R.H. (1929). *A history of financial speculation.* London: Chatto & Windus.

Mueller, G.O.W. (1957). *Mens rea* and the corporation: A study of the Model Penal Code position on corporate criminal liability. *University of Pittsburgh Law Review, 19,* 21–50.

Nader, R. (1969). Business crime. In D. Sanford (Ed.), *Hot war on the consumer* (pp. 138–140). New York: Pitman.

Needleman, M.L., & Needleman, C. (1979). Organizational crime: Two models of crimogenesis. *Sociological Quarterly, 20,* 517–528.

Noonan, J.T. (1984). *Bribes.* New York: Macmillan.

Regier, C.C. (1932). *The era of the muckrakers.* Chapel Hill: University of North Carolina Press.

Roosevelt, T. (1926). The man with the muck-rake. *The work of Theodore Roosevelt* (pp. 415–424). New York: Scribner's.

Ross, E.A. (1907, January). The criminaloid. *The Atlantic Monthly,* pp. 44–50.

Ross, I. (1980, October 1). How lawless are big companies? *Fortune, 102,* 56–72.

Schrager, L.S., & Short, J.F., Jr,. (1978). Toward a sociology of organizational crime. *Social Problems, 25,* 407–419.

Schwendinger, H., & Schwendinger, J. (1970). Defenders of order or guardians of human rights? *Issues in Criminology, 5,* 123–157.

Scott, W.R. (1912). *The constitution and finance of English, Scottish and Irish Joint-Stock companies to 1720.* Cambridge, UK: Cambridge University Press.

Sedgwick, R. (1970). *The House of Commons, 1715–1754.* London: Her Majesty's Stationery Office.

Shapiro, S.P. (1984). *Wayward capitalists: Target of the Securities and Exchange Commission.* New Haven: Yale University Press.

Sharrock, R. (1954). *John Bunyan.* London: Hutchinson.

Shover, N., Clelland, D.A., & Lynxwiler, J. (1986). *Enforcement or negotiation: Constructing a regulatory bureaucracy.* Albany: State University of New York Press.

Sutherland, E.H. (1940). White-collar criminality. *American Sociological Review, 5,* 1–12.

———. (1949). *White collar crime.* New York: Dryden.

Tarbell, I.M. (1904). *The history of the Standard Oil Company.* New York: McClure, Phillips.

Tavoulareas v. Piro. 1985. 759 Fed. Rptr. 2n 90 (D.C. District).

Tomkins, M.F. (1974). *Ida M. Tarbell.* New York: Twayne.

Turner, J.S. (1970). *The chemical feast.* New York: Grossman.

Vaughan, D. (1983). *Controlling unlawful organizational behavior: Social structure and corporate misconduct.* Chicago: University of Chicago Press.

Walton, C. (Ed.). (1977). *The ethics of corporate conduct.* Englewood Cliffs, NJ: Prentice-Hall.

CHAPTER TWO

Defining Corporate Crime:
A Critique of Traditional Parameters

Stephen E. Brown
Chau-Pu Chiang

Criminologists have traditionally studied crime from a narrow legalistic framework, treating it as a problem unique to the lower class. For example, Tappan (1947:100) defines *crime* as "an intentional act in violation of the criminal law" and *criminals* as persons "held guilty beyond a reasonable doubt." These definitions illustrate the influence of law in defining the scope of criminology. The assumption that crime is primarily a lower-class problem, however, has permeated criminological thought throughout most of this century.

This ideological bias has resulted in a legalistic and classist perspective that has largely ignored the problem of corporate crime. As Sutherland (1949:9) noted, "This bias is quite as certain as it would be if the scholars selected only red-haired criminals for study and reached the conclusion that redness of hair was the cause of crime." Arguing that criminologists should study any *punishable* behavior (whether by criminal, regulatory, or civil sanctions), Sutherland provided the intellectual foundation for studying corporate criminality. He further noted that criminologists "should be completely free to push across the barriers of legal definitions" (Sutherland & Cressey, 1974:21). This position reflects the heart of the criminological vision necessary to guide an expansive examination of corporate criminality.

Conflict theorists have argued even more assertively that the parameters of criminological inquiry must not be restricted by prevailing legal definitions of crime. The Schwendingers (1975:133–134), for example, redefine crime in terms of human rights, which they identify as

> the fundamental prerequisites for well-being, including food, shelter, clothing, medical services, challenging work and recreational experiences, as well as security from predatory individuals or repressive and imperialistic social elites.

Any infringement of these rights should be labeled and reacted to as a crime.

Thus competing definitions of crime can be conceptualized as falling along a continuum that extends from a very narrow legalistically constrained meaning to a very broad conception based on human rights (Brown, Esbensen, & Geis, 1991). A recent shift in perspective toward the broader end of this continuum has resulted in awareness of the huge body of previously ignored crime. Criminologists increasingly are scrutinizing a broader range of avoidable and socially harmful behavior, the bulk of which is embedded in the business world.

This ideological shift began in earnest during the 1970s (Clinard & Yeager, 1980; Geis, 1985). Yet the flagitious practices of the upper class have not escaped periodic criticism. While the so-called "muckrakers" exposed the egregious iniquities of the robber barons and other members of the upper class (Lewis, 1920; Ross, 1907; Sinclair, 1906; Steffens, 1904; Tarbell, 1904), Sutherland (1949) was the first criminologist to study corporate deviance systematically. He also understood the social and political barriers that prevent criminalization of avoidable and socially harmful acts committed by corporations pursuing their economic interests.

Corporations may, for example, lobby successfully against legal controls of deceptive advertising, pollution, or unsafe working conditions. If these efforts fail or appear too costly, clever inventions that emasculate legal controls of socially harmful behavior may be substituted. A class bias in the criminal law may be manifested in the requirement of proving *intent* in order to gain a criminal conviction (Hopkins, 1981).

The creation of administrative or regulatory law, and the substitution of fines and injunctions for more punitive criminal sanctions, also exemplifies corporate influence. Moreover, power can be used to influence the frequency and intensity with which existing legal controls are applied. Corporations (especially, the media) also control information, thereby altering perceptions of the nature and scope of harmful corporate activity (see Evans & Lundman, 1983).

Corporate crime differs from the harmful behavior of "street" offenders in ways other than the obvious disparity in the power of perpetrators. The structure of corporations renders identification of the intent of specific corporate offenders more difficult. Likewise, harms are more difficult to link directly to the corporation and its officers, while the impact of corporate misanthropy is extremely difficult to fully assess. Finally, many lay persons, justice system personnel, and criminologists identify with the upper class because legitimate commonalities are perceived to be much greater. Members of the lower class, especially people of color, are frequently perceived as possessing a criminal master status (Becker, 1963). However, because corporate offenders display middle-class characteristics (e.g., a nuclear family, values, planning, communication skills, grooming, educational attainment, etc.), it is difficult to label them as criminals.

Because of these impediments to understanding this genre of upper-class deviance, a new conceptual framework is needed to assess the nature and extent of corporate crime. A chronological review of the literature outlines an emerging direction for thinking about corporate crime. The following section identifies several major theses in this new conceptual scheme.

A Conceptual Framework

Prevailing notions of crime "do not refer to those behaviors that objectively and *avoidably* cause us the most harm, injury, and suffering" (Box, 1983:13). While estimates of the extent of corporate crime vary, most observers agree that the scope of the problem far exceeds that of conventional street crime (Coleman, 1989; Reiman, 1990).

Much of the current debate about the general topic of white-collar crime centers on defining the white-collar or corporate *criminal*. Not since the Sutherland-Tappan exchange almost fifty years ago has much printed space been devoted to defining what constitutes white-collar or corporate *crime* (see Shapiro, 1990). The most meaningful and exhaustive enumeration of the extent of corporate crime recognizes the limiting effects of prevailing legal definitions of crime. A broader definition of crime includes acts that violate existing criminal, civil, and administrative or regulatory law, as well as an array of "harmful but avoidable" behaviors that lack legal or moral stricture, but for which "there is good reason why the act should be against the law" (Levenbook, 1982:49). The latter category of socially harmful behavior can be thought of as "evils . . . for which no law has yet been created" (Frank, 1985:43).

Thus, we would place harmful corporate behavior into one of three categories:

1. Acts that are violations of existing criminal law.
2. Acts that are violations of existing civil and regulatory law.
3. Acts that are harmful but for which no legal remedy yet exists.

This typology incorporates Sutherland's (1945) definition of a "white-collar crime" in that the act need not be punished, but rather must be *punishable*. We extend Sutherland's definition by including acts that *should* be punishable according to our liberalized definition of crime.

We are mindful of the criticisms that this definition is bound to provoke. Tappan would probably chastise us as he did Sutherland by stating that

> [t]he rebel may enjoy a veritable orgy of delight in damning as criminal most anyone he pleases; one imagines that some experts would thus consign to the criminal classes any successful businessman. . . . The result may be fine indoctrination or catharsis achieved through

blustering broadsides against the "existing system." It is not criminology. It is not social science. (Tappan, 1947:99)

We reject arguments of this kind because a great deal of corporate crime is a violation of existing law (statutory and case law) but is not treated as such by the criminal justice system. Moreover, existing official measures of crime (Uniform Crime Reports and National Crime Surveys) do not require conviction of the perpetrator in order to count an act as criminal. Most important, criminologists should not be bound by prevailing legal definitions of crime. In a political economy such as ours, traditional parameters of criminality serve to maintain the interests of the dominant class through the process of labeling (Becker, 1963). Thus, official gauges of crime are invalid measures of crime because they fail to include organizational and occupational crimes.

Our liberalized definition of crime also includes a broader denotation of victimization. Both corporate and conventional criminality result in primary, secondary, and tertiary victimization. There can be no doubt that the seriousness of harms produced by corporate crime far outweigh those that result from conventional crime. While more people are killed and injured and more money is stolen as a consequence of corporate crime, perhaps the most dismal corollary is the realization that victimization by corporations is as inevitable as death itself. While many individuals can take steps to minimize the probability of being a victim of street crime, *there is no way to prevent being a victim of corporate crime.*

Corporate crime is also detrimental to society, though not in the traditional sense of the term. Some level of conventional crime may be functional in that it produces social boundaries (Durkheim, 1964; Erikson, 1966). However, corporate crime is dysfunctional because it lacks the social opprobrium necessary to foster solidarity. By undermining the social structure, corporate malfeasance destroys hope for an egalitarian society. The violation of trust implicit in corporate crime may create cynicism toward the law and other social institutions (Cullen, Maakestad, & Cavender, 1987; Edelhertz & Overcast, 1982).

Although the harm created by corporate crime is difficult to quantify, we suggest that the true impact of corporate crime can best be understood from a liberal definition of crime and its concomitant victimization. We thus define *crime* as *any intentional or avoidable act committed by an individual, an organization, or a political entity that in any way diminishes either the quality or quantity of another individual's life.* The case histories that follow exemplify our views on corporate crime.

Crimes That Are Punishable

Harms from Economic Crimes

Among criminologists, and increasingly among the general public, there is widespread recognition that the economic costs of corporate crime exceed those of conventional street crime. Yet the magnitude of the gap is difficult to estimate. Even government computations place the frequency ratio of corporate to street crime at more than 20:1 (Clinard & Yeager, 1980). Just one corporate crime episode—the savings and loan scandal—will cost the American public $325 to $500 billion according to government estimations, but as high as $1.4 trillion or over $5,000 for every American household by other estimates (Snider, 1991).

The prevalence of economic corporate crime emerged as an issue in Sutherland's (1949) work. Examining the life records (averaging forty-five years) of seventy corporations, Sutherland found that all had official records of offenses, averaging fourteen per corporation. Limiting the count to criminal convictions, he found that 60 percent of the corporations in the sample had records, averaging four convictions each. Sutherland argued that this recidivism rate warranted labeling the majority of corporations as "habitual criminals."

More recently, Clinard and Yeager (1980) examined federal administrative, civil, and criminal actions against 582 corporations in a two-year period (1975 and 1976), finding that 60.1 percent had actions brought against them (an average of 2.7 violations per corporation). Like Sutherland, they found criminal activity to be concentrated among a small segment of corporations. Of all corporations studied, 8 percent were responsible for 52 percent of the violations officially reported. However, neither Sutherland's, nor Clinard and Yeager's, work addressed the avoidable harms caused by corporations that are not "crimes" in the legal sense.

Corporate crimes that result in economic harm are pervasive, costly, and take diverse forms. The following sections review both older and recent examples of this form of offense. They were selected to illustrate the full range of victims and offenses that correspond to our conceptualization of crime.

An Antitrust Case. Gilbert Geis' (1967) case study of the 1961 antitrust convictions for conspiring to fix the costs of heavy electrical equipment serves as a classic example of economic crime as defined by criminal code. Deliberate violations of the Sherman Antitrust Act by manufacturers of heavy electrical equipment inflated the prices paid by public utility systems who ultimately passed the cost of generating electricity on to consumers.

High-ranking officers of General Electric, Westinghouse, and other electric equipment manufacturers carefully developed a *modus operandi* for divvying up the market at noncompetitive or "corporate socialism" prices. By previous agreement, each company was allowed to submit the "low" bid on a certain portion of jobs.

Their secret meetings, called "choir practice," were attended by a roster of key officers from each company referred to as the "Christmas card list." The meetings were held either in private locations or at trade shows (where their association would not raise suspicion) and included very careful steps to hide their activities. The co-conspirators agreed on "low" bids for industrial equipment.

As a result of a complaint filed by the Tennessee Valley Authority, a major regional public utility group, federal indictments were issued for twenty-nine corporations and forty-five individuals. Criminal convictions of the corporations resulted in nearly $2 million in fines. Seven executives, including four vice-presidents, were sentenced to thirty days in jail. Geis compared the criminal sanction that General Electric received to be no more effective than a $3 parking ticket to a person earning

$175,000 a year. Even the $160 million in civil penalties was tax deductible, thereby minimizing the impact of further sanctions on General Electric's profitability.

Medicaid Fraud. A scheme for double billing prescriptions to Medicaid resulted in a criminal (misdemeanor) conviction of Revco Drug Stores of Ohio (Vaughan, 1980). Developed by two executives concerned with losses from rejected claims, the crime involved an efficient *modus operandi* that ultimately was detected only by coincidence. A temporary staff was hired to generate bogus prescription claims by resubmitting previously paid ones ("models"), changing only the date and transposing the last three digits within a six-digit prescription number. Revco acquired over half a million dollars before detection, and upon conviction the company was required to repay the gains along with a $50,000 fine. The two executives responsible for the scheme were each fined $1,000.

This is a case of a corporation victimizing a government entity. The responsible executives rationalized their activities by assuming the role of victims. Some 50,000 rejected claims for reimbursement from Medicaid had accumulated. Two Revco executives concluded that it would be cost prohibitive to correct and refile them, so they decided to resubmit an equal number of successful claims to acquire the funds they believed the state "owed" Revco. In short, the executives rationalized that Revco was the victim of incompetent claim screening by the state Medicaid unit and concluded that the illegal double billing scheme was the only way to recover their losses.

Bilking Investors and Taxpayers. The most costly corporate crime to date is the savings and loan fiasco that came to light after national elections in early 1989. These crimes victimized government agencies, legitimate investors, savings and loan employees, American taxpayers, and other corporations.

The savings and loan industry (S&L's) lost money during the 1970s because of the gap between the rates at which institutions loaned and borrowed money, the latter being higher than the former. The economic conditions during this period undermined the fiscal health of the industry. The demise of the industry was virtually assured by deregulation in the 1980s that allowed the following:

- Removal of restrictions on interest rates.

- Increasing depositor protection from $40,000 to $100,000 per deposit.

- Liberalization of loan policies.

- Allowing unlimited deposits arranged by brokers.

- Removal of regulations that dispensed corporate control among a large group of stockholders.

- Federal government guarantee of losses from investments by S&L's.

Many members of Congress and the Reagan Administration subscribed to the belief that a free market is a self-regulating one. As a result, legislation was enacted and policies were implemented that precipitated a series of actions, 70 to 80 percent of which were criminal in nature and that will eventually cost taxpayers $200 billion over the next decade (Calavita & Pontell, 1990).

The failure to adequately regulate the savings and loan industry provided opportunities for unlawful risk-taking, collective embezzlement, and coverups by executives and government officials (Calavita & Pontell, 1990). A substantial segment of the savings and loan industry ultimately degenerated to a fraudulent scam.

> Overnight, ailing savings and loans could obtain huge amounts of cash to stave off their impending insolvency. But the miracle drug had a downside. Like a narcotic, the more these institutions took in brokered deposits, the more they depended on them, and the more they were willing to, and had to, pay to get them. As brokerage firms shopped across the country for the best return on their money, thrifts had to offer ever-higher interest rates to attract them. And, like a drug, the most desperate institutions needed the most and paid the highest interest rates. In a perverse contortion of the theory of the survival of the fittest . . . , in this environment it was the weakest thrifts that grew the fastest. (Calavita & Pontell, 1990:317)

Clearly, there were economic inducements, compounded by structural deficiencies, that resulted in the most costly corporate crime in American history. These structural problems played a substantial role in the ultimate collapse of the savings and loan industry.

On the eve of the collapse, the House Committee on Government Operations noted that "the best way to rob a bank is to own one" (cited in Calavita & Pontell, 1990). Collective embezzlement is the "looting" or "robbing" of one's own bank. High-ranking corporate officers conspired to funnel corporate money to support exorbitant life-styles. This type of criminal activity occurred on a grand scale in the savings and loan industry and was one of the major sources of its failure.

While specific deficiencies or fraudulent practices were widespread in the industry, efforts to "cover up" after the fact were also pervasive. Techniques for covering up developed in conjunction with the various risk-taking and collective embezzlement schemes, becoming part and parcel of the larger problem.

The causal implications of the scandal-plagued industry are considerably more somber due to the significant role played by the government in developing a criminogenic economic structure. While industrial capitalism requires raw materials and a surplus labor pool in order to produce goods and services, profits from finance capitalism result from "fiddling with money" (Calavita & Pontell, 1990). The events that took place in the savings and loan industry may only be a prelude to future crimes in the evolving "casino" economy because the most fundamental underlying structural sources of the scandal, combined with government protection, remain unaltered.

Harms from Violent Crime

Violent crime is portrayed as a problem unique to the lower class. Occasionally, lower-class predators do stray into middle-class enclaves, wreaking havoc à la Willie Horton. The Federal Bureau of Investigation, the leading source of official crime data in the United States, propagates the myth that violent crime is synonymous with the lower class (Bureau of Justice Statistics,

1981), thereby shunning the entire issue of violent corporate crime. The media likewise tends to depict violent crime in this class-biased context.

Yet the public has increasingly come to view violence by corporations as a significant component of our overall crime problem (Cullen, Link, & Polanzi, 1982; Schrager & Short, 1980). As Geis and Meier (1977:19) noted, we have witnessed "an emerging ethos insisting that persons be accorded every reasonable opportunity to remain alive and healthy until cut down by uncontrollable forces." Shifting tides of public opinion about corporate violence are a reflection of the fact that violence is an alterable ideological construct (Box, 1983).

Nearly 1.5 million violent street crimes, including approximately 20,000 cases of murder and non-negligent manslaughter, occur in the U.S. each year. As frightening as is the magnitude of this violence, it is far exceeded by corporate violence (Brown et al., 1991; Frank, 1985; Hills, 1987; Reiman, 1990; Snider, 1991). More than 100,000 workplace deaths, two million workplace injuries, and 30,000 deaths caused by defective products occur each year in the U.S. While some of these truly represent "accidents," many are a result of violations of existing laws and regulations, while others fit our category of avoidable harms. For example:

- Over 125 people were killed in the collapse of an unlawfully maintained West Virginia dam (Stern, 1976).

- Large numbers of people were killed and seriously injured in automobiles with faulty motor mounts, though General Motors was aware of the defect and refused for a five-year period to recall its cars for repair (Frank, 1985).

- 140,000 birth defects resulted when pharmaceutical manufacturers withheld unfavorable laboratory test results and marketed Bendectin (a drug to reduce nausea and vomiting in pregnant women) (Dowie & Marshall, 1980).

- Over 100,000 asbestos workers will die from lung cancer, 35,000 from mesothelioma, and 35,000 from asbestosis

(Coleman, 1989). Workers and consumers continue to be exposed to asbestos despite conclusive scientific evidence of its lethal effects.

- 26 coal miners died in 1976 Scotia mine explosions, following 652 citations for violations of safety laws and regulations. More than 500 additional safety violations were cited in the year following the deaths of these miners. (Caudill, 1977)

The following sections examine in more detail other cases that represent violations of existing laws. They are subdivided by victim groups.

Consumers

The Ford Pinto Case. On August 10, 1978, a horrible automobile crash took the lives of three young girls driving a 1973 Ford Pinto. For the first time in American history, the state did not attribute an automobile death either to a mistake or to outright recklessness on the part of a driver. Instead, an Indiana county prosecutor charged Ford Motor Company with reckless homicide. Cullen et al. (1987) characterized this willingness to secure a criminal indictment of a corporation for failing to correct a dangerous defect in a consumer product as "a sign of the times." The case has proven to be a milestone in the mobilization of criminal law as a response to the problem of avoidable consumer injuries and deaths.

According to Dowie (1979), there were at least 500 burn deaths caused by Pinto crashes. Prior to releasing the Pinto on the market, executives at Ford allegedly knew that the gas tanks of the vehicles were vulnerable to rupturing and exploding upon low-impact rear-end collisions. The refusal to redesign the Pinto's fuel system, however, saved the company $137 million, which was balanced against a projected loss of $49.5 million in damage suits for deaths, injuries, and property loss (Dowie, 1979; Cullen et al., 1987; Green, 1990). Based upon this calculation, Ford decided not to make the improvements that could have prevented those anticipated outcomes.

In the 1980 trial, the defendants' attorneys argued that Ford was not a "person" who could be responsible for committing a reckless homicide. The court, however, rejected the argument by defining "person" to include corporations and other organizations (Cullen et al., 1987; Green, 1990). While Ford was acquitted on March 13, 1980, of criminal charges in the deaths of Judy, Lyn, and Donna Ulrich, the case established precedents important to the protection of consumers from violent corporate misconduct. In another case, a civil jury concluded that Ford placed profit over safety and awarded a Pinto crash victim over $125 million in 1978 (Green, 1990).

The Pharmaceutical Industry. Some 3,000 drugs are on the U.S. market, with over 1.5 billion prescriptions written annually (Gorman, 1992). A plethora of medical devices constitute another large segment of the pharmaceutical industry. While the industry has made immense contributions to the health standards enjoyed in developed countries, it has also provided fertile ground for both economic (e.g., price-fixing) and violent corporate crime.

Historically, the pharmaceutical industry has operated within the context of a relationship with the Food and Drug Administration (FDA) that can best be characterized as an honor system. The firms proposing the introduction of medical products have conducted tests and presented results that the FDA has accepted. But the recent controversy surrounding silicone breast implants led FDA Commissioner David Kessler to conclude that "the honor system is out the window" (Gorman, 1992:43). Retreat from this honor system to closer monitoring by regulatory agencies would represent an important step in protecting pharmaceutical consumers from avoidable risks due to fraudulent or improper research reports.

The crisis can be traced to 1973, when Dow Corning Corporation announced that safety tests showed four beagles remained in "normal health" after receiving silicone implants, providing the scientific support that led to some two million women receiving implants in the past two decades (Breast implants, 1992). In 1991, however, reports indicating that the research claims were inaccurate began to surface. Rather than remaining in "normal health," one of the dogs died and another developed a tumor after insertion of the implants.

Internal documents of Dow Corning suggested that the company had been aware of implant problems since the mid-1970s and withheld the information for nearly twenty years. A former Dow Corning engineer, who resigned from the company in protest in 1976, has played the role of "whistle blower" by maintaining that the silicone breast implants the company sold could rupture and leak, posing a serious health risk (Smart, 1992).

Another recent example of potential violent victimization of consumers by the pharmaceutical industry is the sleeping pill Halcion marketed by Upjohn Company. Halcion sales in 1991 were $240 million (Gorman, 1992), but reports have been circulating since the summer of 1991 that Upjohn deliberately failed to report side effects such as paranoia and memory loss in their 1973 study, resulting in a ban of the drug in four countries and a reduction in allowable doses in three others (Cowley, 1992).

Even more incriminating is the emergence of evidence that a 1982 study incorporated a substantial quantity of data falsified by Dr. William C. Franklin, an Upjohn researcher. Upjohn officials denied this report, prompting the FDA director of evaluations of new drugs to characterize the Upjohn position as "stunning . . . incomplete, inaccurate in part and generally misleading" (Cowley, 1992:58).

A final example of the pharmaceutical industry selling unsafe products is the Dalkon Shield sold by A.H. Robbins Company in the 1970s. This intrauterine birth control device was declared safe by Robbins and used by 2.2 million women in the United States and 4.5 million worldwide (Green, 1990; Mintz, 1988). In reality, using the device exposed women to high risk of an infection known as pelvic inflammatory disease (PID), sterility, spontaneous abortions, giving birth to children with major congenital defects, and death. Eighteen Dalkon Shield deaths were documented in the United States, and Mintz (1988) suggested that hundreds, perhaps thousands, occurred in other countries. He (1988:38) concluded that "Robbins knowingly and willfully put corporate greed before human welfare; suppressed scientific studies that would ascertain safety and effectiveness; concealed hazards from consumers . . . ; assigned lower value to foreign lives than to American lives. . . ."

Workers

Some portion of the 100,000 workplace deaths and 2 million injuries occurring annually in the United States can be attributed to criminal actions of the employers as defined by existing laws. Traditionally, such misconduct has only been addressed by regulatory agencies such as the Occupational Safety and Health Administration (OSHA). In recent years, however, state and local prosecutors have begun to use the criminal law as an instrument for responding to workplace violence (Bixby, 1990). One notable example of this trend is the 1991 death of twenty-five workers in a North Carolina chicken plant fire.

Imperial Food Products. A 1991 fire in a North Carolina chicken plant run by Imperial Food Products claimed twenty-five lives. Investigation following the fire revealed that the plant had no alarms or sprinkler system and that emergency exits were locked. Efforts of victims to force the doors open before being overcome by smoke were evident. The company was fined $800,000 for the safety violations and charged with twenty-five counts of manslaughter. Only four months after those employees perished, another Imperial plant, located in Cumming, Georgia, was fined $144,500 by OSHA for more than a dozen safety violations (North Carolina . . . , 1992). This repetition of endangering employees shortly after the manslaughter charges echoes Sutherland's application of the habitual criminal concept to corporations.

The Public

Even more difficult to assess than violent corporate actions directed toward consumers and workers are those that victimize the general public. While it is clear that environmental pollution causes many health problems and deaths, it is difficult to establish the causal connection between specific illnesses and deaths and decisions by corporations to engage in illegal pollution. Pollution by corporations that impacts public health, like corporate misconduct that victimizes consumers and workers, has historically been addressed only by regulatory law in the United States. Only recently have criminal actions been initiated against some environmental polluters in this country.

The Love Canal. One of the most infamous cases of environmental pollution by a corporation was the Love Canal disaster that surfaced in the late 1970s. Hooker Chemical Company, a subsidiary of Occidental Petroleum, purchased a tract of land near Niagara Falls, New York, in the late 1930s. For about fifteen years they used the abandoned Love Canal as a dump site for hundreds of tons of chemicals and chemical wastes (Tallmer, 1987). The site was then given to the Niagara Falls School Board in 1953 and used for school construction. Hooker allegedly had failed to notify the school board that the land had served as a chemical dumping site. Then, in 1958, three children were burned by toxic wastes, but the history of chemical dumping was still not released until the chemicals began leaking into homes in the late 1970s (Coleman, 1989). The ultimate causal linking of this pollution to disproportionate levels of miscarriages and birth defects led to a mass evacuation of 239 families from the Love Canal at a cost to taxpayers of some $200 million (Coleman, 1989).

Champion International Corporation. A 1992 ruling by a U.S. District Court set an important precedent for victims of corporate pollution. Brooks (1992) reported that a judge had denied a motion by Champion Fibers, a North Carolina paper plant, to stop suits filed against the corporation by cancer victims. The case involves a couple who had lived all their lives on the Pigeon River and had regularly consumed fish from it. Judge Hull concluded that for over eighty years Champion had dumped dioxin and other carcinogens into the river "not by accident, but as a routine byproduct of its business." Brooks (1992) notes that the judge went on to conclude that "to rule otherwise effectively closes the door to anyone who . . . has had long term exposure to the carcinogens." While only opening the door for expanded civil liability of corporate polluters who victimize the public, it at least represents a trend to hold corporations more legally accountable for imposing avoidable harm on the general public.

Crimes That *Should* Be Punishable

Patterns of avoidable harm by corporations are distressingly common. They take the form of violations of both criminal and regulatory law as well as wrongs that should be prohibited by law but are not. Much of the latter variation of corporate crime is based upon the devaluation of foreign lives. The practice of "dumping" allows corporations to continue to reap profits from the sale of products determined by U.S. regulatory agencies to be unsafe.

Dumping in Third-World Countries

The phenomenon of "dumping" relies upon the vulnerability of third-world countries. Consumers in these locales serve as targets for the distribution of unsafe products due to their greater need for a variety of products and the dearth of consumer protection. The Dalkon Shield, for example, was withdrawn from the U.S. market after it had killed at least eighteen women, but Robbins then sold (dumped) this dangerous product in some 40 third-world countries (Braithwaite, 1984).

Infant formula is another infamous example of the "crime" of corporations dumping unsafe products on unsuspecting third-world people. The powdered formula created a great risk for children in third-world countries due to the lack of access to clean water, the poor financial condition, and the illiteracy of the consumers. Third-world customers often mixed the powder with contaminated water, were too poor to mix the amount of formula needed, or could not read or fully comprehend the instructions. Consequently, many infants suffered or died as results of infections, diarrhea, and malnutrition (Ermann & Clements, 1987). The corporate offenders, however, denied that their product or marketing strategies were responsible, instead attributing the illnesses and deaths to parental neglect and an array of social problems.

In 1974, the Interfaith Center on Corporate Responsibility (ICCR), started to collect information on the issue of infant formula use in third-world countries (Ermann & Clements, 1987). In 1975, the ICCR began meeting with the U.S. infant formula producers but was unable to reach an agreement with them. In 1976, they filed suit against Bristol-Myers, a major manufacturer of infant formula, and reached a settlement to curb mass advertisement and other marketing strategies.

The Dalkon Shield and infant formula are only two examples of a widespread phenomenon, claiming countless third-world victims of deadly drugs, chemicals, pesticides, flammable clothing, and countless other products. Dowie's (1979) investigations for *Mother Jones* reveal the cunning of corporate dumpers in avoiding negative publicity and, in some cases, legal constraints:

> THE NAME CHANGE: When a product is withdrawn from the American market, receiving a lot of bad publicity in the process, the astute dumper simply changes the name.

> THE LAST MINUTE PULLOUT: When it looks as if a chemical being tested by the Environmental Protection Agency won't pass, the manufacturer will withdraw the application for registration and then label the chemical "for export only." That way, the manufacturer doesn't have to notify the importing country that the chemical is banned in the U.S.

> DUMP THE WHOLE FACTORY: Many companies, particularly pesticide manufacturers, will simply close down their American plants and begin manufacturing a hazardous product in a country close to a good market.

> THE FORMULA CHANGE: A favorite with drug and pesticide companies. Changing a formula slightly by adding or subtracting an inert ingredient prevents detection by spectrometers and other scanning devices keyed to certain molecular structures.

> THE SKIP: Brazil—a prime drug market with its large population and virulent tropical diseases—has a law that

says no one may import a drug that is not approved for use in the country of origin. A real challenge for the wily dumper. How does he do it? Guatemala has no such law; in fact, Guatemala spends very little each year regulating drugs. So, the drug is first shipped to Guatemala, which becomes the export nation.

THE INGREDIENT DUMP: Your product winds up being banned. Don't dump it. Some wise-ass reporter from *Mother Jones* will find a bill of lading and expose you. Export the ingredients separately—perhaps via different routes—to a small recombining facility or assembly plant you have set up where you're dumping it, or in a country along the way. Reassemble them and dump the product. (Dowie, 1979:25)

The Tobacco Industry

The violent consequences of marketing tobacco products are unique because, unlike poorly designed automobiles or inadequately researched drugs and pharmaceutical devices, "they are life-threatening when used as intended by the manufacturer" (National Cancer Institute, 1991). A review of research evidence concerning the harmful effects of tobacco (Brown, 1984) revealed a wide range of both short- and long-term health consequences. These findings have continued to accumulate and have been highly consistent, identifying tobacco smoking as the primary health problem in the United States (National Cancer Institute, 1991), causing the loss of about 300,000 lives annually (Clark, 1988). This death toll is several times the loss of life attributed to street crime and all other corporate misconduct combined.

The relatively recent discovery of the harmful effects of tobacco (only beginning in the 1950s and 1960s) has led to shifts in public views toward the product. Both a 1987 Gallup poll (National Cancer Institute, 1991) and a 1992 Associated Press poll (Non-smokers worry, 1992) found that a majority of all Americans favored a ban on smoking in public places. Despite an emerging consensus to legislate controls on tobacco products, the industry has resisted such regulations, spending $3.6 billion in 1990 on advertisement campaigns.

Not all victims of the tobacco industry fall into the category of consumers. Secondhand or environmental smoke has been found to carry even more carcinogens than mainstream smoke (Apostolides & Lebowitz, 1982; Breathing Other . . . , 1978; Guerin, 1980; U.S. Department of Health, Education and Welfare, 1979) and epidemiological analyses have revealed that nonsmokers with heavy exposure to other's smoke are considerably more likely to die of cancer than those with lesser levels of environmental exposure to tobacco smoke (Hirayama, 1981; Miller, 1978; Trichopoulos et al., 1981). The Environmental Protection Agency has recommended that "secondhand tobacco smoke" be labeled a known human carcinogen, exposure to which results in as many as "300,000 cases of respiratory illness and 3,000 cases of lung cancer annually" (Cloud, 1992).

Most tobacco consumers differ from patrons of other products in at least one of two ways. Tobacco is addictive and "90 percent of cigarette-smoking initiation is complete by age 21" (National Cancer Institute, 1991). Consequently the tobacco industry targets youth in their marketing strategies despite legal prohibition of selling to minors and advertising regulations that condemn the practice of directing advertisements to youth. *Rolling Stone* ads featuring "Smooth Joe Camel," free cigarettes at rock concerts, and sponsorship of car races are examples of efforts to bring youth into the market. Once addicted the consumer has less freedom of choice than consumers of most products.

A second very large group of tobacco consumers who differ from most consumer groups are third-world people who serve as victims of another variation of dumping. In the face of declining U.S. markets, attributed to increasing awareness of the dangers of smoking, tobacco conglomerates have identified developing countries as growth markets. In the absence of educational campaigns concerning the health risks of smoking and controls on advertising, these markets have grown rapidly. Shifting sales of this life-threatening product to other countries preserves corporate profits even while U.S. sales decline.

Although forty-five of fifty states have passed legislation placing constraints on smoking (National Cancer Institute, 1991) and the majority have done so through criminal statutes, cigarette manufacturers have only been subjected to regulatory actions. Following Sutherland's rationale, however, corporate violations of regulations (e.g., advertising violations) constitute corporate crime. The avoidable loss of life from tobacco use exceeds that attributed to any other form of corporate activity; as a result, our definition of corporate crime identifies tobacco sales as the most pervasive violent offense in the United States.

Workers

Many Americans have recently been victimized by one of the most pernicious corporate practices. The current euphemisms for this practice are "downsizing," "reorganization," or "corporate takeover." Regardless of the terminology, the end result is that workers are continually sacrificed in order to enhance corporate profits. While the practice of maximizing the size of the excess labor pool is as old as capitalism itself, recognition of the ramifications of this practice is just beginning.

The direct impact of the loss of employment is relatively easy assess. Homes and other possessions repossessed or sold can be counted, while surveys can determine the number of delayed purchases. The number of people without health insurance or who are underinsured can also be measured with some degree of accuracy. However, the magnitude of the psychological impact of loss of employment can never be adequately evaluated. Dislocation from family and friends, heightened tensions among family members, and increased stress on the former "breadwinner" are all manifestations of corporate misanthropy.

Yet the harm from "downsizing" or "reorganization" is not limited to the lives of the displaced workers. The victimization extends to corporations and to society. An example from a recent newspaper editorial illustrates the problem.

A man who is vice-president is told his position is being eliminated as part of reorganization. "It's nothing personal," he's told, even though he's the only one who's been "reorganized." He is devastated. It takes him two weeks to tell his grown kids. Even now, as new offers are pouring in, you can hear the bitterness of the lesson he's learned. "From now on, I'm doing what's best for me instead of worrying about the company first." (Gabriel, 1992, November)

Obviously, the relationship between employer and employee is affected by this type of exploitation. The question is how does this abuse in the workplace affect familial and social relationships? Does this "me-first" attitude lessen concern for humanity?

While this type of exploitation is not a crime in the traditional sense of the term, there can be little doubt that the quality of life of displaced workers and their families is greatly diminished. Therefore, along with racism, sexism, and classism, exploitation of workers should be considered a crime according to our definition.

Summary and Conclusions

This chapter has described the extent of corporate crime, contending that it grossly exceeds the scope of conventional street crime in terms of both quantity and impact. This level of seriousness holds true for both violent and property offenses and includes the victimization of consumers, workers, and the general public. The magnitude and seriousness of corporate crime merits considerably more attention than previously accorded. Perhaps this chapter will provide encouragement and direction toward redefining *crime* to include the harmful behavior of corporations.

The preceding examples of harmful corporate behavior illustrate the kinds of acts that are currently punishable and those that *should be* punishable. Our conceptual scheme goes beyond violations of existing criminal, civil, and administrative law to include *avoidable* harms. This inclusion sharpens the focus on violent activities of corporations that victimize employees, consumers, and the global community. This broader definition is essential to understanding and managing the problem of crime in general (Schwendinger & Schwendinger, 1975).

Understanding the full scope of crime will require acknowledgment of the role that law plays in shaping social reality. Our revised definition explicitly recognizes the relativity of law to the prevailing definition of crime. The progress in understanding and responding to corporate crime in recent years is a reflection of that relativity. The increasing number of criminal prosecutions of corporate offenders signifies evolutionary change in the administration of law. We are witnessing a shift toward a broader conceptualization of the legal and social responsibilities of corporations. However, some of the recent research suggests that while the number of prosecutions of white-collar offenders has increased, the median sentence imposed against them has decreased (Hagan & Palloni, 1986). We do not know if this trend is also true for corporate criminals (i.e., both the corporation *and* its executives). The task of the criminological community is to continue debate over the definition of crime that will facilitate expanded study of the avoidable harms that plague society.

Several recommendations are outlined in this chapter. These exhortations are based on the premise that criminology needs to shift its focus from corporate criminals to a more careful explication of corporate crime. In so doing, it has been argued that avoidable harm should serve a central role in defining crime and the social reality of crime vis-à-vis law should be explicitly acknowledged. Theory and research need to incorporate an international perspective because the true parameters of crime (i.e., avoidable harm) can only be understood outside the context of national boundaries. The international scope of crime, for example, was illustrated in the pharmaceutical, chemical, and tobacco industries. Finally, many criminologists will not be satisfied with the development of an adequate framework for studying the full gamut of corporate crime, but they will want to explore policy implications of the liberalized definition. Expanding the traditional parameters of corporate crime inquiry and policy analysis holds the potential to revolutionize theory, research, and practice within the discipline.

Understanding Corporate Criminality

REFERENCES

Apostolides, A.Y., & Lebowitz, M.D. (1982). Involuntary smoking and lung cancer: The health consequences of smoking. *Report of the Surgeon General*. Washington, DC: U.S. Government Printing Office.

Becker, H.S. (1963). *Outsiders: Studies in the sociology of deviance*. New York: Free Press.

Bixby, M.B. (1990). Was it an accident or murder? New thrusts in corporate criminal liability for work place deaths. *Labor Law Journal*, July, 417–423.

Box, S. (1983). *Power, crime, and mystification*. London: Tavistock.

Braithwaite, J. (1984). *Corporate crime in the pharmaceutical industry*. London: Routledge and Kegan Paul.

Breast implants: Assigning blame. (1992, January 27). *U.S. News & World Reports*, p. 17.

Breathing other people's smoke. (1978). *British Medical Journal, 2*, 453–454.

Brooks, J. (1992, March 25). Judge agrees to hear victims' family's case. *Johnson City Press*, p. 3.

Brown, S.E. (1984, October). *Involuntary smoking: A case of victims without crime*. Paper presented at the meeting of the Mid-South Sociological Association, Monroe, LA.

Brown, S.E., Esbensen, F., & Geis, G. (1991). *Criminology: Explaining crime and its context*. Cincinnati: Anderson.

Bureau of Justice Statistics. (1981). *Dictionary of Criminal Justice Data Terminology* (2nd ed.). Washington, DC: U.S. Government Printing Office.

Calavita, K., & Pontell, H.N. (1990). "Heads I win, tails you lose": Deregulation, crime, and crisis in the savings and loan industry. *Crime & Delinquency, 36*, 309–341.

Caudill, H.M. (1977). Dead laws and dead men: Manslaughter in a coal mine. *Nation, 226*, 492–497.

Clark, M. (1988, May 30). Getting hooked on tobacco: Is nicotine as addicting as cocaine or heroin? *Newsweek*, p. 56.

Clinard, M.B., & Yeager, P.C. (1980). *Corporate crime*. New York: Free Press.

Cloud, J. (1992, July 23). Secondhand smoke from tobacco called carcinogen by panel. *Wall Street Journal*, p. A3.

Coleman, J.W. (1989). *The criminal elite* (2nd ed.). New York: St. Martin's.

Cowley, G. (1992, February 17). Halcion takes another hit: Tainted data played a key role in FDA approval. *Newsweek*, p. 58.

Cullen, F.T., Link, B.G., & Polanzi, C.W. (1982). The seriousness of crime revisited: Have attitudes toward white-collar crime changed? *Criminology, 20*, 82–112.

Cullen, F.T., Maakestad, W.J., & Cavender, G. (1987). *Corporate crime under attack: The Ford Pinto case and beyond*. Cincinnati: Anderson.

Dowie, M. (1979). Pinto madness. In J. Skolnick & E. Currie (Eds.) *Crisis in American institutions* (pp. 23–41). Boston: Little, Brown.

Dowie, M., & Marshall, C. (1980). The Bendectin cover-up. *Mother Jones, 5*, 43–56.

Durkheim, E. (1964). *The division of labor in society*. New York: Free Press.

Edelhertz, H., & Overcast, T.D. (1982). *White-collar crime: An agenda for research*. Lexington: D.C. Heath.

Erikson, K.T. (1966). *Wayward puritans: A study in the sociology of deviance*. New York: John Wiley.

Ermann, M.D., & Clements, W.H. (1987). The campaign against marketing of infant formula in the third world. In M.D. Ermann & R.J. Lundman (Eds.), *Corporate and governmental deviance* (pp. 209–229). New York: Oxford University Press.

Evans, S.S., & Lundman, R.J. (1983). Newspaper coverage of corporate price-fixing. *Criminology, 21*, 529–541.

Frank, N. (1985). *Crimes against health and safety*. New York: Harrow and Heston.

Gabriel, J. (1992, November). Squandering our most precious resource. *The Commercial Appeal*, p. 21.

Geis, G. (1967). The heavy electrical equipment antitrust cases of 1961. In M. Clinard & R. Quinney (Eds.), *Criminal behavior systems*. New York: Holt, Rinehart and Winston.

———. (1985). Criminological perspectives on corporate regulation: A review of recent research. In B. Fisse & P.A. French (Eds.), *Corrigible corporations & unruly law* (pp. 62–84). San Antonio, TX: Trinity University.

Geis, G., & Meier, R.F. (Eds.). (1977). *White-collar crime: Offenses in business, politics, and the professions* (rev. ed.). New York: Free Press.

Gorman, C. (1992, February 10). Can drug firms be trusted? *Time Magazine*, pp. 42–44.

Green, G.S. (1990). *Occupational crime*. Chicago: Nelson-Hall.

Guerin, M.R. (1980). Chemical composition of cigarette smoke. In B. Gio & F.G. Bock (Eds.), *A safe cigarette?* (Banbury Report 3) (pp. 191–204). Cold Spring Harbor, NY: Cold Spring Harbor Laboratory.

Hagan, J., & Palloni, A. (1986). "Club fed" and sentencing of white-collar offenders before and after Watergate. *Criminology, 24*, 603–622.

Hills, S.L. (Ed.). (1987). *Corporate violence: Injury and death for profit*. Totowa, NJ: Rowman and Littlefield.

Hirayama, T. (1981). Non-smoking wives of heavy smokers have a higher risk of lung cancer: A study from Japan. *British Medical Journal, 282*, 183–185.

Hopkins, A. (1981). Class bias in the criminal law. *Contemporary Crises, 5*, 385–394.

Levenbook, B.B. (1982). Bibliographical essay/criminal harm. *Criminal Justice Ethics, 1*, 48–53.

Lewis, S. (1920). *Main street*. New York: Harcourt, Brace.

Miller, G.E. (1978). The Pennsylvania study on passive smoking. *Journal of Breathing, 41*, 5–9.

Mintz, M. (1988). At any cost: Corporate greed, women, and the Dalkon Shield. In S.L. Hills (Ed.), *Corporate violence: Injury and death for profit* (pp. 30–40). Totowa, NJ: Rowman and Littlefield.

National Cancer Institute. (1991). Strategies to control tobacco use in the United States: A blueprint for public health action in the 1990s. (NIH Publication No. 92–3316). Washington, DC: U.S. Government Printing Office.

Non-smokers worry about health. (1992, March 25). *Johnson City Press*, p. 11.

North Carolina chicken plant hit with additional fines of $144,500. (1992, January 28). *Johnson City Press*, p. 20.

Reiman, J. (1990). *The rich get richer and the poor get prison* (3rd ed.). New York: Macmillan.

Ross, E.A. (1907, January). The criminaloid. *The Atlantic Monthly, 99*, 44–50.

Schrager, L.S., & Short, J.F., Jr. (1980). How serious a crime? Perceptions of organizational and common crimes. In G. Geis & E. Stotland

(Eds.), *White-collar crime: Theory and research* (pp. 14–31). Beverly Hills: Sage.

Schwendinger, H. & Schwendinger, J. (1975). Defenders of order or guardians of human rights? In I. Taylor, P. Walton, & J. Young (Eds.), *Critical criminology* (pp. 113–146). Boston: Routledge and Kegan Paul.

Shapiro, S. (1990). Collaring the crime, not the criminal: Reconsidering "white-collar crime." *American Sociological Review, 55,* 346–365.

Sinclair, U. (1906). *The jungle.* New York: Doubleday and Page.

Smart, T. (1992, January 27). This man sounded the silicone alarm in 1976. *People Magazine,* p. 34.

Snider, L. (1991). The regulatory dance: Understanding reform processes in corporate crime. *International Journal of the Sociology Law, 19,* 209–236.

Steffens, L. (1904). *The shame of the cities.* New York: McClure, Phillips.

Stern, G.M. (1976). *The Buffalo Creek disaster: The story of the survivor's unprecedented lawsuit.* New York: Random House.

Sutherland, E.H. (1945). Is "white-collar crime" crime? *American Sociological Review, 10,* 132–139.

———. (1949). *White collar crime.* New York: Dryden.

Sutherland, E.H., & Cressey, D.R. (1974). *Principles of criminology* (9th ed.). Philadelphia: Lippincott.

Tallmer, M. (1987). Chemical dumping as a corporate way of life. In Stuart L. Hills (Ed.), *Corporate violence: Injury and death for profit* (pp. 111–120). Totowa, NJ: Rowman and Littlefield.

Tappan, P.W. (1947). Who is the criminal? *American Sociological Review, 12,* 96–102.

Tarbell, I.M. (1904). *The history of Standard Oil Company.* New York: Macmillan.

Trichopoulos D., Kalandidi, A., Sparros, L., & MacMahan, B. (1981). Lung cancer and passive smoking. *International Journal of Cancer, 27,* 1–4.

U.S. Department of Health, Education, and Welfare. (1979). *Smoking and health: A report of the surgeon general.* Washington, DC: U.S. Government Printing Office.

Vaughan, D. (1980). Crime between organizations: Implications for victimology. In G. Geis & E. Stotland (Eds.), *White-collar crime: Theory and research* (pp. 77–97). Beverly Hills, CA: Sage.

CHAPTER THREE

Assessing Victimization from Corporate Harms

B. Grant Stitt
David J. Giacopassi

- One hundred and thirty Americans die every day in automobile crashes. Many of those deaths are caused by vehicle defects and are preventable by using available vehicle crashworthiness designs.

- More than 1,000 Americans die every day from cigarette-induced disease.

- Over the next 30 years, 240,000 people—8,000 per year, one every hour—will die from asbestos-related cancer.

- The Dalkon Shield intrauterine device seriously injured tens of thousands of women who used it.

- 100,000 miners have been killed and 265,000 disabled due to coal dust (black lung) disease (Mokhiber, 1988: 3–4).

- The Environmental Protection Agency (EPA) estimated that in 1987, 2.7 billion pounds of toxic chemicals were released in the air. Over 220 cancer deaths per year in the Los Angeles area alone are predicted from the mix of air pollutants from industrial sources, highway fuels, and small businesses (U.S. Senate Subcommittee on Environmental Protection, 1989:1–2).

- People have always worried about threats over which they have little or no control—the Black Death, the disease that decimated colonial populations, and floods, earthquakes, and famines. Today, organizations can create events or products at least as threatening as those created by the natural environment (Clarke, 1989:2).

To be a citizen of the United States is to be a victim of corporate harm. Yet corporate harm is not, nor should it necessarily be equated to, corporate crime. Material acts are not without consequence. Given our state of technological development and the realization that we do not reside in a risk-free world, it is unreasonable to believe that corporations can operate without some risk to consumers, some danger to workers, and some damage to the environment. How, then, can the consequences of corporate conduct be evaluated to distinguish between crimes (civil and criminal) and unintentional (nonnegligent) harm? Since both categories of acts result in harm, how should claims of victimization be assessed?

In order to answer these questions, we must define the terms "victim" and "corporate crime." If this were a simple task, there would be consensus among criminologists as to an appropriate definition. There is not. Yet how we choose to define corporate crime will determine the scope and breadth of victimization that can result. As Packer (1968:364) stated regarding the volume of crime, "We can have as much or as little as we please, depending on what we choose to count as criminal."

Corporate Crime: The Definitional Problem

Mokhiber (1988:11) noted that corporate wrongdoing frequently is adjudicated in civil court, not criminal court. Corporate transgressions commonly result in civil suits not indictments, where consent decrees culminate in neither admission nor denial of guilt. However, Mokhiber pointed out that, "many corporate misdeeds that fall outside the narrow definition of crime as 'conviction' qualify as crimes in a more fundamental sense of the word, in that they contain the essential characteristic of crime" (1988:11).

That characteristic, according to Sutherland, is that the behavior is "prohibited by the State as an injury to the State and against which the State may react, at least as a last resort, with punishment" (1983:46). This corresponds to the definition provided by Samaha, "Crimes according to legal theory are whatever legal theory clearly defines, prohibits and prescribes a punishment for" (1987:9). From these definitions of crime, three conditions must exist: (1) a specific act must be defined by a specific law to be a crime; (2) the law must prohibit the act (in a few cases, behaviors are prescribed such as adequate testing of products or providing adequate warning labels on potentially hazardous drugs); and (3) a penalty or sanction must be decreed for violation of the law. Such a conception of crime, as Sutherland pointed out, does not require that the act *be punished*, only that it *be punishable*.

Clinard and Yeager, however, defined corporate crime as "any act committed by corporations that is punished by the state, regardless of whether it is punished under administrative, civil or criminal law" (1980:16). This definition is clearly different from Sutherland's strictly legalistic definition in two ways. First, it requires that punishment must take place. This is a reactive definition requiring recognition by some governmental authority and formal processing of the guilty party or parties. The objective fact that the violation took place does not suffice for the act to be considered a "corporate crime." Second, this is a considerably broader definition because it extends to violations of administrative and civil infractions as well as breaches of the criminal law.

Clinard and Yeager justified this expanded definition by saying that unless it is used, "it is not possible to consider violations of law by corporations in the same context as ordinary crime" (1980:16). Clinard (1990) provided a more specific rationale for such an expanded definition when he noted that the public's perception of corporate violations is that they are "noncriminal" and, thus, not serious in nature due to their relative infrequency as criminal prosecutions.[1] Clinard specifically stated that this expanded conception of corporate crime "has been adopted by many as the only way to bring the law violations of corporations into the same perspective as those of ordinary criminal offenders" (1990:15).

This inclusive definition is further justified because corporate power and influence have caused legislatures to provide a wide range of administrative and civil penalties or remedies such as warnings, injunctions, consent decrees, and noncriminal monetary settlements in lieu of criminal penalties (Clinard, 1990). Clinard still implied that even with the inclusion of civil and administrative violations, official recognition and action by governmental authorities are still required for a corporate action to be considered an instance of "corporate crime."

Similar to the Clinard and Yeager position is the conceptualization of corporate wrongdoing as instances of corporate deviance. This notion can be traced back to issues raised by C. Wright Mills (1956,1959) where he challenged sociologists to study organizational deviance. Ermann and Lundman (1982) studied the development of this conceptualization and its organizational perspective on behavior and specified two conditions that such behavior must meet. First, "the action must be contrary to norms maintained by others outside the organization," and second, "the action must be supported by internal operating norms of the organization" (Ermann & Lundman, 1982:7).

The obvious characteristic of this behavior is that it benefits the organization rather than just the individual or individuals involved. This is the same type of consideration that separates "corporate crime" from the general category of "white-collar crime" (Clinard & Quinney, 1973). Of little consideration is the issue of harm, the factor of central importance for victimization. From the corporate deviance perspective, there is no necessary dependence on either criminal, civil, or administrative laws or rules. What is essential is the attribution of the label "deviant."

For the purposes of identifying victims, the attribution of deviance as a label is extremely subjective and relativistic. Labeling depends on such factors as who commits the act in question, who views the act, who is harmed or perceives the harm, how society and its institutions react, and numerous other possibilities. The issue of the attribution of deviance ultimately depends on what is defined as normative. If, for example, virtually everyone is driving 65 miles per hour in a 55-mile-per-hour zone, breaking the law is not deviant, however driving at the legal maximum speed of 55 may be so labeled. Similarly, if all of the dairies in a state are in collusion and are fixing the prices on milk, then none is deviant, but all are monetarily victimizing the public.

Substantial confusion emerges when the concepts "corporate crime" and "corporate deviance" are used in the same discussion. For example, in his discussion of corporate deviance and corporate victimization, Shichor stated:

> In addition, this summary of classification schemes may have a practical value in policy-making aimed at curbing corporate deviance. The fact that effects of corporate violations in terms of victimization and harm are very widespread (indirect, secondary and tertiary victimization) could spur renewed efforts for educating the public about the extent and the consequences of corporate crime. (1989:82)

It is not clear why if one wished to educate the public regarding victimization resulting from corporate crime, one would not also wish to educate them about victimization resulting from what must be the broader category—corporate deviance. With these concerns in mind, it is surprising that the term corporate deviance is still used in the context of "corporate violations, corporate harms, corporate victimizations and corporate victims" as is done by Shichor (1989). Given this confusion, perhaps the solution lies in the conceptualization of the issue on the basis of victimization.

Another intriguing conceptualization is presented by Shapiro (1990) in her attempt to "liberate" the concept white-collar crime from its identification with the perpetrators to the quality and character of their misdeeds. Shapiro contended that the focus on the offender, particularly his/her social status, has been wrought with problems. The focus on the offender has hindered our understanding of the act itself, as well as the role of organizational processes and macro social forces that are at work. Shapiro further stated:

> The related concepts of white-collar crime, corporate, and occupational crime have created an imprisoning framework for contemporary scholarship, impoverishing theory, distorting empirical inquiry, oversimplifying policy analysis, inflaming our muckraking instincts, and obscuring fascinating questions about the relationship between social organization and crime. (1990:362)

She suggested that instead we study these offenses as instances of abuse of trust and in so doing "develop a conception of trust, and specify the nature of acts proscribed by norms of trust" (Shapiro, 1990:347). Her conception of trust involves viewing relationships in society in terms of fiduciary roles. She suggested we examine "how fiduciaries exploit the structural vulnerabilities of trust relationships through deception, self-interest, and, to a lesser extent, incompetence" (1990:350). Clearly, this conceptualization goes beyond violations of the criminal law and encompasses civil and administrative violations as well as violations of expectations covered in the broadest normative sense. Also, harm does not necessarily result from all violations of trust.

The Schwendingers (1975) called for an even broader definition of crime by arguing that violations of basic human rights should be the focus of criminology. They believed the operative legalistic definitions reflect the interests of the political and economic elites to the detriment of the majority in society. By limiting criminological study to infractions of official rules—whether criminal, civil or administrative—the vast majority of serious social injuries inflicted on the powerless remain beyond the pale of criminological inquiry. This point is certainly well taken; however, the "human rights" conceptualization as suggested by the Schwendingers is fraught with problems due to the complexity of defining human rights.

The definitional issues discussed above have inescapable implications for any analysis of corporate crime victimization. Although the Clinard and Yeager proposition for an expanded definition of corporate crime seems justified, Sutherland's specification that the act merely be punishable as opposed to the requirement that it be punished seems more appropriate if victimization is the concern. Clearly, there can be victims where there is no perpetrator who is caught and punished. The absence of a reaction is not a consideration relevant to the objective fact of victimization. The deviance, violation of trust, and human rights perspectives each justifiably call for an extension of traditional study of corporate crime but are themselves vague and extraordinarily difficult to measure empirically. Therefore, another alternative should be considered with the conceptual focus on the victim.

The Attribution of Victimization

Who are the victims of corporate crime? In order to address this problem, we must define the concept of victim. Originally, the term "victim" referred to "a person or animal who was put to death as a sacrifice to a supernatural power or deity" (Stitt, 1988:90). Today, however, the word victim has taken on a far broader meaning. Feinberg (1984:117) noted that the term now refers to "a person who suffers any kind of serious misfortune (and not just death or physical injury), whether through cruel or oppressive treatment by other persons, or from any kind of hard circumstances." We say that individuals can be victimized in numerous ways, such as being the victims of natural events (i.e., earthquakes or tornadoes), victims of disease or accidents, victims of war, poverty, or discrimination, or victims of crime. If we expand the definition of corporate crime to include violations of civil and administrative law, then we are no longer speaking of just corporate crime victimization.

Given this situation, it is suggested we substitute *corporate harm* for *corporate crime* and study the broader class of individuals and groups harmed by corporate acts. By making this change, we can accurately discuss victims of corporate actions as members of a common classification. At the same time we can either be concerned with only those situations where corporations have been reacted to by official reactors (the criminal justice system, civil courts, or administrative agencies), as Clinard and Yeager (1980) prefer, or we can focus on the objective factual harms generated by corporate actions, regardless of whether they are recognized and reacted to by the state.

Viano, in his discussion of major issues in research and public policy in victimology, presented the following definition of victim:

> [A] victim is any individual harmed or damaged by another or by others who perceived him- or herself as harmed, who shares the experience and seeks assistance and redress, and who is recognized as harmed and possibly assisted by public, private, or community agencies. (1989:4)

There are two key terms in this definition that deserve examination, perception, and harm. By requiring that the victim perceives harm done to him or herself, Viano creates a situation where recognition or self-labeling is necessary for victimization to occur. This is highly subjective and rules out many forms of victimization because victims may never know that they have been adversely affected by actions of corporations, most notably in areas such as environmental pollution or pathogenic conditions of the work environment. For purposes of social action such as intervention, aid, and support of victims, this self-perception aspect is no doubt important; however, from an etiological standpoint, requiring this criterion is untenable.

More important is the criterion of harm. Harm, it will be remembered, is the sole justification that John Stuart Mill (1859/1962) proposed warranted government's limitation of individual freedom. Unfortunately, he did not provide a definition of harm. Feinberg suggested that if this harm principle is to be applied, we must specify clearly how harm or a harmful condition is to be understood (1984:31–32). A broad and inclusive definition of harm was proposed by Stitt (1988). The following definition of possible wrongful setbacks of interest that constitute harm and thus renders one the status of victim shall apply in the present discussion:

> It will be assumed that a harm shall have occurred if (a) an individual is physically harmed (e.g., murder, assault or rape); (b) an individual's property is harmed (e.g., theft, or vandalism); (3) an individual is psychologically harmed

(e.g., threat of physical injury, trauma or fright); (d) an individual is socially harmed (e.g., exploitation, debasement, slander or libel); or (e) an individual's freedom is taken away (e.g., kidnapping or false imprisonment). (Stitt, 1988:92)

Beyond the notion of harm to the individual is the more abstract notion of social harm. In this vein, Feinberg distinguished two types of harm to "public interest." Exemplars of the first type of harm are "those produced by generally dangerous activity that threatens no specific persons nameable in advance, but almost anyone who happens to be in a position to be affected" (1984:223). Examples of such harms would include the manufacture and distribution of unsafe products, fraudulent advertising, unsafe work conditions, and discriminatory employment practices.

The second type of harm is to "widely shared, specific interest" (Feinberg, 1984:223). This type of harm involves "contamination of the environment and spreading of distrust" and includes air, water, and other forms of environmental pollution. Conceivably, this type of harm might have no immediate detrimental effect, but it could result in unknown and untold long-term ecological devastation.

For each of Feinberg's harms to public interests, it is individuals that ultimately are affected either physically, monetarily, or psychologically. An excellent case in point is the devastation that resulted from the dumping of 20,000 tons of more than 200 different chemical substances by the Hooker Chemical and Plastics Corporation over the course of many years into the abandoned Love Canal. The company had filled the canal with clay and sold it to a city school board. By the late 1970s, the effects became apparent to over 1,200 homeowners in the then developed area. Birth defects, spontaneous abortions, liver disorders, rare kidney diseases, and numerous other ailments could be traced to this irresponsible corporate action. Needless to say, residents suffered considerable monetary harms associated with the horror of living in the middle of a hazardous waste-disposal field. Additionally, the residents experienced great psychological trauma and will continue to for years to come. Clearly, the community as a whole, as well as individual members, were victimized.[2]

It might seem at this juncture that the definitional problems have been resolved. However, the task of specifying who are the victims of corporate actions remains. The difficulties become more apparent if the existence of "victimless crimes" is acknowledged (Schur, 1965; Schur & Bedau, 1974; Stitt, 1988). If we speak strictly of corporate crime, it is possible to conceptualize corporate crime without victims (i.e., the willing purchase of untested drugs for conditions for which there are no known cures). If, however, we do as suggested above and are concerned only with corporate harms, then the attribution of victimization may be greatly simplified. Analyzing harm as it applies to the concept "victimless crime," Stitt suggests:

> Ultimately, an important aspect of a definition of harm must be that it is an unwanted or unsought-after consequence. Therefore, if an individual freely chooses to participate in an action where he knew injuries might befall him he is not, for legal purposes, harmed if injuries result. In Feinberg's terms, his interests are not wrongfully set back, because he has chosen this outcome. (1988:92)

Of crucial importance in many instances of corporate victimization are the issues of knowingly and willingly consenting while possessing an awareness of the consequences (dangers or hazards involved) that might ensue.

The idea that truly informed consent can negate a claim to victimization is of central importance if we utilize an expanded definition of "corporate crime" including civil and administrative as well as moral violations. In our system of criminal law, crimes are considered as offenses against the state, and not individuals, though individuals are most often the direct victims. Under civil law, it is individuals or groups who are the direct victims, and under administrative law, it is the system that is somehow victimized, though indirectly it is individuals who are harmed. Dix and Sharlot noted that:

> the criminal law has not looked favorably upon the proposition that the perpetrator of a crime should be excused because the 'victim' consented to the injury before the fact or agreed, after the fact, to accept financial

compensation in lieu of pursuing criminal charges. (1980:588)

The individual under our system of law is not in the position to excuse public wrongs. However, for private wrongs (torts), where the victim's rights are at stake, the consent of the victim may mitigate or even relieve the defendant of liability.

The definition of victim provided by Viano (1989) makes no mention of the issue of consent. However, the notion of consent must play a critical role in the attribution of victimization. If, for example, an individual is warned that cigarette smoking can be dangerous to one's health, that it is addicting, and that it may lead to cancer, emphysema, or other health problems, and the individual goes on to smoke and suffers these adverse consequences—how can he or she claim to have been victimized? They may indeed suffer serious consequences, but their claim to victim status is negated by their informed consent. Harm, in the victimization sense, can only come to individuals who (1) do not give their informed consent, (2) are incapable of making a reasonable judgment, or (3) are forced or deceived into participation in a situation that results in adverse consequences to them.

Types of Corporate Harm

Because of the variety and complexity of behaviors potentially involved in corporate harm, its analysis becomes exceedingly complex. Forms of corporate harm have been variously analyzed by categorizing types of behaviors resulting in harm, types of harm generated by corporate actions, and types of victims.

Clinard and Yeager (1980) identified six main types of illegal corporate behavior. Administrative violations involve a corporation's noncompliance to legally mandated requirements, such as failure to construct pollution control facilities or failure to provide adequate information required by regulatory agencies. Environmental violations involve corporate behaviors resulting in legally proscribed levels of pollution or other harmful environmental practices. Financial violations involve monetary or securities transactions prohibited by law (bribery, securities fraud, tax violations) or omission of legally required activities of a financial nature (as failure of a corporation to record adequately terms of various types of transactions). Labor violations include employment discrimination, violation of occupational safety rules, unfair labor practices, and wage and hour violations. Manufacturing violations involve the production of products that are ineffective, defective, or dangerous. Unfair trade practices encompass behavior ranging from false advertising to price fixing to monopolistic practices (Clinard & Yeager, 1980:113–116).

While the Clinard and Yeager typology of violations is extensive and represents most forms of corporate misbehavior, other researchers have emphasized the types of corporate actions that are potentially most serious and disruptive to society. Cullen, Link, and Polanzi (1982), for example, specified a form of corporate crime termed "government corruption," where corporations bribe government officials and thereby undermine our system of government. A second form of particularly injurious corporate harm was termed "violent white-collar offenses" by Cullen, Link, and Polanzi (1982) and "corporate violence" by Hills (1987). These offenses occur when defective or dangerous corporate practices or products result in death or serious injury to a corporation's workers or customers. While both government corruption and violent offenses may be subsumed under categories in Clinard and Yeager's classification system, Cullen and associates believed the significant nature of the behavior should be the focal point of a classification system dealing with types of corporate harm.

Other researchers have focused on the type of harm itself. Meier and Short (1982) identified physical, financial, and moral harms as types of harm associated with corporate misbehavior. Clearly, in the mind of the public, financial harm has been associated most prominently with corporate wrongdoing. Price fixing, monopolistic practices, price gouging, windfall profits, and a variety of other terms indicate the public's familiarity with corporate attempts to maximize profits. Sutherland and Cressey noted that "the extraordinary development of fraud in modern life has been an aspect of the drive for profits" (1974:44).

McCaghy (1980) argued that profit maximization is the most prominent reason for corporate deviance. Similarly, most academic research of corporate crime has focused on economic loss rather than physical harm (Schrager & Short, 1978).

However, increasingly, physical harm is being linked to corporate crime. Prominent cases such as the Ford Pinto, Dalkon Shield, and the Bhopal-Union Carbide disaster all represent death or serious injury in the mind of the public. Cullen, Maakestad, and Cavender (1987) argued that as the physical danger associated with corporate crime penetrates the public's consciousness, the public's conception of corporate crime changes, and the public increasingly views corporate crime as "serious business."

While financial and physical harms are now commonly associated with corporate crime, other types of harm have less tangible consequences. The damage to moral climate identified by Meier and Short (1982:27) refers to the broader consequences of corporate deviance. Sutherland (1949) long ago noted that one of the most serious consequences of white-collar crime is that it resulted in destruction of trust in social institutions and "the erosion of the moral base of our society." Meier and Short elaborated on this theme, linking corporate crime to increased social alienation, decreased social confidence, and damage to society's "moral climate and social fabric" (1982:35–36). Specifically, Meier and Short noted that because of the high social standing and respectability of those involved,

> these violations create cynicism and foster the attitude that "if others are doing it, I will too." More fundamentally, it is held that white-collar crime threatens the [trust] that is basic to community life, e.g., between citizens and government officials, professionals and their clients, businessmen and their customers, employers and employees, and even more broadly, among members and between members and nonmembers of the collectivity. (1982:27–28)

Though these comments were made with regard to white-collar crime in general, they clearly apply most fundamentally to large trusted corporations, many of which are virtually institutionalized in our society. Though broadly perceived as a social harm, this harm is manifested at the individual level by the psychological consequences that can result from corporate wrongdoing. Where loss of trust connotes a hesitancy in establishing or continuing a business relationship with a corporation, "loss of trust" does not adequately convey the psychological consequences of victimization.

In a study of the bankruptcy of an industrial banking corporation, Shover, Fox, and Mills (1991) identified a significant number of victims who were characterized as "devastated" by the institution's failure. The devastation was less financial than psychological as several of the victims were characterized as despondent, having suffered "inestimable psychological suffering," and characterizing their lives as having been "destroyed" as a result of the experiences (1991:14). While clearly not all victims of corporate deviance suffer extreme psychological consequences, it nevertheless appears common enough and of sufficient importance to merit recognition.

The last means of categorizing corporate harm is by type of victim. Sellin and Wolfgang (1964) identified three general types of victims of crime that are appropriate to an analysis of victims of corporate crime. Primary victimization occurs when an individual suffers physical harm or financial loss as a direct consequence of illegal activity. Secondary victimization generally refers to commercial establishments or organizations. The victimization is impersonal, commercial, and collective but not so diffuse as to include the community at large. Tertiary victimization extends to the larger community and includes environmental, administrative, and governmental offenses.

McCaghy (1980) distinguished three types of victims of corporate crime: the general public, consumers, and employees. Crimes against the general public include such offenses as restraint of trade or bribery of public officials. Crimes against consumers range from false advertising to the manufacture of ineffective or dangerous products. Crimes against employees most typically involve violations of workplace safety requirements. McCaghy argued that the workplace environment is, in fact, one of the most hazardous yet is one of the least recognized dangers in society (1980:197).

Shichor (1989) added, but failed to elaborate on, a fourth type of victim of corporations, the owners (stockholders) of corporations that engage in corporate crime. Because of the nature of most large corporations, stockholders have little direct knowledge and no hands-on experience in the daily operation of the corporation. Corporate officers, government regulators, auditors, and accountants are entrusted by shareholders to perform their duties in a diligent and law-abiding manner. When this fails to happen, the consequences for the shareholders can be substantial, including the bankruptcy of the corporation and total loss of investment by thousands of shareholders. Although shareholders theoretically provide oversight of the corporate directors, this is equivalent to *caveat emptor* and holding retail customers of corporations responsible for the purchase of defective merchandise. In reality, the stockholders can also be victimized by corporate wrongdoing.

The Paradox of Victimization

If victims of street crime are neglected and generally relegated to a secondary status in the criminal justice process, victims of corporate crime are almost totally invisible with no perceptible impact on the functioning of the criminal justice system. Several authors have suggested reasons for the absence of official recognition for victims of corporate crime.

First, corporate crime is seen as resulting almost exclusively in minor and diffuse harm. Rarely is this harm believed to affect individuals significantly, either physically or monetarily. Thus, while overcharging a few cents per gallon for gasoline may result in millions of dollars of profit for oil companies, it does not substantially impact the financial condition of ordinary citizens.

Second, the difficulties in identifying and investigating corporate crime are immense. Most often, the culpable acts are committed in private and are not open to public or even law enforcement scrutiny. The corporate bureaucracy isolates the executive in the same way the hierarchical structure of organized crime protects its leaders from incrimination. As a result, rarely can criminal intent be demonstrated and linked to specific individuals within the corporation. Thus, civil and administrative remedies are most frequently sought with the corporation as the defendant.

In addition to lack of access, law enforcers often lack the specialized technical skills necessary to detect or investigate corporate crimes, such as environmental pollution or accounting irregularities. Furthermore, the effect of corporate wrongdoing may occur in places distant from the locus of corporate power, as was the case of the Union Carbide plant in Bhopal, India, where the explosive release of 40 tons of deadly gases into the atmosphere resulted in 200,000 injuries—30,000 to 40,000 of them classified as serious—and the deaths of up to 5,000 inhabitants.[3]

Third, Evans and Lundman (1983) maintained that corporations escape public condemnation because the media "fail to provide frequent, prominent, and criminally oriented coverage" of corporate crime (1983:530). The media deflect attention from corporate crime to more dramatic types of crime that involve both a sinister offender and a "senseless" act of violence. While corporate crime can have similar components, frequently it involves complex legal and technical violations of the law not understood fully by either the news reporter or the average reader. Cases involving corporations can drag on for years without ever resulting in a definitive conclusion that makes it difficult for the media to cover and to convey adequately the issues to the public. Consequently, news media images of crime generally exclude corporate crime, while the images of street crime help to initiate and sustain public stereotypes of crime, criminals, and victims that are further amplified by television and film.

Fourth, corporations are politically powerful entities. Through political action committees (PAC), corporations can channel enormous sums of money to elect state and federal legislators who are sympathetic to big business. From January 1987 through June 1988, corporate PACs provided over $36 million to various political campaigns (Novack, 1989:108). These funds, along with the lobbying efforts of corporations and their trade organizations, insure that business executives have access to legislators and their staffs in order to express their sentiments whenever corporate interests are threatened.

Finally, corporations can hire the best legal talent and develop specialized legal expertise that can provide the corporation with a dominant position in dealing with individual complainants and shaping government regulations. Galanter (1974) argued that corporations have become adept at influencing the laws and regulations that govern their activities. As "repeat players," corporations have long-term views that allow them to "play for the rules." Since corporations are involved in numerous disputes over time, they can be selective in the cases they litigate, vigorously pursuing only those cases that have a high likelihood of resulting in favorable precedents, settling others before reaching court and thereby avoiding the establishment of unfavorable precedents. All of these factors combine to diminish the role and visibility of corporate crime and its victims.

As a result, little research has been conducted on the reactions of victims to corporate crime. Research has indicated that reactions common to all types of victimization include feelings of shock, anxiety, helplessness and depression (Frederick, 1980; Horowitz, 1980; Janoff-Bulman, 1985). Janoff-Bulman and Frieze (1988) identified an increased sense of vulnerability, a heightened perception of the world as lacking in meaning and order, and a diminished view of oneself as common in all types of victimization. These reactions are heightened to the degree that, prior to victimization, the individuals believed themselves to be invulnerable and in control of their own fates.

Janoff-Bulman (1985:500) noted that while the shattering of basic assumptions about an "illusion of invulnerability" provides a means of analyzing all forms of the victimization experience, the consequences of criminal victimization differ in several important ways from the consequences of noncriminal victimization.[4] Criminal victimization typically involves an offender who commits an act intended to cause harm to an individual singled out for victimization. Noncriminal victimizations, due to disease or acts of nature, lack the criminal intent as well as the element of victim selection. Consequently, criminal victimization induces both greater self-doubt and increased awareness of hostility and unpredictability as elements of an individual's social reality. Fisher (1984:167) found that criminal victimization "most radically traumatized . . . the victim's sense of community."

Several aspects of corporate crime distinguish its victimizations from that of more traditional forms of criminal activities. Primary among these distinctions is that harm is frequently (although not necessarily) less focused and more diffuse (secondary and tertiary victimizations). Individuals may experience injury, but the impact of harm is typically lessened for any particular individual. Second, due to the inability to establish criminal intent, corporations and not individuals are the defendants in the resulting criminal and civil cases. The organization is held to blame and its procedures faulted, but the organization is not perceived as evil. Third, the motivation underlying the harm-inducing behavior is not intentionally to maim or injure. McCaghy (1980) asserted that profit maximization is the single most compelling factor behind corporate deviance. While this motivation clearly can lead to injury or even death, physical harm is not the intent driving the behavior. Janoff-Bulman argued that technological disasters often involve a guilty party, but "one would not claim . . . that the specific intention involved in dam failures, power plant failures, or toxic waste disposal was to harm other people" (1985:501). Due to the absence of a "ruthless design," the consequences of the act are most often less traumatic psychologically to the victim. Fourth, individuals are not selected for victimization by the corporation. As a consequence, the victim's perception of involvement is less problematic since the victim does not question the personal attributes that might have led to being selected for victimization. Instead, the victimization is seen as the result of an unfortunate confluence of circumstances that placed the victim in jeopardy.[5]

The Government's Role in Corporate Victimization

Built into the criteria governing regulation of harmful corporate actions is a balancing of potential individual harm and public interest. Regulatory agencies weigh the harm generated by the corporate actions against such factors as the economic impact sanctions would exact from the corporation, as well as hardships imposed upon the wider community. For example, the Toxic Substances Control Act of 1977 specifies that regulators, in fulfilling the primary purpose of the statute, should not "impede unduly or create unnecessary economic barriers to technological innovation" (Thomas, 1982:104). OSHA regulations similarly include economic impact as a factor to be considered in enforcement of safety standards in the workplace (Thomas, 1982). In effect, greater tolerance is exercised by the government when assessing potential harm generated by corporations since factors other than the harm are considered when assessing the harm-inducing behavior.

This governmental forbearance of harmful corporate behaviors extends to the sanctioning process as well. Regulatory agencies institutionalize the belief that criminalization of corporate harm results in an adversarial process that hinders effective regulation by decreasing cooperation, thereby increasing the potential for continued abuse (Scholz, 1984). Consequently, when corporate harm requires government intervention, the regulatory agencies do not initially seek to punish but to elicit compliance under the assumption that cooperation and goodwill are essential to effective corporate regulation (Snider, 1990). It is only when the cooperative model has failed and substantial harm has resulted that the criminal process is initiated (Shapiro, 1985).

Although several authors have advocated a cooperative or an "enforced self-regulation" model as the most effective means of corporate regulation (Braithwaite, 1982; Scholz, 1984), several problems are apparent from a victimization perspective. First is the unproven assumption that formal and public governmental actions against corporations have no deterrent value. Fisse and Braithwaite (1983:313) concluded that since corporations are dependent upon the goodwill of the public, disclosure of corporate misdeeds is appropriate, particularly for "egregious cases where emphatic stigmatizing is necessary for the purposes of specific or general deterrence."

A second problem of the self-regulation model is that of "capture" where the cooperative relationship leads to the co-optation of the regulators by the regulated (Braithwaite, 1982; Snider, 1990). Another form of capture is when the industry becomes influential in determining the composition of the regulations. The lobbying efforts of the Business Roundtable, for example, appear influential in requiring a "knowing" instead of a "reckless" state of mind in most instances of criminal liability. Similarly, the Business Roundtable argued against including "reckless failure to supervise" as a sufficient condition to permit individual criminal liability of corporation executives, arguing that it would result in conviction "without consciousness of or participation in the wrongdoing" (Senate Judiciary Committee, 1987:7).

While many believe this phenomenon of capture to be a modern development, Pepinsky and Jesilow have described the situation in 1882 when a former railroad attorney became attorney general and helped establish the Interstate Commerce Commission's regulation of railroads. The attorney general wrote at that time to the president of the Burlington Railroad that the Interstate Commerce Commission

> can be of great use to the railroads. It satisfies the popular clamor for government supervision of railroads, at the same time that supervision is almost entirely minimal. The part of wisdom is not to destroy the commission, but to utilize it. (Pepinsky & Jesilow, 1988:68)

Corporations apply their political power directly as Clinard (1990) noted in his discussion of abuses of the democratic process. Clinard pointed out that corporations, "conscript the political process for their own benefit through their large financial contributions, both legal and illegal" (1990:6). Powerful cabinet and regulatory agency positions are often held by former top corporate executives, and this influence coupled with strong lobbying and substantial, and often illegal, campaign contributions causes politicians to listen when the corporations speak (Clinard, 1990).

A third problem of the regulatory process as it now exists is that some intentional harm to citizens is tolerated by the government if this harm is committed by a corporate entity. The level of harm is not specified but is clearly tolerated up to the point that the harm inducing behavior elicits a punitive regulatory response. In effect, a threshold level of victimization is institutionalized in government regulatory mechanisms. At the very least, concern must be raised at the apparent double standard applied to "suite crime" versus "street crime" in relation to both offender and victim.

Reiman (1990) has written that the definition of crime should include any intentional act that is harmful to society. He argued that there is no moral justification for treating indirect harm—the type of harm most likely to result from corporate actions—as less evil than the one-on-one harm characteristic of ordinary criminal conduct. Yet the government's response to corporate harm is clearly based on a different model than that utilized in assessing noncorporate criminal conduct. It is a model that recognizes victimization through intentionally generated harm, yet does not incorporate, except in extreme circumstances, attribution of criminal responsibility to the intentionally induced victimization. It seems that regulatory agencies are generally inclined to invoke the criminal process only when corporate acts are so egregious as to undermine confidence in the capitalist system.

Conclusions

We began with the idea that not all harm committed by corporations is blameworthy. McCaghy (1980:299) has similarly observed that when studying corporations, academics must guard against sweeping indictments of the entire economic system as one based on exploitation *vis à vis* profit maximization. Yet most would agree with Geis and Edelhertz that "the history of attitudes toward . . . controllers of production processes is . . . to show a tendency of legislators and courts to ignore or be permissive toward the acquisitive excesses of such persons in their occupational roles" (1973:989).

White has written that the corporation should be viewed as a "collective citizen." As such, it has the same responsibilities and should be held to the same standards of conduct as other citizens. White concludes that

> to say that a corporation's only goal is to make money would be to define the business corporation . . . as a kind of shark that lives off the community rather than as an important agency in the construction, maintenance, and transformation of our shared lives. (1985:1416)

Consistent with this broader view of the corporation, the present analysis has argued that studying victims of corporate harm may be a superior strategy to studying the incidence of corporate crime through official reports. Definitions of criminal, civil, or administrative wrongs and the imposition of appropriate sanctions are hindered by numerous political, economic, and social realities. It is doubtful that these realities will change; therefore, it is questionable whether criminologists will ever be able to study effectively corporate crime or its variations.

By shifting the unit of analysis from corporate crime to victims of corporate harm, several advantages accrue. Victimization can be defined by objective criteria that avoid the criminal/civil/administrative distinctions, negate issues of intent, and obviate the need for criminologists to access unavailable or closely guarded corporate data.

While the proposed shift in focus extends the analysis beyond the normal realm of criminological inquiry, it has the advantage of studying all corporate actions that result in harm that, arguably, is the real concern of society. Furthermore, since a single act of corporate harm can affect a variable number of citizens in the society, studying acts of corporate harm is not as socially relevant as analyzing the consequences of these acts for the citizenry.

The shift in focus to an analysis of corporate harm has solid criminological underpinnings. From Sutherland's decision to include civil and criminal infractions in his classic study of white-collar crime (1949), to the exhortations of Chambliss (1989) to study "state-organized crime," to the Schwendingers' (1975) concern that we focus on "human rights," criminologists are going beyond the traditional bounds of criminological research.

Similarly, Elias has argued that victimology, by accepting "official or criminological definitions" of crime, is doing a disservice to victims (1985:5). He stated that a new victimology is needed based on "human rights" since traditionally, "the definitions we have chosen, or at least accepted, represent neither 'natural' nor 'scientific' nor 'popular' boundaries" (Elias, 1985). Viano presented the possibility of expanding the traditional scope of victimology when he wrote that "whether victims of natural disasters, war, environmental pollution, the closing of a factory . . . how one is harmed is irrelevant . . . what counts is being harmed"[6] (1989:4).

Clearly, both criminology and victimology are expanding their realms of inquiry relative to corporations. As Bellah and associates argued in *The Good Society* (1991), "The corporation must be held accountable to larger constituencies—the communities that have given it tax advantages and public facilities, suppliers and customers, a general public that expects from it ecological responsibility, ethical practice, and fair dealing." (Bellah et al., 1991:102). It appears appropriate, if not inevitable, that criminology and victimology should join to bring the corporation into full democratic accounting.

NOTES

1. Several studies contradict the view that the public perceives crime as minor. See Cullen, Maakestad, and Cavender (1987) for a discussion of the public's perception of corporate crime.

2. For a discussion of communities as victims of corporate crimes, see Meyer (1981).

3. Exact casualty and injury figures will never be known due to inadequate disaster response. For example, many families reportedly buried their dead before they could be counted. Also the effects of long-term complications such as infertility and the carcinogenic, mutagenic, or teratogenic effects cannot be calculated.

4. It should be noted that Janoff-Bulman's description of criminal victimization is not broad enough to include many types of corporate crime. Noncriminal victimization includes harm caused by diseases, accidents, and natural disasters.

5. Some criminologists argue, counter to Janoff-Bulman's (1985) views, that if the full extent of the harms caused by corporations were known, the public would experience a greater fear of victimization from corporate crime than street crime precisely because the harm is generated by established, trusted, and powerful social entities (Meier & Short, 1982; Reiman, 1990).

6. Viano recognized that by extending the term "victim" to encompass those who suffer from such things as corporate harm, he was vulnerable to charges that he was politicizing the field of victimology. However, he observed that "social research is inescapably political, although usually (and ironically) only the research aimed at changing the system is so labelled" (1983:54).

REFERENCES

Bellah, R., Madsen, R., Sullivan, W., Swidler, A., & Tipton, S. (1991). *The good society*. New York: Alfred A. Knopf.

Braithwaite, J. (1982). Enforced self-regulation: A new strategy for corporate crime control. *Michigan Law Review, 80*, 1466–1507.

Chambliss, W. (1989). State-organized crime. *Criminology, 27*(2), 1983–208.

Clarke, L. (1989). *Acceptable risk? Making decisions in a toxic environment*. Berkeley: University of California Press.

Clinard, M.B. (1990). *Corporate corruption*. New York: Praeger.

Clinard, M.B., & Quinney, R. (1973). *Criminal behavior systems: A typology* (2nd ed.). New York: Holt, Rinehart and Winston.

Clinard, M.B., & Yeager, P.C. (1980). *Corporate crime*. New York: Free Press.

Cullen, F.T., Link, B.G., & Polanzi, C.W. (1982). The seriousness of crime revisited: Have attitudes toward white-collar crime changed?" *Criminology, 20*(1), 83–102.

Cullen, F.T., Maakestad, W.J., & Cavender, G. (1987). *Corporate crime under attack: The Ford Pinto case and beyond.* Cincinnati: Anderson.

Dix, G.F., & Sharlot, M.M. (1980). *Basic criminal law.* St. Paul: West.

Elias, R. (1985). Transcending our social reality of victimization: Toward a new victimology of human rights. *Victimology, 10,* 5–25.

Ermann, M.D., & Lundman, R.J. (Eds.). (1982). *Corporate and governmental deviance* (2nd ed.). New York: Oxford University Press.

Evans, S.S., & Lundman, R.J. (1983). Newspaper coverage of corporate price-fixing. *Criminology, 21*(4), 529–541.

Feinberg, J. (1984). *The moral limits of criminal law.* Vol. 1. *Harm to others.* New York: Oxford University Press.

Fisher, C. (1984). A phenomenological study of being criminally victimized: Contributions and constraints of qualitative research. *Journal of Social Issues, 40,* 161–177.

Fisse, B., & Braithwaite, J. (1984). *The impact of publicity on corporate offenders.* Albany: State University of New York Press.

Frederick, C. (1980). Effects of natural vs. human-induced violence. *Evaluation and Change, 7,* 71–75.

Galanter, M. (1974). Why the "Haves" come out ahead: Speculations on the limits of legal change. *Law and Society Review, 9*(1), 95–160.

Geis, G., & Edelhertz, H. (1973). Criminal law and consumer fraud: A sociological view. *The American Criminal Law Review, 11*(4), 989–1010.

Hills, S.L. (Ed.). (1987). *Corporate violence: Injury and death for profit.* Totowa, NJ: Rowman & Littlefield.

Horowitz, M.J. (1980). Psychological response to serious life events. In V. Hamilton & D. Warburton (Eds.), *Human stress and cognition* (pp. 235–263). New York: Wiley.

Janoff-Bulman, R. (1985). Criminal vs. noncriminal victimization: Victims' reactions. *Victimology, 10*(1–4), 498–511.

Janoff-Bulman, R., & Frieze, I. (1988). A theoretical perspective for understanding reactions to victimization. *Journal of Social Issues, 39*(2), 1–17.

McCaghy, C.H. (1980). *Crime in American society.* New York: Macmillan.

Meier, R.F., & Short, J.F., Jr. (1982). The consequences of white-collar crime. In H. Edelhertz & T.D. Overcast (Eds.), *White-collar crime: An agenda for research* (pp. 23–49). Lexington, MA: D.C. Heath.

Meyer, P.B. (1981). Communities as victims of corporate crimes. In B. Galaway & J. Hudson (Eds.), *Perspectives on crime victims* (pp. 33–43). St. Louis, MO: C.V. Mosby.

Mill, J.S. (1859/1962). On liberty. In M. Warnick (Ed.), *John Stuart Mill* (pp. 126–250). New York: New American Library.

Mills, C.W. (1956). *The power elite.* New York: Oxford University Press.

———. (1959). *The sociological imagination.* New York: Oxford University Press.

Mokhiber, R. (1988). *Corporate crime and violence.* San Francisco: Sierra Club Books.

Novack, J. (1989). Influence for sale. *Forbes, 143,* 108–109.

Packer, H. (1968). *The limits of the criminal sanction.* Stanford, CA: Stanford University Press.

Pepinsky, H.E., & Jesilow, P. (1988). *Myths that cause crime.* Cabin John, MD: Seven Locks.

Reiman, J. (1990). *The rich get richer and the poor get prison* (3rd ed.). New York: Macmillan.

Samaha, J. (1987). *Criminal law.* St. Paul: West.

Scholz, J. (1984). Voluntary compliance and regulatory enforcement. *Law & Policy, 6*(4), 385–404.

Schrager, L.S., & Short, J.F., Jr. (1978). Toward a sociology of organizational crime. *Social Problems, 25*(4), 407–419.

Schur, E.M. (1965). *Crimes without victims.* Englewood Cliffs, NJ: Prentice-Hall.

Schur, E.M., & Bedau, H.A. (1974). *Victimless crimes: Two sides of a controversy.* Englewood Cliffs, NJ: Prentice-Hall.

Schwendinger, H., & Schwendinger, J. (1975). Defenders of order or guardians of human rights? In I. Taylor, P. Walton, & J. Young (Eds.), *Critical criminology* (pp. 113–146). London: Routledge & Kegan Paul.

Sellin, T., & Wolfgang, M.E. (1964). *The measurement of delinquency.* New York: Wiley.

Senate Judiciary Committee. (1987, April 17 and May 8). *Hearings on oversight of the problem of white collar crime.* Washington, DC: U.S. Government Printing Office.

Shapiro, S.P. (1985). The road not taken: The elusive path to criminal prosecution for white collar offenders. *Law and Society Review, 19*(2), 179–217.

———. (1990). Collaring the crime, not the criminal: Reconsidering the concept of white-collar crime. *American Sociological Review*, *55*(3), 346–365.

Shichor, D. (1989). Corporate deviance and corporate victimization: A review and some elaborations. *International Review of Victimology*, *1*, 67–88.

Shover, N., Fox, G.L., & Mills, M. (1991). *Victimization by white-collar crime and institutional delegitimation*. Manuscript submitted for publication.

Snider, L. (1990). Cooperative models and corporate crime: Panacea or cop-out? *Crime & Delinquency*, *36*(3), 373–390.

Stitt, B.G. (1988). Victimless crime: A definitional issue. *Journal of Crime and Justice*, *11*(2), 87–102.

Sutherland, E. [1949] (1983). *White-collar crime: The uncut version*. New Haven: Yale University Press.

Sutherland, E., & Cressey, D. (1974). *Principles of Criminology* (9th ed.). Philadelphia: J.B. Lippincott.

Thomas, J. (1982). The regulatory role in the containment of corporate illegality. In H. Edelhertz & T. Overcast (Eds.), *White-collar crime: An agenda for research* (pp. 88–112). Toronto: D.C. Heath.

U.S. Senate Subcommittee on Environmental Protection. (1989). *Hearing on Clean Air Amendments of 1989* (S.Hrg. 101–331, Pt.1). Washington, DC: U.S. Government Printing Office.

Viano, E. (1983). Violence, victimization and social change: A sociocultural and public policy analysis. *Victimology*, *8*, 54.

———. (1989). Victimology today: Major issues in research and public policy. In E. Viano (Ed.), *Crime and its victims: International research and public policy issues* (pp. 3–14), Proceedings of the Fourth International Institute on Victimology. New York: Hemisphere.

White, J.B. (1985). How should we talk about corporations: The languages of economics and citizenship. *Yale Law Journal*, *94*, 1416–1425.

CHAPTER FOUR

Public Perceptions of Corporate Crime

T. David Evans
Francis T. Cullen
Paula J. Dubeck

At the turn of the century E. A. Ross (1907) expressed his dismay over society's failure to punish and control rich and powerful "criminaloids." Perceiving extreme public indifference toward this new "variety of sin," Ross (1907:viii) declared that citizen reactions in "today's warfare on sin . . . are about as serviceable as gongs and stink-pots in modern battle." Similarly, about three decades later Sutherland (1940) complained that the public was not aroused by white-collar crime. Echoing Sutherland's sentiments thirty years hence, the President's Commission on Law Enforcement and the Administration of Justice (1968:158) concluded that "the public tends to be indifferent to business crime or even to sympathize with the offenders who have been caught."

Many early commentators on white-collar crime were discouraged about the prospects of controlling such illegality because they linked public apathy, based on ignorance of the enormous costs of upperworld crime, with minimal punishment. Ross (1907:59) believed, for example, that socially irresponsible business practices escaped "both punishment and ignominy" because public sentiment supported neither criminalization nor vigorous enforcement of existing codes. Sutherland (1940:11) also held that upperworld criminality went unpunished "because the community is not organized solidly against that behavior."

In contrast to Ross and Sutherland, other observers are neither puzzled nor dismayed by the fact that upperworld crime escapes public censure or heavy legal sanctioning (Kadish, 1977; Wilson, 1975). Kadish (1977) claimed, for example, that criminal sanctions are ineffective deterrents of white-collar crime because public sentiment against such offenses is weak (cf. Packer, 1968). Similarly, Wilson (1975:x), contrasting white-collar with common crime, asserted that "predatory street crime is a far more serious matter [to most citizens] than consumer fraud, antitrust violations. . . ."

Although Ross and Sutherland diverge from Kadish and Wilson on the issue of why members of the public are relatively indifferent to elite criminality, or indeed if citizens should be concerned about it at all, the views of all four commentators converge in the conclusion that the "public is 'condoning, indifferent, or ambivalent' toward business crime" (Conklin, 1977:17). The appeal of this perspective, however, may be based on a misreading of empirical reality. Research to be reviewed below indicates that the public is—and may have always been— indignant about the misdeeds of white-collar criminals and willing to exact harsh punishments, including criminal sanctions, for some white-collar and corporate crimes.

In this chapter, we first review findings of empirical research on public attitudes—perceptions of seriousness and deserved punishment—toward white-collar and, especially, corporate crime. Second, we focus on understanding public attitudes in the context of broader social and cultural shifts. We argue that contemporary attitudes toward business crime as a "hazard" (Meier & Short, 1985) can be more fully understood within the contexts of changing perceptions of risk, declining confidence in public and private institutions, and new demands for equitable treatment within the criminal justice system. Finally, we consider the prospects for continued public concern about business illegalities and the impact that such apprehensions may have on criminal justice policy and practice.

Evaluating Corporate Crime

Public attitudes toward white-collar and corporate crime have usually been examined by asking respondents to either rate the seriousness of such crimes relative to common crimes or to recommend appropriate levels of punishment. Although most reviewers of the literature have considered seriousness and punishment studies together, there is reason to believe that the two constructs are not interchangeable measures of moral indignation. Just as perceptions of crime seriousness are complex and determined by a number of factors (Sykes & Blum-West, 1978), it is likely that punishment attitudes are also complicated and may not be directly inferable from judgments of seriousness. Indeed, Rossi, Simpson, and Miller (1985:89) found that "there is not a one-to-one relationship between the seriousness measures of crimes and desired sanctions but rather . . . seriousness is modified by the characteristics of offenders and victims and by the consequences of the crimes in question."

Further, while a crime may be quite serious to a respondent in the abstract, perceptions of "just desserts" may depend on specific mitigating or aggravating circumstances of the crime event (Frank, Cullen, Travis, & Borntrager, 1989; Grabosky, Braithwaite, & Wilson, 1987) Therefore, while recognizing that seriousness and punishment ratings are related indicators of public concern about white-collar crime, we treat these constructs separately.

Let us add one other introductory comment. Whether asked by researchers to rate seriousness or suggest punishments, the public is normally presented with crime inventories in which white-collar offenses engaged in for individual gain have been mixed with corporate offenses. As a subset of white-collar crime, corporate illegalities are collective and organized endeavors with the primary goal of profit or other benefit for the corporation. Since white-collar and corporate crimes have not been clearly distinguished in the literature, we review public attitudes on these two forms of upperworld crime together, making special reference to corporate offenses where possible.

The Public View:
Seriousness of Corporate and White-Collar Crime

Although they may be separate constructs, it is reasonable to assume that a perception of "seriousness" is a necessary condition for criminalization and punishment of conduct. The "consensus model" of criminal justice also makes the point that since the public does not consider white-collar crime to be as serious as street crime, harsher punishment should be reserved for the latter. For these reasons, we first review the literature on seriousness.

Violent Corporate and White-Collar Crime

A 1969 Harris poll provided a glimpse of the public's sentiment toward violent corporate crimes when it found that a manufacturer of an unsafe automobile was regarded with much more disapproval than a mugger (68 percent for the automaker versus 22 percent for the mugger). When distinctions by impact have been made—as in this case—surveys have routinely found that the public is most alarmed about business practices that cause or threaten physical harm as contrasted with those having only economic impacts.

Seriousness studies, however, have not always differentiated reactions to white-collar crime by the level of harm. In a pre-Watergate study, in which 200 Baltimore residents rated 140 offenses, white-collar crimes were perceived as less serious than all other categories except public order crimes (Rossi, Waite, Bose, & Berk, 1974). Even victimless offenses were perceived as more serious. Not surprisingly, Rossi et al. (1974) concluded that the public does not regard white-collar crimes as particularly serious.

In their reanalysis of Rossi et al.'s (1974) data, Schrager & Short (1980:16) noted that although the "economic harm caused by organizational illegality is often recognized to far exceed the costs of common crime . . . little as yet is known about the physical harm." After separating organizational offenses from the entire group of white-collar items in the inventory, they found that organizational crimes with physical impacts were perceived as much more serious than those with economic impacts. In comparing upperworld to common crimes, they also found that organizational and ordinary crimes with similar impact—physical or economic—were considered equally severe as evidenced by the association of their seriousness rankings.

The strategy of distinguishing types of white-collar crimes also was followed by Cullen, Link, and Polanzi (1982) in their replication of Rossi et al.'s (1974) work. After differentiating the twenty-two white-collar offenses amenable to classification, Cullen et al. (1982) found that the public was relatively unconcerned about such types of crime as price fixing, defrauding consumers, and income tax fraud. The strongest moral condemnation was reserved for violent corporate crimes, crimes against a business organization (embezzlement), and governmental corruption. Although the twelve top-ranked crimes by seriousness involved homicides by persons, "knowingly selling contaminated food which results in death" was rated the thirteenth most serious of all crimes listed and was ranked ahead of three forms of homicide. As further evidence of the public's concern about corporate crimes with serious physical impacts, "causing the death of an employee by neglecting to repair machinery" and "manufacturing and selling drugs known to be harmful to users" were ranked as more serious than two forms of homicide.

An important insight of the Cullen et al. (1982) and Schrager and Short (1980) studies is that public response to white-collar crime is not unitary. The highest ratings are reserved for white-collar offenses which cause or threaten physical harm (cf. Sykes & Blum-West, 1978). An analytical approach which recognizes distinctions by the nature of the consequences of the act is necessary because "people appear to evaluate [the seriousness of] both common and organizational offenses in terms of impact" (Schrager & Short, 1980:26).

Other observers have also found this same pattern when the public ranks crimes by seriousness, indicating that the factor of harm to individuals supersedes categorical crime labels when crimes with comparable impacts are rated. Sinden (1980) found, for example, that the violent act of an "employer failing to repair machinery which results in the death of a worker" was seen as more serious than vehicular homicide, armed robbery, and bank robbery.

In another recent seriousness study, Goff and Nason-Clark (1989) replicated Rossi et al.'s (1974) research with a Canadian sample. Their respondents rated white-collar crimes higher than the original sample, but lower than the Cullen et al.(1982) sample. They too found, however, that higher seriousness ratings were assigned to crimes involving physical harm, regardless of the crime category. And those crimes which cause actual physical harm were rated higher relative to others which only pose the threat of harm.

As even further evidence of this pattern, a national crime seriousness survey found that, consistent with other more local surveys, violent white-collar crimes are considered very serious (Wolfgang, Figlio, Tracy, & Singer, 1985). In fact, respondents rated violent corporate crimes as more serious than some forms of homicide. For example, "factory pollution of a municipal water supply resulting in the death of twenty people" was rated as more serious than "stabbing another person to death" or some other forms of intentional interpersonal violence.

There is limited evidence that this pattern of seriousness ratings holds up cross-nationally. A 1986 survey of Australian attitudes toward white-collar crime revealed that industrial pollution which kills ("A factory knowingly gets rid of waste in a way that pollutes the city water supply. As a result one person dies") and industrial negligence injury ("A worker had his leg caught in an unguarded piece of machinery because the employer knowingly failed to provide safety measures. As a result the worker lost his leg") were rated just below the most severely rated crimes of stabbing another to death and heroin trafficking (Grabosky et al., 1987). Both acts of intentional, violent corporate crime were considered more serious than armed robbery, or child and spousal abuse.

Not only is the public concerned about corporate crime, especially of a violent nature, but it also appears that public sentiment toward corporate illegalities is increasing in severity. The mean seriousness score of Cullen et al.'s (1982) sample for the twenty-four white-collar crimes in their offense inventory was significantly higher than that discovered by Rossi et al. (1974). The respondents also ranked nineteen out of twenty-four white-collar offenses higher than the respondents in the previous study. Perhaps most importantly, when the overall findings were compared to the earlier study, it was found that white-collar crime was the "only category to show a substantial change . . . in the direction of greater seriousness" (Cullen et al., 1982:92).

Contrary to claims that citizens are unconcerned about the effects of white-collar crime, it is clear from our review that—while they may not realize its full extent and costs—the public is not indifferent to violent corporate crimes. There is a growing realization among criminologists and the public that "physical costs—the toll of lives lost, injuries inflicted, and illnesses suffered—are perhaps the gravest and certainly the most neglected of the damages that corporate lawlessness imposes on the American people" (Cullen, Maakestad, & Cavender, 1987:67).

Physical victimization of workers, consumers, and the general public is accomplished through workplace hazards, the production and marketing of unsafe products, and the operation of polluting manufacturing and construction facilities. The potential for physical victimization is not lost on the public; as shown above they are mindful of and morally indignant about corporate acts which result in actual or probable injury, illness, or death. And, as will be shown below, citizens are increasingly willing to invoke harsh sanctions against corporate actors whose illegalities impose such harms on the public.

Violations of Trust

Although less than their concern about violent corporate crime, seriousness studies suggest that the public reserves varying degrees of moral condemnation for acts which may result in both monetary loss and the corruption of trust (e.g., embezzlement, bribery, and selling fraudulent securities). It appears that citizens may be apprehensive about these types of white-collar offenses because the resulting breaches of trust damage interpersonal relationships. Ultimately, such violations also damage institutional trust and the social fabric (Short, 1984).

As an example of the public's pulse on these matters, a 1969 Harris poll revealed that a price fixer was regarded as worse than a burglar. Similarly, even though Cullen et al. (1982) found that violent corporate illegalities were rated as much more serious than any other type of white-collar crime, offenses against a business organization (e.g., embezzlement) were considered the second most serious of the white-collar crimes. Finally, Wolfgang et al. (1985) reported that several forms of bribery were considered relatively serious compared to moderate thefts ($1,000) and some types of interpersonal violence.

The Public View:
Punishment of Corporate and White-Collar Crime

The findings of punishment studies tend to support the general finding from seriousness studies that the public is especially concerned about white-collar and corporate offenses which pose actual or threatened physical harm or undermine trust.

Violent Corporate and White-Collar Crime

Newman's (1957) study of violations of the Food, Drug, and Cosmetic Act found the public calling for harsher penalties than those actually invoked. While an example of a violent corporate crime with potential impact on consumer health, contamination of consumer goods—like many other crimes with direct economic impacts—also represents a violation of trust and fiduciary responsibilities to the public. Such crimes illustrate situations where businesses disregard their implicit general obligation for public welfare—or at least to refrain from doing harm—and government reneges on its oversight regulatory responsibility.

As corroboration of the theme of public intolerance of violent white-collar crimes and willingness to punish, Hawkins (1980) found that of the twenty-five crimes rated by his sample, punishment of a "hotel owner for ignoring of a fire alarm which resulted in 100 people being burned" ranked just below an "automobile hit and run" and above "rape of a babysitter by a 50 year-old man." This same study also found that in the punishment rankings, a "farmer selling contaminated grain" was rated just below rape and ahead of killing of parents and sisters.

In a comparative study of punishment attitudes in eight different countries, including the United States, Scott and Al-Thakeb (1977) reported that the public recommended more severe penalties for an "executive of a drug company who allows his company to manufacture and sell a drug knowing that it may produce harmful side effects for most individuals" than for auto theft, larceny, burglary, aggravated assault, and robbery. Scott and Al-Thakeb's findings support two rather consistent patterns found in other surveys: violent corporate crimes against persons are judged more harshly than economic crimes, and perceptions of culpability are important factors in punishment judgments.

In their Australian replication of Scott and Al-Thakeb's work, Broadhurst and Indermaur (1982) found a similar pattern in the ordering of sanctions considered appropriate for corporate offenses. The negligent drug company executive, for example, was found deserving of more prison time than a person who commits robbery or aggravated assault and only slightly less time than a rapist. This finding suggests that respondents are more indignant with regard to violent white-collar crimes than those with an economic impact only, and that they are more punitive toward violent corporate crime than any type of property crime.

The ability of the public to differentiate in the dispensing of "just deserts" among types of white-collar and corporate crime was also demonstrated by Cullen, Clark, Link, Mathers, Niedospial, and Sheahan (1985). Even though their crime inventory contained mostly white-collar offenses, the average sentence recommended by respondents was 5.3 years and more than 60 percent of the sample favored incarceration across all offenses. This outcome suggests that the public has little reluctance to impose criminal sanctions against a type of offense that has been viewed by some social commentators as relatively unserious to the general public. Of the forty-one predominantly white-collar and corporate offenses, the public allocated the third harshest punishment for "knowingly manufacturing and selling contaminated food that results in death." This act was superseded in suggested penalty only by the "assassination of a public official" and "killing a police officer in the course of a terrorist hijacking of a plane," and it ranked ahead of homicide committed during an argument, armed robbery of a bank, and rape.

The evidence seems clear that the public makes distinctions by impact among corporate crimes and is willing to sanction most harshly, those crimes, common or white-collar, which cause or pose the highest risk of physical victimization. As with seriousness ratings, the public is also willing to mete out relatively harsh punishment for violations of public trust—an issue we address below.

Violations of Trust

In an early survey of punishment attitudes Gibbons (1969) found that 87.7 percent of the public favored prison terms for embezzlers, 69.8 percent for anti-trust violators, and 42.9 percent for false advertisers. The theme of intolerance of breaches of trust was further revealed when Wilson and Brown (1973) reported that their Australian sample was willing to punish "fraudulent misappropriation of company funds by a director" more harshly than any of the other property crimes except armed robbery of a bank ($10,000). Fraudulent misappropriation of funds was also given higher punishment ratings than vehicular homicide or assault which results in hospitalization of the victim. Reed and Reed (1975) also found that embezzlement and the sale of fraudulent securities were as likely to elicit recommendations for imprisonment as was bank robbery.

Citizens of countries other than the United States are also quite willing to criminally sanction violations by persons in positions of trust. With the exception of the United States, where a bank robber was dealt with only slightly more harshly, respondents in a cross-national survey approved of stiffer sentences for personal appropriation of government funds than for robbery (Newman, 1976). In another comparative study, respondents suggested a penalty for oil price fixing that was higher than for burglary, larceny (felony) or auto theft (Scott & Al-Thakeb, 1977). As further confirmation of the public's concern about trust violations, Cullen et al. (1985) found that a lawyer's embezzlement from a client's account was given a higher punishment than that given for "assault with a gun on a stranger." Thus it appears that such crimes, committed by individuals for personal gain or on behalf of corporations, are not deemed trivial or deserving of less punishment than many "serious" street crimes.

As a summary of public sentiment on punishment of general white-collar crime, Cullen, Clark, Mathers, and Cullen (1983) found that nearly 90 percent of the respondents in their sample believed that white-collar criminals, as a group, were treated too leniently. Respondents believed that upperworld criminals "have gotten off too easily" and "deserve to be sent to jail for their crimes just like everyone else" (Cullen et al., 1983:485). Whether labeled "street crime" or "suite crime," it appears that the public judges crimes with comparable impact equally.

We have reviewed a compelling body of evidence which tends to refute the charge that the public is indifferent to the effects of corporate crime and will not support "getting tough" with white-collar and corporate criminals (see also Braithwaite, 1982; Braithwaite, 1985; Cullen & Dubeck, 1985). Even so, the assessment should not be taken to imply that citizens now fully appreciate the complexity or the magnitude of the "corporate crime problem." It is unlikely that the public has relinquished its belief that violent street crime is the most serious type of crime and deserving of the heaviest punishment, relative to any type of corporate crime. While meaningful attitudinal changes appear to have occurred, it would be too much to assert that most citizens' thinking about the nature of crime has undergone a truly fundamental transformation (Cullen et al., 1987).

Public Response in Context

Going beyond rankings of seriousness or punishment attitudes, some recent work has attempted to specify the conditions which shape public responses to white-collar and corporate crime. Contextualizing corporate crimes provides the potential for determining the circumstances under which public attitudes might change or be more or less severe. More finely specifying the conditions of the criminal event and motivations of offenders also offers the prospect of a clearer modeling of the process whereby seriousness ratings are transformed into punishment attitudes.

Two recent studies have attempted to specify punishment ratings by presenting respondents with mitigating information and by portraying the perpetrators as individual or corporate actors. Frank et al. (1989) used crime vignettes to compare business executives and the general public on the use of civil and criminal sanctions against a corporate entity or individual executives. The vignettes allowed the researchers to examine punitive attitudes based on varying levels of culpability and harm. They found that, when the act was committed with knowledge and recklessness, the public supports criminal sanctioning of executives and corporate entities regardless of the harm involved. The sample even more strongly supported such sanctions in cases of clear culpability *and* physical harm. Even so, the general public was more willing than business executives to criminally sanction offenders. Both the general public and the executives were reluctant to invoke criminal, as opposed to civil, penalties against individual managers.

In another example of providing contextual information about the crime event, Hans and Ermann (1989) presented their respondents with two scenarios involving injury to employees: one portrayed the perpetrator as a corporation and the other as an individual. In general and relative to individuals, corporations were judged to be more morally wrong and more reckless, held to a higher standard of responsibility than the individual, and deserving of harsher civil and criminal punishment.

What Is the Public View on
Corporate and White-Collar Crime?

From studies of punishment attitudes and seriousness rankings, a clear pattern emerges that the public is not tolerant of elite criminality. Two types of impact of such crimes appear to be most shocking to the public, with resultant disapproval: harm or the threat of harm to life, health, or safety of persons and violations of trust and fiduciary obligations. It is also clear that violent corporate crimes are regarded as much more morally reprehensible and deserving of severe treatment—even criminal sanctioning—than those involving only economic damage or common property crimes.

Among white-collar and corporate crimes, violence against and by the government, embezzlement, and corporate violence are perceived as the most serious offenses. While respondents generally feel that corporate crime is sanctioned too lightly, such individual and organizational white-collar crimes as tax evasion and false advertising are considered relatively trivial. Although the mental state of the offender, including attributions of intent and recklessness, have seldom been provided to respondents, it may be an important factor in seriousness rankings or recommended levels of punishment (Sebba, 1980; see Riedel, 1975, for a contrary view). The elements of culpability and harm may also interact to produce higher seriousness ratings and harsher penalties for corporate crimes. If respondents believe that the offender acted with intent, they perceive greater harm and, thus, may rate the act as more serious than a situation where intent is absent.

Finally, although the evidence is far from conclusive, it appears that the public is more willing to sanction corporate offenders as an entity than individual business executives (Frank et al., 1989; Hans & Ermann, 1989). Such "contextualizing" of the offense raises the possibility that aggravating and mitigating circumstances may be found to play a role in actual punishment decisions and, thus, should be considered in empirical analyses.

While it is likely that individual attitudes are situationally determined and influenced by characteristics of the offender, including status as an individual or corporation and culpability, public opinion is formed in a broad social and cultural context. In the following sections, we examine the influences of changing social forces on public attitudes about white-collar and corporate crime.

The Social Context of Public Attitudes Toward Corporate Crime: Shifting Moral Boundaries

Public attitudes and opinions are embedded in social and cultural contexts. In the following sections, we discuss three of the important contexts in which public sentiments on corporate crime are formed and sustained. The first context involves public perceptions of risk and assessments of tolerable and fair levels of risk from hazards, including those engendered by corporate crime. The second contextual condition to be considered is public confidence in business and government. We argue that the recent steep decline in confidence in these two major institutions has negative effects on public attitudes toward corporate crime. The third and final context, related to confidence and risk, consists of a new demand for equality of treatment in the criminal justice system. This has led to the widespread perception that the law is not neutral, but disproportionately benefits the rich and powerful, including corporate criminals.

The Changing Context of Risk: Perception and Acceptability

The public's concern about and response to elite crime is conditioned in part by the perceived level of harm and risk of victimization. Meier and Short (1985) have recently recast crime, especially white-collar law-breaking, as a type of hazard. Hazards pose harm to persons, property, and the "structure of interpersonal and institutional relationships in a community" (Meier & Short, 1985:389). Risks are "measures of the likelihood of specific hazardous events leading to certain adverse consequences" (Kates & Kasperson, 1983:7027).

As a hazard, then, corporate crimes pose dangers to persons and things they value. Identification of hazards, including corporate crime, assessments of risk probabilities connected with the hazards, and acceptable levels of risk are all socially and culturally constructed, not based solely on inherent features of the risk event (Clarke, 1988; Douglas & Wildavsky, 1982; Johnson & Covello, 1987; Nelkin, 1985; Slovic, 1987). Furthermore, quantitative and technical assessments of risk do not capture the "variations in the perception of similar risks in different social, cultural, and institutional contexts, and among different social groups" (Nelkin, 1985:16). Before an act, such as corporate crime, can be considered serious, it must be identified as a hazard with an unacceptable risk of harm to society or personal victimization.

When Ross and Sutherland were observing and evaluating public attitudes and responses to white-collar crime, natural and human-made hazards, including those arising from corporate crimes, were accepted with relative equanimity by today's standards. In the routine course of "doing business," workers and consumers were injured or killed, but such harm was typically accepted as an expected feature of employment or daily life (Friedman, 1985).

Dramatic changes have taken place recently in the United States concerning tolerance for risk and identification of hazards. Americans now fear "nothing much . . . except the food they eat, the water they drink, the air they breathe, the land they live on, and the energy they use" (Douglas & Wildavsky, 1982:10). Worry about crime and victimization could be added to the list of hazards feared by Americans (Hindelang, Gottfredson, & Garofalo, 1978; National Opinion Research Center, 1987; Warr, 1987).

The identification of hazards, responsibility for their management and control, and tolerance of the risks associated with hazards have all changed in recent years. Demands for "total justice" (Friedman, 1985) and the increasing use of the law to settle disputes are largely the result of changes in attitudes and beliefs about the causes and controllability of hazardous events, about attributions of culpability, about entitlement to

equity before the law, and about restitution for harm done—
issues we explore below.

Numerous observers have recently expressed alarm over
the apparent rise in the use of law and the courts to settle
disputes. They refer to a "law explosion" in an increasingly
"litigious society" which is wasteful of resources, stifles
innovation, and hampers economic development (Huber, 1988;
Lieberman, 1981). As Friedman (1985:4) has commented, "the
feeling is that there is a runaway legal system in this country, a
system out of control." Friedman insists, however, that changes
in the legal system in the last century merely reflect the evolution
of two new social norms. The first norm is the expectation of
equity under the law; the second norm involves complete
restitution for injuries and losses suffered. The combination of
the equity and restitution norms is what Friedman calls the
expectation of, even demand for, "total justice."

The new conceptions of risk and liability associated with
"total justice" tend to shift the burden from workers to
employers and from consumers to manufacturers, marketers,
and providers of services (Friedman, 1985; Hans, 1989). This new
norm of justice considerably weakens an employer's or
manufacturer's defense that the victim bears at least partial
responsibility (contributory negligence) for injuries incurred in
the course of employment or the use of a product. What might
have earlier been termed an "accident," is redefined as criminal
conduct. Contamination of the air, water, and soil, once viewed
as a tolerable side effect of production, is now seen as an affront
to public morality. The expectation, or at least tolerance, of
victimization by industrial accidents, pollutants, unsafe working
conditions, and hazardous products is no longer the norm. The
new standard is based on beliefs and values about compensation
for damages: all victims deserve fair treatment and
compensation and, insofar as possible, to be made "whole"
again.

Changes in norms regarding culpability and liability for
damages hinge on a related belief that crises and calamities are
controllable and thus preventable. Under the new rules of
justice, a safe environment—relatively free of risk, uncertainties,
and victims—is believed attainable and desirable (Fairlie, 1989;

Wildavsky, 1988). In this context, workers and consumers alike are more willing to press their claims, civil and criminal, in courts of law. If "accidents" can be foreseen, so the reasoning goes, they can be prevented or at least managed so as to mitigate and minimize damage.

Such strict liability standards for business lead to the identification of more hazards in modern life that are not simply due to "bad luck" or "fate." Someone or some organization can now be held blameworthy and accountable for the consequences. Many hazards of daily life that were once tolerated are no longer accepted with complacence and resignation. Levels of risk associated with these hazards which were routinely tolerated in the past are no longer defensible. The moral boundaries between victims and perpetrators have shifted.

The changes in legal culture resulting from demands for "total justice" are undoubtedly linked to changes in public attitudes toward corporate crimes. The difference between labeling an event a "normal accident" (Perrow, 1984) or a "crime" with subsequent potential for litigation depends largely on the public's view about the controllability of events and assignment of responsibility when things go out of control. Only when culpability and intentionality could be clearly assigned to corporate entities was it likely that the harmful consequences of a corporate act could be interpreted as criminal. As a result, businesses are now less able to shift or externalize responsibility and liability for their crimes.

This shifting of liabilities arising from risks associated with corporate activity is no longer acceptable to the American public. As a result, corporate actions which cause actual harm or pose threats of such harm are judged more harshly and are, in some cases, seen for the first time as profound affronts to public morality. With increasing demands for "total justice," the public is less accepting of risk over which it often has little direct control; citizens are much more likely to condemn corporate entities and business executives to whom risk management and control have been yielded. In short, they are beginning to perceive some types of corporate crimes not as accidents, or due to negligence or oversight, but as serious transgressions deserving of severe punishments.

Confidence in Institutions, Risk Perceptions, and the Public's Attitude toward Corporate Crime

Organizations, public and private, are increasingly responsible for the measurement of risk and management of hazards. This change has tended to shift the burden of risk from individuals to organizations (Clarke, 1988) and heightened demands for "total justice." Increasingly, organizations create, filter, and distribute risk (cf. Clarke, 1988; Perrow, 1984; Stallings, 1990). Hohenemser, Kasperson, and Kates (1980:2) note that "while individuals have some choice and control over the hazards they face, their responses are substantially constrained." Individuals are often forced to involuntarily—or unknowingly—assume the consequences of a hazard about which they lack sufficient information to make informed decisions. To offset these individual limitations, risk management has increasingly shifted from individuals to business and government. During the same period that sensitivity to hazards and perceptions of risk have increased, confidence in the very institutions charged with managing risk and ensuring safety appears to have declined. The organizations that are expected to mitigate the consequences of hazards, including those arising from corporate crime, are increasingly viewed with suspicion and mistrust (Lipset & Schneider, 1983). Goldfarb (1991:22) claims that when cynicism replaces trust in institutions, citizens come to believe that "all those in authority justify their actions through elaborate rationalizations of privilege [and the] principles upon which authoritative actions are at least sometimes based will disappear."

To be effective in managing risk and taking "authoritative actions," business and government must preserve confidence and legitimacy. Acceptable levels of risk for the public are influenced by the credibility, and ultimately legitimacy, of organizations responsible for the control of risk. As Meier and Short note (1985:391),

> ... perceptions of risk, including judgements as to the acceptability of a particular risk, are a foundation of the

degree to which the institutions which are responsible for the assessment and management of risks are trusted.

If the leaders of these institutions cannot be trusted and if risk assessment and regulatory agencies lose legitimacy, the norm of trust is gradually supplanted by the norm of "total justice." Americans are less tolerant of risk from many sources, in part at least because trust in major institutions appears to have dramatically declined in recent times.

Based on their review of polling data over a number of years, Lipset and Schneider (1983:42–43) reported that confidence in business leaders fell from 55 percent in 1966 to 27 percent in 1971. Anti-business sentiment is part of a larger pattern of "cynicism toward all major institutions in American society" (Lipset & Schneider, 1983:44). In contrast to a period when business and its leaders were trusted to act in the public interest while serving their own private interests, by the early 1980s people began to assume that "business people . . . will act in a socially responsible way only when the public interest coincides with their self-interest" (Lipset & Schneider, 1983:382). This belief creates a more hostile social environment for business.

According to Lipset and Schneider, a long and sustained period of "good news" will be necessary to offset the lasting institutional damage from the political and social turmoil of the late 1960s and early 1970s. During this period, the nation experienced a number of events that challenged confidence in major institutions and the ideals of democracy. These included the demands of women, racial and ethnic minorities, and gays for equitable treatment and full inclusion in American society; the Vietnam War and the ensuing bitter and divisive protest of our continued involvement; immoral business practices; and political scandals such as the Watergate affair.

Writing in 1983, Lipset and Schneider believed it was unlikely that the deep mistrust of business and other major social institutions was a "transitory event" or that the business community will quickly regain a position of sufficient trust to insulate it from suspicion and public scrutiny. In fact, there has been even more "bad news" about misdeeds in high places in the last decade, including the savings and loan crisis and extensive reports of insider trading and other chicanery and fraud in the securities industries (Bruck, 1988; Calavita & Pontell, 1991; Day, 1989; Pizzo, Fricker, & Muolo, 1989; Shapiro, 1984; Stevens, 1987; Stewart, 1991; Winans, 1986).

Not surprisingly, since Lipset and Schneider's (1983) massive synthesis of public opinion data, recent surveys indicate that confidence in government and business is at historically low levels. An updated review found that the

> confidence gap did not end with the 1980 election of Ronald Reagan, nor did it disappear during the upbeat era. Confidence in major institutions and leaders, which had fallen dramatically during the Carter "malaise" years, 1978–1980, actually reached its lowest point in 1983. (Lipset & Schneider, 1987:419)

Although Reagan was attempting to restore confidence in business, it was trust in government that benefited most from his tenure. In fact, "there has been little tendency to return to the appreciation of big business shown in polls taken in the 1960s" (Lipset & Schneider, 1987:426).

Also indicative of anti-business sentiment is the response of Americans when asked how often they felt that "individuals and corporations commit white-collar crimes to make a dishonest profit for themselves or their companies." With a choice of three categories (very often, occasionally, or hardly ever), a majority answered very often and 96 percent answered either very often or occasionally (Opinion Roundup, 1986:22). Furthermore, in the same survey, a majority said they believe American corporate executives are dishonest (Opinion Roundup, 1986:22). Finally, between 1976 and 1988 the public's favorable rating (high or very high) of honesty and ethics among business executives declined from 20 percent to 16 percent (The Gallup Poll, 1988:19).

Gallup polls (Gallup & Newport, 1991) from 1988 to 1991 also indicate a continuation in the downward trend of confidence in big business as an institution, with corresponding declines in other institutions. Americans who indicated that they have "a great deal" or "quite a lot" of confidence in business fell during this period from 25 percent to 22 percent. Among the eleven institutions rated in 1991, confidence in business was tied with organized labor, and both institutions received more favorable ratings than only Congress (18 percent).

We hasten to note that such cynicism about business is not rooted in opposition to capitalism or free enterprise. Despite their firm belief in capitalism and general opposition to excessive government intervention in the economy, a clear majority of Americans expressed the belief that government *should* intervene in the economy to regulate pollution, price fixing, safe products and services, safe working conditions, and fair employment practices (Roper & Miller, 1985:14).

From their review, Lipset and Schneider (1983:290) concluded that what Americans fear most is concentrated power in business or government. Similarly, Page and Shapiro (1992:144) found that "many citizens are especially suspicious of big business, which is seen as a source of high prices and profits, and excessive power." Thus, it appears that Americans have little confidence in business or government, and desire a political economy in which government intervenes deeply enough in business affairs in order to insure fair competition and protection of health, safety, and welfare. The public is "simultaneously skeptical of business and skeptical of government; they worry about the power of corporations, and also worry about what would happen if they failed" (Dionne, 1991:326).

Competent government regulation is one means whereby privately imposed risk can be managed in the public interest. Diminished confidence in industry and government, however, leads to lower public trust in the ability or willingness of organizations to manage or regulate risks in accord with public safety. On the other hand, if the public believes—has faith—that risk is well managed and controlled by business or government regulators, businesses operate with a degree of immunity to public scrutiny and are able to draw "credits" against public trust to offset damages to their reputations as the result of corporate wrongdoing. The public is willing to give business the benefit of the doubt when confidence in the institution and business executives is high.

Unfortunately for big business, as shown above, the reputation of business firms and executives has been tarnished in recent years and neither are held in high esteem. Thus lowered trust in business and government institutions may well increase the probability of perceiving higher risks from white-collar and corporate crimes and rating them as relatively serious.

Confidence in government institutions, particularly regulatory agencies, may also indirectly impact on seriousness ratings and punishment attitudes. Mistrust of business and lack of confidence in business leaders and management may be ameliorated if the public believes that government regulators assigned oversight responsibility are performing competently in the public interest. The assessment and management of risk in that case is entrusted to government regulators. As shown above, however, trust in this "backup" system of social control has declined, and, consequentially, the norm of trust has been gradually supplanted by the norm of "total justice."

The Rule of Law and Public Attitudes Toward Corporate Crime

The norm of "total justice," which includes the expectation of equal treatment under the law, arose in part from declining trust in institutions during the 1960s and 1970s. This trend, including diminished trust in the criminal justice system, challenged the legal ideals of equal and fair treatment.

Despite what many have termed a "litigation explosion," Friedman (1985) contends that the recent expansion of the work of the courts has been more qualitative than quantitative. And, "on the whole, lawyers do not lead, they follow" in responding to the demand for their services which comes from outside the legal system (Friedman, 1985:25). Demands for qualitative changes are produced by changes in values, attitudes, and other ideas about the law, including how the criminal justice system should respond to previously excluded groups.

According to Friedman (1985:43) American legal culture has changed so that there is an "expectation of fair treatment, everywhere and in every circumstance," as part of a larger pattern of a "pervasive expectation of fairness . . . substantive as well as procedural." The campaign for civil rights raised the question of fair treatment under the law by focusing on the legal ideals of neutrality, autonomy, and formal rationality. Demands for equal justice challenged the legitimacy of law and the social order by calling attention to class and race inequities in the use of the state's social control apparatus. While poor people went to prison, rich and powerful, mostly white, upperworld criminals were seldom criminally sanctioned and almost never incarcerated. The revelation of such unequal treatment caused the public to wonder why "harms inflicted by the poor [should be] subject to penal sanctions but not those inflicted by the advantaged" (Cullen et al., 1983:490).

The apparent laxness in the control of upperworld criminality, in stark contrast to the vigorous pursuit of common and street criminals, highlighted the essential dualism in the criminal justice system. A heightened sensitivity to this unequal treatment under the law was produced by the movement for civil and equal rights. The lenient sanctioning of elite criminals was made even more apparent and intolerable to members of less privileged groups. The public's response of outrage and indignation over the lack of criminal sanctions against E. F. Hutton for its check-kiting scheme is illustrative of this sentiment (Cullen et al., 1987:340; Hans & Ermann, 1989). "The legal apparatus was playing favorites; disclosures of that bias undermined the law's neutrality and thus challenged its legitimacy" (Cullen et al., 1987:13).

Prosecutions of rich and powerful business and political leaders, following the Watergate crimes, not only reaffirmed the efficacy of the legal apparatus but also served to "reassert the ideology of equal justice and neutrality of law" (Cullen et al., 1987:12). The prosecutions, thus, constituted an effort by the state to reestablish the legitimacy of its authority and remedy the legitimation crisis that arose, in part, from the operation of a dual system of justice. In turn, these prosecutions heightened public sensitivity to the delicts of the rich and powerful.

Demands for equity under law are part of the larger pattern of cultural changes which led to the supernorm of "total justice." Just as such demands challenged the very foundations of the legal system, they also helped focus attention on the fact that the poor, powerless, and excluded members of society were unable to redress grievances through the system. Worse still, their contacts with the system highlighted the existence of two systems of justice, two standards of law and order. This recognition itself may have led to further declines in confidence in business and industry, which represented the interests of the rich and powerful. It also led to demands for further changes in substantive and procedural justice. The hazards and attendant risks produced by corporate America could no longer be ignored.

Changing Public Conceptions: Implications for Criminal Justice Policy

It is clear that the public is not indifferent to flagrant abuses of public morality or trust by rich and powerful criminals and business establishments. Increasing sensitivity to corporate crime, demands for "total justice," and diminishing faith in public and private institutions—these all converge to support the use of criminal law as one device for controlling corporate wrongdoing and restoring order and trust in the business community (Cullen et al., 1987).

The ideological support of the public, expressed in a willingness to invoke criminal sanctions against corporate criminals, helps remove at least one barrier to successful prosecution of culpable executives and corporate entities. As shown in an analysis of the Ford Pinto case, shifting moral boundaries resulting from a larger social movement against corporate crime helped to facilitate prosecution of the case. In general,

> . . . prosecutions of corporate offenders became more prevalent when private citizens, academics, and members of the legal profession began to lose confidence in the trustworthiness of elites, were sensitized to issues of equal justice before the law, and broadened their view of what "crime" might entail. (Cullen et al., 1987:319)

We have argued throughout this paper that ideas have consequences—the public mood, reflected in lowered tolerance of risk, increased demands for "total justice," and the resulting changing definitions of "crime" and punishment translates into encouragement of and support for more stringent scrutiny of corporate behavior. Citizens are increasingly intolerant of flagrant affronts to public morality by business and are willing to support the mobilization of the state's control machinery to contain corporate crime.

The convergence of a "confidence gap," general demands for "total justice," and specific appeals for equal treatment under the law during the 1960s and 1970s made it possible—perhaps even necessary—for the state to respond to the crimes of the elite in order to restore legitimacy in the legal system. The ensuing prosecutions and publicity generated from the pursuit of corporate crime sensitized citizens by reminding them of the huge costs of such crime (see Benson, Cullen, & Maakestad, 1990; Benson, Maakestad, Cullen, & Geis, 1988; Cullen et al., 1987 for detailed information on prosecution of corporate offenses and trends in local prosecutions). The dialectic has been set in motion—increased public sensitivity leads to greater sanctioning which, in turn, sensitizes the public to the extent and costs of the corporate crime problem (Cullen et al., 1987). We see no indication of a reversal of this long-term trend, nor do we see changes in the social or cultural context which would reduce the anxiety of the American public about the risks which are imposed on them by corporate crimes.

REFERENCES

Benson, M.L., Cullen, F.T., & Maakestad, W.J. (1990). Local prosecutors and corporate crime. *Crime and Delinquency, 36,* 356–372.

Benson, M.L., Maakestad, W.J., Cullen, F.T., & Geis, G. (1988). District attorneys and corporate crime: Surveying the prosecutorial gatekeepers. *Criminology, 26,* 505–518.

Braithwaite, J. (1982). Challenging just deserts: Punishing white-collar criminals. *The Journal of Criminal Law and Criminology, 73,* 723–763.

————. (1985). White collar crime. *Annual Review of Sociology, 11,* 1–25.

Broadhurst, R., & Indermaur, D. (1982). Crime seriousness ratings: The relationship of information accuracy and general attitudes in Western Australia. *Australian and New Zealand Journal of Criminology, 15,* 219–234.

Bruck, C. (1988). *The predator's ball: The inside story of Drexel Burnham and the rise of the junk bond raiders.* New York: Penguin Books.

Calavita, K., & Pontell, H.N. (1991). "Other people's money" revisited: Collective embezzlement in the savings and loan insurance industries. *Social Problems, 38,* 94–112.

Clarke, L. (1988). Explaining choices among technological risks. *Social Problems, 35,* 22–35.

Conklin, J.E. (1977). *"Illegal but not criminal": Business crime in America.* Englewood Cliffs, NJ: Prentice-Hall.

Cullen, F.T., Clark, G., Link, B., Mathers, R.A., Niedospial, J.L., & Sheahan, M. (1985). Dissecting white-collar crime: Offense type and punitiveness. *International Journal of Comparative and Applied Criminal Justice, 9,* 15–28.

Cullen, F.T., Clark, G.A., Mathers, R.A., & Cullen, J.B. (1983). Public support for punishing white-collar crime: Blaming the victim revisited? *Journal of Criminal Justice, 11,* 481–483.

Cullen, F.T., & Dubeck, P.J. (1985). The myth of corporate immunity to deterrence: Ideology and the creation of the invincible criminal. *Federal Probation, 49,* 3–9.

Cullen, F.T., Link, B.G., & Polanzi, C.W. (1982). The seriousness of crime revisited: Have attitudes toward white-collar crime changed? *Criminology, 20* (1), 83–102.

Cullen, F.T., Maakestad, W.J., & Cavender, G. (1987). *Corporate crime under attack: The Ford Pinto case and beyond.* Cincinnati: Anderson.

Day, K. (1989). When hell sleazes over: Judgment day for S & L slimeballs. *The New Republic,* March 20, p. 26.

Dionne, Jr., E.J. (1991). *Why Americans hate politics.* New York: Simon & Schuster.

Douglas, M., & Wildavsky, A. (1982). *Risk and culture: An essay on the selection of technological and environmental dangers.* Berkeley: University of California Press.

Fairlie, H. (1989). Fear of living: America's morbid aversion to risk. *The New Republic*, January 23, pp. 14–19.

Frank, J., Cullen, F.T., Travis, L.F., III, & Borntrager, J. (1989). Sanctioning corporate crime: How do business executives and the public compare? *American Journal of Criminal Justice, 13*, 139–169.

Friedman, L.M. (1985). *Total justice*. New York: Sage.

Gallup, G., & Newport, F. (1991, October). Confidence in major U.S. institutions at all-time low. *Gallup Poll Monthly*, pp. 36–37.

The Gallup Poll. (1988, December). *Honesty and ethical standards* (pp. 1–40). (Report No. 279). Princeton: Author.

Gibbons, D. (1969). Crime and punishment: A study of social attitudes. *Social Forces, 47*, 391–397.

Goff, C., & Nason-Clark, N. (1989). The seriousness of crime in Fredrickton, New Brunswick: Perceptions toward white-collar crime. *Canadian Journal of Criminology, 31*, 19–33.

Goldfarb, J.C. (1991). *The cynical society: The culture of politics and the politics of culture in American life*. Chicago: University of Chicago Press.

Grabosky, P.N., Braithwaite, J.B., & Wilson, P.R. (1987). The myth of community tolerance toward white-collar crime. *Australian and New Zealand Journal of Criminology, 20*, 33–44.

Hans, V.P. (1989). The jury's response to business and corporate wrongdoing. *Law and Contemporary Problems, 52*, 177–203.

Hans, V.P., & Ermann, M.D. (1989). Response to corporate versus individual wrongdoing. *Law and Human Behavior, 13*, 151–166.

Harris, L. (1969, June 6). Changing morality: The two Americas. *Time*, pp. 26–27.

Hawkins, D.F. (1980). Perceptions of punishment for crime. *Deviant Behavior: An Interdisciplinary Journal, 1*, 193–215.

Hindelang, M.J., Gottfredson, M.R., & Garofalo, J. (1978). *Victims of personal crime: An empirical foundation for a theory of personal victimization*. Cambridge, MA: Ballinger.

Hohenemser, C., Kasperson, R.E., & Kates, R. (1980, March). *A structural model of technological hazards*. Paper presented at the meeting of the Society for Toxicology.

Huber, P.W. (1988). *Liability: The legal revolution and its consequences*. New York: Basic.

Johnson, B.B., & Covello, V.T. (1987). *The social and cultural construction of risk: Essays in risk selection and perception*. Boston: Reidel.

Kadish, S. (1977). Some observations on the use of criminal sanctions in enforcing economic regulations. *University of Chicago Law Review, 30*, 423–449.

Kates, R.F., & Kasperson, J.X. (1983). Comparative risk analysis and technological hazards (A review). *Proceedings of the National Academy of Science, U.S.A., 80*, 7027–7028.

Lieberman, J.K. (1981). *The litigious society.* New York: Basic.

Lipset, S.M., & Schneider, W. (1983). *The confidence gap: Business, labor, and government in the public mind.* New York: Free Press.

———. (1987). *The confidence gap: Business, labor, and government in the public mind* (rev. ed.). Baltimore: Johns Hopkins University Press.

Meier, R.F., & Short, J.F., Jr. (1985). Crime as hazard: Perceptions of risk and seriousness. *Criminology, 23*, 389–399.

National Opinion Research Center. (1987). *General social surveys (1972–1987).* Chicago: Author.

Nelkin, D. (1985). *The language of risk: Conflicting perspectives on occupational health.* Beverly Hills: Sage.

Newman, D.J. (1957). Public attitudes toward a form of white-collar crime. *Social Problems, 4*, 228–232.

Newman, G. (1976). *Comparative deviance.* New York: Elsevier.

Opinion roundup: An erosion of ethics? (1986, November–December). *Public Opinion,* pp. 21–28.

Packer, H. (1968). *The limits of the criminal sanction.* Stanford, CA: Stanford University Press.

Page, B.I., & Shapiro, R.Y. (1992). *The rational public: Fifty years of trends in American's policy preferences.* Chicago: University of Chicago Press.

Perrow, C. (1984). *Normal accidents: Living with high risk technologies.* New York: Basic.

Pizzo, S., Fricker, M., & Muolo, P. (1989). *Inside job: The looting of America's savings and loans.* New York: McGraw-Hill.

President's Commission on Law Enforcement and Administration of Justice. (1968). *Challenge of crime in a free society.* Washington, DC: U.S. Government Printing Office.

Reed, J.P., & Reed, R.S. (1975). "Doctor, lawyer, indian chief": Old rhymes and new on white collar crime. *International Journal of Criminology and Penology, 3*, 279–293.

Riedel, M. (1975). Perceived circumstances, inferences of intent and judgments of offense seriousness. *The Journal of Criminal Law and Criminology, 66*, 201–209.

Roper, B.W., & Miller, T.A.W. (1985, August–September). Americans take stock of business. *Public Opinion*, pp. 12–15.

Ross, E.A. (1907). *Sin and society: An analysis of latter-day iniquity.* Gloucester, MA: Peter Smith.

Rossi, P.H., Simpson, J.E., & Miller, J.L. (1985). Beyond crime seriousness: Fitting the punishment to the crime. *Journal of Quantitative Criminology, 1*, 59–90.

Rossi, P.H., Waite, E., Bose, C.E., & Berk, R.E. (1974). The seriousness of crime: Normative structure and individual differences. *American Sociological Review, 39*, 224–237.

Schrager, L.S., & Short, J.F., Jr. (1980). How serious a crime? Perceptions of organizational and common crimes. In G. Geis & E. Stotland (Eds.), *White-collar crime: Theory and research* (pp. 14–31). Beverly Hills: Sage.

Scott, J.C., & Al-Thakeb, F. (1977). The public's perception of crime: A comparative analysis of Scandinavia, Western Europe, the Middle East, & the United States. In C. Huff (Ed.), *Contemporary Corrections* (pp. 78–88). Beverly Hills: Sage.

Sebba, L. (1980). Is *mens rea* a component of perceived offense seriousness? *The Journal of Criminal Law and Criminology, 71*, 124–135.

Shapiro, S.P. (1984). *Wayward capitalists: Target of the Securities and Exchange Commission.* New Haven: Yale University Press.

Short, J.F., Jr. (1984). The social fabric at risk: Toward the social transformation of risk analysis. *American Sociological Review, 49*, 711–725.

Sinden, P.G. (1980). Perceptions of crime in capitalist America: The question of consciousness manipulation. *Sociological Focus, 13*, 75–85.

Slovic, P. (1987, April 17). Perception of risk. *Science*, pp. 280–285.

Stallings, R.A. (1990). Media discourse and the social construction of risk. *Social Problems, 37*, 80–95.

Stevens, M. (1987). *The insiders: The truth behind the scandal rocking Wall Street.* New York: G.P. Putnam & Sons.

Stewart, J.B. (1991). *Den of thieves.* New York: Simon & Schuster.

Sutherland, E.H. (1940). White-collar criminality. *American Sociological Review, 5*, 1–12.

Sykes, G.H., & Blum-West, S.R. (1978, March). *The seriousness of crime: A study of popular morality*. Paper presented at the meeting of the Eastern Sociological Society, Philadelphia.

Warr, M. (1987). Fear of victimization and sensitivity to risk. *Journal of Quantitative Criminology, 3*, 29–46.

Wildavsky, A. (1988). *Searching for safety*. New Brunswick: Transaction Publishers.

Wilson, J.Q. (1975). *Thinking about crime*. New York: Basic Books.

Wilson, P.R., & Brown, J.W. (1973). *Crime and the community*. St. Lucia: University of Queensland Press.

Winans, R.F. (1986). *Trading secrets: Seduction and scandal at the Wall Street Journal*. New York: St. Martin's Press.

Wolfgang, M.E., Figlio, R.M., Tracy, P.E., & Singer, S.I. (1985). *The national survey of crime severity*. Washington, DC: U.S. Government Printing Office.

CHAPTER FIVE

Measuring Corporate Crime

Sally S. Simpson
Anthony R. Harris
Brian A. Mattson

Reports of corporations producing unsafe products, maintaining unsafe working conditions, engaging in fraud, price fixing, and even homicide are a fact of life in the 1990s. Whether corporations are increasing their participation in crime or whether the reporting and discovery of illegality is improving is uncertain. But, one thing is clear—citizens and politicians are more concerned with the problem of corporate crime than ever before (Cullen, Maakestad, & Cavender, 1987). Tentative steps are now being taken toward gathering better data from which estimates of the extent and cost of corporate crime can be calculated (U.S. Sentencing Commission, 1991; Wellford & Ingraham, 1990).[1]

Corporate crime measurement, because it involves both individuals and organizational entities and encompasses interdependencies between criminal actors, is an extremely complex matter that requires sophisticated counting techniques. In this chapter, we highlight the complexity of corporate crime and its measurement by: (1) identifying and evaluating current corporate crime data sources; (2) assessing the strengths and weaknesses of proposed alternatives to current sources; and (3) constructing an ideal measure of corporate crime that is rate-based and sensitive to the organizational context in which acts of corporate offending occur.

Before proceeding with measurement issues, however, it is important to cover some definitional terrain. By corporate crime, we mean the "conduct of a corporation, or of employees acting on behalf of a corporation, which is proscribed and punishable by law" (Braithwaite, 1984:6). Typically, criminality is supported, at least in part, by operational norms (Coleman, 1989) and is punishable through criminal, administrative, or civil means (Clinard & Yeager, 1980).

The range of crime types and crime victims covered by this definition is extensive and has prompted diverse classification schemes. To simplify the issue, we classify corporate crimes according to the body of law that defines and regulates illegal acts (Clinard & Yeager, 1980). Victims of these acts can include employees, consumers, the general public, governments, local communities, businesses and other organizations, and stockholders. Like corporate criminal actors, victims of corporate crime can be individuals or collectivities.

The bifurcation of individual and organizational actors/victims is consequential for how crimes are counted and measured. Take, for instance, the decision rule that is employed in cases of insider trading. Michael Milken and his employer, Drexel Burnham Lambert, were each charged with various counts of securities law violation stemming from the same set of illegal activities. Yet, the crime counts may appear as distinct occurrences of crime. Similarly, these cases may show up as criminal, civil, or administrative statistics depending on the origin of the case and/or the kind of remedy sought, e.g., civil or criminal RICO, regulatory investigation. To complicate matters further, victims of this genre of fraud can also contribute to the crime count by seeking class action relief (as collectivities) or through individual civil cases. Obviously, how and who to count as an offender or victim will affect estimates of the incidence of illegality; knowledge about corporate crime will also be influenced by the decision rules that are employed to measure corporate crime.

In the following section, the problem of what and who is counted is discussed in the context of available data sources. We have two goals in our review of these sources. Our primary purpose is informational. We list the kinds of corporate crime data that currently exist and where they can be found. But, in so doing, we also caution the data consumer. Each source offers a particular version of corporate offending that is incomplete at best and misleading at worst.

Current Data Sources

Official Crime Counts

Existing data sources of information related to corporate crime are collected at the municipal, state, and federal levels of government. Recordkeeping at these levels varies in content and methodology, but each provides a unique window on corporate illegal activity.

City and State-level Data. Official police statistics report known cases of fraud, bribery, forgery, some state regulatory violations, and negligent homicide (Department of Justice, 1984:79–81). However, within these *Uniform Crime Report* categories, corporate offenses are mixed in with occupational (i.e., acts by persons who use their occupational position for their own gain through acts of embezzlement, fraud, forgery, and so forth) and conventional crime.[2] For the *UCR* to be useful as a corporate crime data source, one must extract two pieces of information. (1) Did the criminal actor(s) use occupational means to commit the illegal act? (2) Who benefitted from the crime, the employer or employee? Obviously, these definitional requirements are essential to distinguish corporate illegalities from other kinds of offending, but the data are not amenable to such breakdowns.

State level corporate crime data also are collected by the Office of the State Attorney General. A recent survey of Attorneys General found that a majority of states do not have separate white-collar investigative units and that definitions and measurement of these crime types are not well-developed at the state level (Wellford & Ingraham, 1990). Consequently, many states are not substantially involved in the investigation and pursuit of white-collar crimes and criminals. In a minority of states—those characterized by "substantial commercial development"—efforts have been made to identify white-collar (occupational) offenders. But even here, cases overwhelmingly focus on criminal, not civil, violations and may be defined as important because they overlap with organized crime activity (cf., New York State Organized Crime Taskforce, 1989).

Our interviews with the office of the Attorney General in Maryland and Virginia generally support Wellford and Ingraham's findings. In these states, corporate offenses are prosecuted through the Attorney General's office. In Maryland, case records are kept by a white-collar crime investigation unit in which offenders' names, dates, convictions, and dispositions are documented. In Virginia, records are not maintained in any systematic manner that would allow access to corporate crime cases. Neither set of records is easily accessible for research purposes.

Federal-level Data. At the federal level, corporate violations of criminal and civil law are handled by the U.S. Attorney General under the auspices of the Department of Justice. The Attorney General's office maintains regional offices that operate independently under the guise of the Executive Office of the U.S. Attorney General (EOUSA). Generally, case referrals come to the various districts from the Federal Bureau of Investigation and regulatory agencies. Adjudicated cases can be accessed through federal court records. Closed case files are available only by Freedom of Information Act requests and may yield limited information.

The majority of corporate crime cases are administered by federal regulatory agencies.

> The volume and consequence of white collar matters decided by administrative law judges easily outweigh those decided by civil or criminal court judges and matters detected by regulatory agents and resolved by discretionary decisions of their agencies, often loom larger than those detected by criminal enforcement divisions and adjudicated as criminal matters. (Reiss & Biderman, 1980:51)

Federal agencies have the primary role of "policing," investigating, and in some instances sanctioning corporate offenders—individuals and/or organizations (Clinard & Yeager, 1980; Frank & Lombness, 1988). Cases are brought to the attention of regulatory agencies through a variety of proactive or reactive means including site inspections, victim complaints, whistle-blowers, tracking "questionable" trends in stock transactions or industry prices, referrals from other agencies, and so forth.

Once a case is brought into the system, there is no guarantee that formal adjudication will result.[3] Using the Federal Trade Commission[4] as a guide, we show in Table 1 the many decision points through which a case will pass before formal adjudication occurs. Each stage in the regulatory process will carry its own set of potential biases, but it is difficult to assess whether these biases are random or systematic (Green, 1990).

Ideally, each stage of the regulatory process could provide detailed information about the illegal act and the characteristics of offenders. Unfortunately, the typical procedure is to make regulatory records available for public consumption after formal charges are brought. Even at this relatively late stage in the regulatory process, available data are spotty (Clinard & Yeager, 1980).

Not all regulatory agencies approach corporate crime prevention and control in the same manner. Distinct intervention strategies may provide unique data opportunities. The "no action letter" of the Securities and Exchange Commission is one example. Corporations who suspect that they are in violation of SEC guidelines are allowed by the agency to submit written descriptions of the act in question to the SEC enforcement division. Upon review, the SEC then recommends actions to rectify conditions found to be in violation of regulatory code.

The "no action letter" is the first step in a "negotiated" settlement by which the company avoids the stigma and cost of formal processing and the SEC achieves compliance through cooperation. Cases of misconduct discovered through this source are on line and accessible through Westlaw and Lexis. The letters also are available in text format at the Securities and Exchange Commission in Washington, D.C.

Table 1
Federal Trade Commission Case Progression[*]

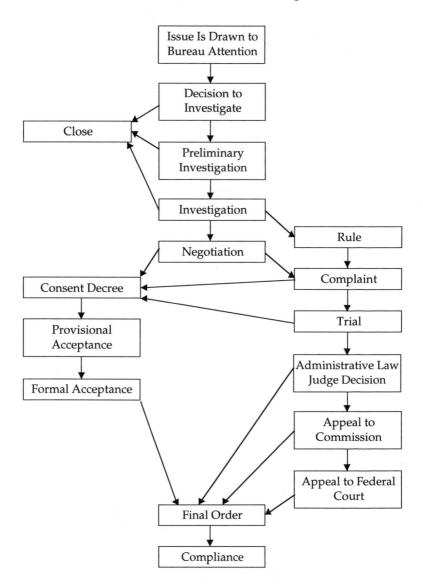

[*]Figure taken from Berney, 1980:12

State and Federal Case Decision Summaries. One of the most comprehensive sources of known corporate illegality are court records (Sutherland, 1949). Citations for all cases in the federal and state courts, numerous federal administrative bodies, and the U.S. District Courts are maintained in *Shepard's Federal Citation Series*. In addition, case reporters are maintained by private publishing agencies (e.g., Commerce Clearing House, Bureau of National Affairs, and Administrative Law). These sources provide full text of administrative and judicial actions, decisions, opinions, and rulings. *Westlaw* and *Lexis* maintain an online database that will generate a list of federal and state case decisions related to a specific subject.

Federal agencies produce case summary information in various forms. Enforcement actions taken by individual agencies are summarized in reports like the *Federal Trade Commission Decisions* and the *Securities and Exchange Commission Decisions and Reports*. In addition, statistical compendia like the American Statistics Index (ASI) provide information on a variety of regulatory activities (Goehlert & Gunderson, 1987).

Court records are an important source of comprehensive information about offenses, but only a small percentage of corporate crimes actually reach the adjudication stage. Thus, there is a great deal of "thick description" about a relatively select group of cases.

Corporate Self-Reports. Regulatory agencies may also require corporations to self-report to stockholders civil litigation, ongoing criminal and administrative investigations, and case outcomes. The corporate 10–K yearly reports to the SEC are an important source of information that can be used to assess the validity of information drawn from other sources. Clinard et al. (1979) used these data to access SEC (e.g., improper reporting procedures) and FTC (e.g., antitrust and unfair reporting practices) proceedings against firms. Additionally, the "Form 10–K was a major source of private, competitor, derivative action, stockholder and class action suits and the only source from which these actions were systematically recorded" (Clinard et al., 1979:62).

Victimization Data. The first national victimization survey was conducted under the auspices of the President's

Commission on Law Enforcement and Administrative of Justice. Although the primary concern of the commission was conventional criminal victimization, respondents were queried about consumer fraud, governmental corruption (specifically, bribery solicitation), and rental building victimizations (Ennis, 1967). Each of these general categories of crime may include corporate offenders, but it is impossible to ferret out corporate offenses from those perpetrated by individuals unassociated with corporations. Thus, this data set is of limited use for scholars investigating corporate offenses.

Limitations of Current Sources

The Dark Figure of Crime

Many of the data sources discussed above share a similar weakness. As officially generated statistics, only a portion of the actual incidence of corporate crime is captured within them. According to Reiss and Biderman (1980:51), "a great many transgressions of law—many similar to those litigated or adjudicated" lie outside the statistical reporting system. Researchers consistently identify this limitation with official data (Clinard et al., 1979; Reiss & Biderman, 1980; Shapiro, 1984; Sutherland, 1949; Wellford & Ingraham, 1990), but can only guess the degree to which officially defined cases are representative of all corporate offending. Clinard and Yeager (1980:112) estimate that their study underestimated corporate offending by as much as one-fourth to one-third.

Sources of Bias in Official Data Sources

An additional problem with official data is that methods used to measure corporate crime are not systematically implemented among agencies. As a result, a single event may be classified differently by individual agencies, counted as more than one event, or not counted as a criminal event at all.

Discretion, too, influences corporate crime measurement. Certainly, some amount of discretion is central to maintaining an efficient justice system. Yet little is known about how discretion actually operates and influences crime counts. It is reasonable to assume that offenses easy to detect and prosecute are more likely to be pursued and thus recorded as infractions. Further, regulatory screening procedures may produce lopsided crime counts. For instance, unfair advertising and merger violations are likely to be uncovered by FTC screening procedures, but other kinds of uncompetitive acts are less likely to be discovered by authorities (Simpson, 1986).

Counts are affected as well by politics (Simpson, 1993; Szasz, 1984), case mobilization (Reiss, 1987), and "corporate capture," i.e., when regulatory decisions reflect the interests of corporations instead of those of the general public. Katzman (1980:27) describes how reactive versus proactive mobilization of cases affects Federal Trade Commission statistics.

> the *reactive approach* relies upon the mailbag as the source of investigations, supports strict enforcement of the laws, and tends to yield conduct cases. Proponents of the *proactive approach* argue that the Bureau of Competition should not only react to the complaints that are directed to the commission but also plan its prosecutorial efforts. . . . The proactive perspective frequently leads to a caseload of ambitious and innovative structural matters that seek to eliminate market power.

Kitsuse and Cicourel (1963) argue that official crime data reveal little about crime, but more about official reactions to crime.

Temporal Considerations

Many cases of corporate crime are sophisticated, complex, and enduring. They involve shifting coalitions of actors (individuals and organizations) and may vary in their degrees of seriousness over time (Reiss & Biderman, 1980). Take the case of a price-fixing conspiracy. If the crime is measured as an event at *time 1*, the data will show a relatively trivial transgression (e.g., a meeting between two competitors to share pricing information).

However, if a conspiracy is discovered after prices have been set for several years at artificially high levels, and all major competitors in an industry are active participants, it is much more difficult to account for all crime participants, victims, and costs—even though the case at *time 2* will reveal a much more consequential instance of offending.

Another important temporal issue involves when to start the crime clock. Official data start the clock with discovery (or some decision point after discovery). Yet, for etiological purposes, one must know when the actual crime occurred (Simpson, 1986). Similarly, onset data is required for the study of crime control. By tracking when corporations offend and whether and how they are punished for their actions, one can assess how organizations respond to formal legal sanctions (see, e.g., Simpson & Koper, 1992).

Availability and Access

Although information about corporate offending may be part of the public record (i.e., publicly available), it may not be easy to access. In some cases, data are not systematically reported in a useable format. In others, access is limited because of the inherent value of the information or because of the potential harm brought about by its disclosure.

Information about corporate misconduct is filtered through a "public record" sieve. Information that is not filtered out can be requested by way of a Freedom of Information Act (FOIA) request.[5] The FOIA sets forth the specific conditions under which information may remain private. FOIA requests are time consuming and not necessarily informative. For instance, the authors' recent inquiry at the Federal Trade Commission found that FOIA requests for case investigative materials would yield little substantive information.

In sum, official data sources—although the primary quantitative sources of information about corporate illegality—are incomplete, redundant, presented in cumbersome ways, suffer from biases, and may be difficult to obtain.[6] In light of these deficiencies, new or more systematic composite measures of corporate crime have been suggested.

Alternative Sources of Corporate Crime Measurement

A White-Collar Crime Index

Wellford and Ingraham (1990:29) argue that a realistic start to a white-collar crime measurement should begin with available statistics. They recommend constructing a national uniform reporting system, based primarily on data gathered through federal agencies. Specifically, the aggregated reporting system would be a composite of data generated by these four federal agencies: the SEC, IRS, OCG, and FBI.[7] They estimate that these agencies account for 60 percent of all federally handled white-collar offenses. In addition, agency screening processes, crime definitions, and measurement are similar enough that data mergers among them are possible. Moreover, detailed information about the criminal event and actor is collected in a systematic matter.

An instance of offending would be "counted" after a case is determined to have merit and an investigation is launched, but prior to the filing of formal charges. At this point, the index would be comparable to conventional crime measures contained in the *Uniform Crime Reports*, a regulatory equivalent of "crimes known to police."

Not all are as enamored with the idea of constructing a white-collar crime index as Wellford and Ingraham (1990). In addition to problems with construct validity (Kitsuse & Cicourel, 1963), Reiss (1987) points out that an aggregate index would be more sensitive to fluctuations in common offenses (such as fraud) and would be misleading as an aggregate indicator of crime trends. He advises "very strongly against the development of aggregate indexes like the UCR Index [to] avoid saying to the citizens of California (or any state) that white-collar crime is going up or down" (Reiss, 1987:75). Additionally, these aggregate data would suffer from all the limitations of official statistics discussed earlier in this chapter.

Surveys

Critics maintain that survey techniques have little utility in the case of corporate offending (Green, 1990; Reiss & Biderman, 1980; Wellford & Ingraham, 1990). However, under limited circumstances, surveys may be useful tools to learn more about corporate offending. For example, surveys can be used to assess conditions under which violating behavior might be contemplated or inhibited (Paternoster & Simpson, in press) or to validate official reports of crime.

Two primary populations are targeted by survey techniques: victims and offenders. The possible strengths and limitations of surveys of corporate crime offenders and victims are reviewed below.

Victimization Surveys. The National Crime Survey (NCS) calculates street crime rates based on the survey responses of crime victims. In most cases of conventional crime, victims are aware that they have been victimized. A lost item may be mistakenly reported as a burglary, or victims may lose track of the actual number of times they were victimized, but for the most part, victims are aware of their victimization. The same cannot be said for corporate victimizations.

It is rare that a corporate crime victim is aware that a victimization has occurred. And, as Reiss and Biderman (1980:92) point out, this knowledge is even more tenuous when the victim is an organization. "Organizational intelligence on victimization itself depends upon a socially organized system for becoming aware of victimization."[8] Organizations armed with detection systems may be atypical of the majority of organizational victims. Thus, in the case of corporate crime, reliance on victimization surveys could result in: (1) misspecifying the amount of corporate offending; (2) over or under reporting certain offenses; and (3) creating misleading composites of the typical corporate offender and victim. Finally, some victimizations may involve consensual activity, decreasing the likelihood of reporting (Reiss & Biderman, 1980).

Another problem with victim surveys is definitional. The amount of crime reported will fluctuate with how criminal activity is defined, i.e., you can have as much or as little crime as the definition allows.

Victimization surveys may be useful in situations where victims are more apt to be cognizant of their victim status. Employees working with dangerous chemicals might be asked whether they had been given proper safety instruction about the materials, and if appropriate safety equipment was available to them; marketing units could be surveyed about how competitors represent their firm's products in advertisements.

Perpetrator Surveys. Perpetrator surveys measure crime by asking individuals to report offenses they have committed, usually within a particular opportunity window (say, the last six months). Like victimization data, self-reports have been successfully used to estimate the hidden figure of crime among conventional offenders.[9] However, the interdependency of much corporate offending—where many actors together produce a crime event—renders a self-report measure less useful. For instance, in the case of a price-fixing conspiracy, individual actors may not know how many criminal participants are involved. Additionally, actors may be unable to estimate their own contribution to the criminal event.

Another problem with self-reported corporate crime is that many illegalities may not be defined as criminal by the event participants. To the extent that participants view technical violations of the law as common business practices, they will be less apt to report participation in an illegal act.

Survey Limitations in General

Illegality may be covered up and actions taken to avoid identification of culpable parties within the organization (Katz, 1979). Survey measures in general will not capture offenses that are consciously concealed. Morever, few sampling techniques exist that draw reliable organizational samples. Sample inclusion probabilities for many corporations are very low. Thus, extremely large and costly samples would be necessary so that diverse offenders and offenses, as well as multiple events, would be represented (Reiss & Biderman, 1980).

The proposed alternatives to official statistics reviewed in this chapter are refurbished conventional crime measures that are then applied to corporate offenders. Inherent in this strategy is an assumption that corporate and conventional offenses are fundamentally the same. As shall be demonstrated, this is a questionable assumption. In fact, the whole problem of counting corporate crime may require reconceptualization.

Constructing a Measurement Ideal

Most studies of corporate crime, particularly those that involve quantitative analysis, have neither relied on a rate-based approach to corporate crime nor have they been concerned with the general issue and problem of corporate crime rates. Undoubtedly, a rate-based approach to corporate offending would be helpful in unraveling questions about crime patterns. For instance, a rate-based measure would allow crime comparisons across companies or over time (e.g., crime at *time 1* for a given firm could be contrasted with its rate at *time 2*).

Therefore, we believe that corporate crime measurement must begin with the issue of crime rates. Rates of crime for corporate offenders, however, must be sensitive to two unique features of illegality within corporations.[10] Rates must take into account the parameters of criminal opportunity (defined as "logical units of opportunity") *and* the fact that each "act" typically involves multiple interconnected actors within a formally organized set of relationships. Rarely an isolated *independent* event, corporate crime is serially produced (i.e., the criminal act is perpetrated by multi-connected actors who are interdependent within the organization).

Building a Rate Measure:
Logical Units of Opportunity and Serial Production

Logical units of opportunity (LUO) are broadly conceived as occasions or situations in which crime might or might not occur. Organizations present a set of crime opportunities that are dependent upon: (1) the objective positioning of the corporation as an entity; and (2) each corporate actor's relative positioning within an organizational hierarchy. Conceivably, every purposive action by a corporation (or its representatives) represents one objective criminal opportunity. The goal of measurement is to "equalize" these opportunities for purposes of comparison.

Similarly, an ideal measure would be sensitive to the interdependence of crime within corporations. Criminality within organizations is a shared event, conditioned by one's organizational power, position, and motivation.[11] But not all organizational actors share equally the responsibility for crime. Consider the occasion of unsafe production. Within a corporation, what is the ability of any one person to stop the reproduction of a known unsafe product? At the assembly line level, a single informed worker may refuse to sign off at the final stage of production, thereby, in a day, limiting production by some small percentage. By the next day, the worker is replaced. At the level of top management, a single informed executive may refuse to sign off on a new round of production, thereby in a day, limiting production by 100 percent. It is putatively very difficult to replace the executive by the next day, however.

In this example, power is hierarchial, but it need not be. In some corporations, especially those comprised of many divisions and subdivisions, the distribution of power may be both horizontal and vertical (Hickson et al., 1971). Division control over a scarce resource (e.g., knowledge) may enable one organizational subunit to commit and cover-up criminality without the knowledge of other units, or one division may force criminality on other divisions as a *fait accompli* (e.g., doctoring the books, falsifying or suppressing product safety tests, rigging bids, and so forth). In these cases, power transcends an individual's organizational position and is embodied in the subunit or division.

Power relations are not intraorganizationally bound. Coercion and subsequent serial production of crime may reach beyond a single firm to include outside persons and organizations. The recent OPM bankruptcy case (Gandossy, 1985) demonstrates how outsiders can share the criminal event.[12]

Whether power relations are examined intraorganizationally (as relationships between individuals or subunits) or interorganizationally (as relationships between individuals, subunits, or corporate wholes), the production of crime within organizations should be understood as a sequence of interdependent acts by decision-makers with varying degrees of power and protective resources.

Incidence and Prevalence Rates of Corporate Crime

The two features of corporate crime discussed above—logical units of opportunity (LUO) and serial production—render problematic the traditional means of constructing crime rates, i.e., rates of crime prevalence and incidence. In the case of street crime, prevalence rates report on the central tendency of a group to commit a crime. Using these rates, we can answer such questions as: "What percent of eighteen- to twenty-four-year-olds committed a robbery last year?" Another common rate measure for conventional crime is the incidence rate. Incidence rates report on the sheer volume of crime produced by a group and allow us to answer questions such as the number of rapes per 100,000 females last year.

For corporate offenders, a particularly troublesome feature of incidence and prevalence rates is defining the appropriate base for our measure.[13] Corporate *prevalence* rates for any relevant unit of analysis (e.g., a corporation, a subunit, salaried versus wage employees, etc.) can vary from 0.00 to 1.00, where 1.00 means that everyone in the population of interest is criminal. So, for example, a prevalence rate measure might be calculated by counting the number of criminals by corporate rank (e.g., 80 percent of upper-management are criminal), or by the amount of crime owned by each employee of a corporation (of 100 total employees, 20 percent are criminal).

Using the LUO implied by street crime incidence rates, we might calculate a corporate crime *incidence* rate based on the total number of corporations, a sort of per capita corporate crime rate (occurrences/number of firms). This measure would tap the sheer volume of corporate crime within a specific time frame, controlling for the number of potential violators. It also assumes that any given analytic unit is essentially equal to all other units of comparison.[14] In the case of organizations (or corporations, more specifically), this translates into the assumption that there is some intrinsic similarity between Chrysler Corporation and Dow Chemical that is shared across, say, retail firms, or even incorporated farmers.

But, like some street crime rates (especially property crime), the measure makes little substantive sense. We have equalized the actors instead of corporate opportunities (LUO). Recognizing this problem, some researchers have constructed incidence rates in terms of relative "productive capacity" (e.g., the number of crimes per corporate profits, sales, or number of employees, cf., Clinard & Yeager, 1980). This approach is interpretatively straightforward (i.e., large firms have more opportunities to commit crime because they engage in more business transactions), but the concept "LUO" is not unidimensional. A transaction-based rate must also take into account how corporate crime opportunities are affected by legal vulnerability (activities subject to more or less law [Black, 1976]), the objective positioning of the firm, the number and type of business transactions, and the company's criminal history (culture and payoffs).

Transaction-Based Serial Rates (GINI-crime)

As currently conceived, incidence and prevalence rates are inappropriate tools in the search for an organizationally power sensitive crime measure. They assume criminal acts are event independent, and unconstrained by any other occurrence/non-occurrence of crime. Because of their lack of interdependency, let's call these types of crime and the rates that are calculated from them "parallel."

Unlike other population aggregates, such as "teenage females," corporations deliberately plan on interdependencies of acts and outcomes. And, equally important, *these interdependencies are conditioned by power distributed within the organization.* We refer to rates that take into account event interdependence as "serial." At the general level, the image of serial acts and outcomes is intuitively powerful in approaching the production of corporate as well as individual crime. Yet, as described thus far, the image is very general in the abstract, let alone very difficult to imagine operationalized. In the following discussion, we try to specify this measurement ideal.

Every rate construction is implicitly based on what is termed a logical unit of opportunity. For street crime, parallel (or event independent) rates implicitly count an individual, in a time period, as such a unit. If, as has been argued, this approach is not rich or dynamic enough to approach an individual's production of crime, it is surely not rich or dynamic enough to approach a corporation's.

Our measurement ideal, or near-ideal, for corporate crime must be baselined against a logical unit of opportunity that can accommodate considerations of serial production arrayed by an organizational power. As a starting point, we propose that this corporate LUO—or rate baseline—be found in business transactions. Transactions may be categorized by an organizational arena, such as the production arena, sales arena, financial arena, and so forth. Any large corporation may engage in thousands or hundreds of thousands of transactions daily, within different arenas. Theoretically, each transaction—each act of doing business—carries the potential for criminality (Hein, 1985). Thus a crime rate for Firm X, in the sales arena, for time period Y, might be calculated as 500 crimes/100,000 sales transactions. Further, transactions that involve principals *external* to the firm may be distinguished from transactions that involve principals solely *internal* to the company.

Baselining crimes against transactions within transaction arenas gives us a foothold in calculating corporate crime rates. But this foothold is at the level of parallel rates; considerations of serial production and power asymmetries are not yet accommodated.

A near approximation of our ideal-type measure of corporate crime is represented by a GINI-like measure of criminal incidence dispersion within any given corporation.[15] Calculation is essentially a two-step affair. First, a shared incidence rate of criminal culpability is determined (based on transaction arena). Second, this distribution is then arrayed by organizational power, with upper-level executives carrying or "owning" the largest share of that incidence rate (Ferrell & Gresham, 1985).

The shared incidence rate is based on an individual's knowledgeable participation in a criminal activity. Knowledge implies legal culpability. To create transaction culpability in an incidence measure, the organizational arena of criminality is isolated and each participant's share of the total number of unsafe products is assigned—assuming that organizational higher-ups are responsible for more of that total. The sum total of the weighted shares of crime can then be used to form the GINI-crime index; the vertical axis reflects the cumulative proportion of crime owned by hierarchically arranged corporate members, while the cumulative proportion of the corporation population comprises the horizontal axis. Unlike a standard GINI-like measure though, where in infinite populations the index varies between 0 and 1 (Allison, 1978), a negative sign for GINI-crime is theoretically possible (Suits, 1977). When the majority of criminal acts cluster near the bottom of the corporate hierarchy, GINI-crime should be negative. Conversely, if corporate executives "own" most of the count, GINI-crime should have a positive value.[16]

The GINI-crime measure is imperfect, but it does achieve a certain symmetry by first embedding the crime count in transactions shared and then weighting culpability by power. We believe that these features make it preferable to other measures that may capture culpability separately (such as weighting individuals by their total compensation)[17] but not transactions, or vice versa (incidence rates based in transaction arena). We especially think that any measure of corporate crime, like the GINI-crime measure, must be sensitive to that which makes corporate crime distinct: (1) organizational and individual transaction opportunities (i.e., logical unit of opportunity); and (2) criminal event-dependence (i.e., serially produced).

Problems with GINI-Crime

A few problems with the measure are worth noting. First, as currently operationalized, the logical unit of opportunity is the criminal transaction itself. In order to accurately gauge corporate criminality as a function of total transaction opportunity, it makes sense to nest the crime count in all possible transactions (criminal or otherwise). Second, GINI-crime does not discriminate degrees of crime seriousness. While not believed to be an inherent problem with the construct,[18] we do not consider it in this discussion. Finally, decisions about how to measure organizational power will influence the serial crime rate. Power has a number of dimensions and can be measured as vertical, horizontal, formal, informal, individual, and/or organizational. If we chose to measure power monotonically (as suggested by Simpson & Harris, 1987), this assumes that power is based on organizational position and that the appropriate level of measurement is ordinal.

While some may prefer ordering to be based in subunits rather than individual position,[19] in either case the crime measure will be a function of the number of units on which it is based. This wreaks havoc with cross-corporation comparisons, as well as creating systematic bias with potential independent variables such as firm size. Say, for example, all fifty managers knew about an instance of price fixing in Firm A. Likewise, in Firm B, every manager knew that their firm was price-fixing. However, because firm B has one hundred managers instead of fifty, it will have a higher crime rate and a positive coefficient for firm size.[20]

The ordinal level of measurement becomes problematic when individual power rankings are used as multipliers to calculate each participant's power-based share of the serially produced crime. Ordinal measurement qualities have now assumed interval level qualities. Further, it is quite possible that one function (e.g., linear) is appropriate for some firms (say relatively small, undiversified companies with homogeneous product lines), but not others (conglomerates, for example). We suspect this to be the case, but note that even if power relationships within corporations are arranged conveniently in ascending order such that $Power_1 < Power_2 < \ldots Power_n$, an inequality measure must characterize every set of possible P_1's (Allison, 1978:866). Clearly, more theorizing is necessary to identify the "proper" quantitative representation among and between organizational power positions.

Conclusions

What counts as crime and how to capture the elements of the phenomenon in measurement are fundamental to any analysis of corporate crime, whether it be theoretical or empirical. In this chapter, we describe available data and the various counting techniques employed in the construction of these sources (as well as their limitations). Like others, we find much about which to be critical in this literature. We hope that these criticisms prove helpful for data consumers who use and draw conclusions from these problematic sources.

Yet, in order for significant scholarship to take place in the corporate crime area, it is necessary to move away from traditional counting techniques—approaches that find their legitimacy in assumptions about conventional *not* corporate crime. As a theoretical step in that direction, we offer a GINI-like measure of criminal incidence dispersion that accounts for differences in organizational opportunities, power, and act-actor interdependencies. We recognize that this measure is by no means a perfect choice. However, in a world where actual measurement cannot match theoretical ambition, we would for the moment at least settle for more discussion. For surely, an approach to corporate crime rates like the one suggested here would be likely to generate causal analyses far more "tuned-into" the realities of serial production and power in corporate life than previous approaches.

NOTES

1. Currently, the Senate Judiciary Committee is investigating available data sources to better estimate the extent of corporate offending.

2. Extracting occupational offenses from *UCR* crime categories is no easy task and many researchers have been criticized for their reliance on these data to formulate criminological theory (see, e.g., Simon, 1975;

Hirschi and Gottfredson, 1987; Daly, 1989; Steffensmeier, 1989; Gottfredson and Hirschi, 1990).

3. For instance, in her study of 2000 individual and organizational violations between 1948 and 1972, Shapiro (1984:48) found that 45 percent of known offenders were not formally prosecuted by the Securities and Exchange Commission.

4. Created in 1914 by Congress, the Federal Trade Commission has the power to investigate and adjudicate (issue cease-and-desist orders) cases of unfair methods of competition.

5. The Freedom of Information Act is detailed in Title 5, U.S.C. Section 552.

6. Case studies and indepth interviews with corporate employees are also important sources of information about corporate crime (e.g., Geis, 1967; Clinard, 1983; Vaughan, 1983; Benson, 1984; Braithwaite, 1984; Simpson, 1992b; Yeager and Kram, 1990). Many of our criticisms about crime counts, however, apply as well to these kinds of data.

7. These agencies are selected in part because "each has developed sophisticated management information systems that track matters referred to them" (Wellford and Ingraham, 1990:31).

8. GAO and OMB investigations of computer fraud disclosed that most agencies were not organized either to secure their information system against fraud or to detect it when it occurred.

9. Victimization and perpetrator surveys have their share of problems even when examining more conventional crimes (cf., O'Brien, 1985)

10. Our remarks are relevant too for other instances of organizational offending in which power hierarchies are present and illegal acts are attenuated across actors.

11. Weber's (1968:I,53) distributive definition of power seems most reasonable here. Power is the probability that one actor within a social relationship will be in a position to carry out his or her will despite resistance. Yet, we find Parsons' (1960:199–225) addendum useful. Power also may be enhanced *collectively*, whereby persons cooperatively gain power over others through social organization (cf., Mann, 1986).

12. As shown in Calavita and Pontell's (1990) recent discussion of collective embezzlement (or "looting") in the savings and loan scandals, extra-organizational participation in criminal events can also be a feature of occupational crime.

13. Problems with defining the numerator in our base-rate (i.e., what to count as a crime event) were addressed earlier in this chapter.

14. For street crime, incidence rate measures are based on the assumption that within a given year each individual in the population shares the same crime possibility.

15. A GINI-Index is most commonly used to measure societal income inequality as a distribution of total family income across the percentage of all families in that society (Levy, 1988: 227-229). The GINI-coefficient is calculated by contrasting a perfectly equal distribution (e.g., 5 percent of the families control 5 percent of total family income; 10 percent of families control 10 percent of total family income, and so forth) with the share of income actually controlled by all families.

16. Careful attention must be paid to the distribution of power-based serial rates within the corporation. The GINI-summary measure is potentially misleading if crime is shared disproportionately by actors at the bottom and top of the firm. In this situation, the final GINI-score will approximate zero.

17. A technique suggested by Paul Goldman.

18. One could easily calculate distinct GINI-crime measures by seriousness in the same way that conventional measures distinguish degrees of harm.

19. Differences in subunit power could be distinguished empirically by examining organizational contingencies, managerial succession, or subunit control of organizational resources. See, e.g., Fligstein, 1987; Hickson, et al., 1971; Perrow, 1972.

20. We are indebted to Harold Barnett and David Jacobs for some of these observations and criticisms. See also, Allison, 1978.

REFERENCES

Allison, P.D. (1978). Measures of inequality. *American Sociological Review,* *43,* 865–880.

Benson, M.L. (1984). The fall from grace: Loss of occupational status as a consequence of conviction for a white-collar crime. *Criminology,* *22,* 573–593.

Berney, J. (1980). *Legislative and administrative contexts of Federal Trade Commission data: A white-collar crime data project case study.* Washington, DC: Bureau of Social Science Research, Inc.

Black, D. (1976). *The behavior of law.* New York: Academic.

Braithwaite, J. (1984). *Corporate crime in the pharmaceutical industry.* London: Routledge and Kegan Paul.

Calavita, K., & Pontell, H.N. (1990). "Heads I win, tails you lose": Deregulation, crime, and crisis in the savings and loan industry. *Crime and Delinquency, 36,* 309–341.

Clinard, M.B. (1983). *Corporate ethics and crime: The role of middle management.* Beverly Hills, CA: Sage.

Clinard, M.B., & Yeager, P.C. (1980). *Corporate crime.* New York: The Free Press.

Clinard, M.B., Yeager, P.C., Brissette, J.M., Petrashek, D., & Harries, E. (1979). *Illegal corporate behavior.* Washington, DC: U.S. Government Printing Office.

Coleman, J.W. (1989). *The criminal elite: The sociology of white-collar crime* (2nd ed.). New York: St. Martin's.

Cullen, F.T., Maakestad, W.J., & Cavender, G. (1987). *Corporate crime under attack: The Ford Pinto case and beyond.* Cincinnati: Anderson.

Daly, K. (1989). Gender and varieties of white-collar crime. *Criminology, 27,* 769–793.

Department of Justice. (1984). *Uniform Crime Reporting Handbook.* Washington, DC: U.S. Government Printing Office.

Ennis, P.H. (1967). *Criminal victimization in the United States: A report of a national survey.* Washington, DC: U.S. Government Printing Office.

Ferrell, O.C., & Gresham, L.G. (1985). A contingency framework for understanding ethical decision making in marketing. *Journal of Marketing, 49,* 87–96.

Fligstein, N. (1987). The intraorganizational power struggle: The rise of finance personnel to top leadership in large corporations—1919 to 1979. *American Sociological Review, 52,* 44–56.

Frank, N., & Lombness, M. (1988). *Controlling corporate illegality: The regulatory justice system.* Cincinnati, OH: Anderson.

Gandossy, R.P. (1985). *Bad business.* New York: Basic Books.

Geis, G. (1967). The heavy electric equipment antitrust case of 1961. In M.B. Clinard and R. Quinney (Eds.), *Criminal behavior systems: A typology* (pp. 139–150). New York: Holt, Rinehart, and Winston.

Goehlert, R., & Gunderson, N. (1987). *Government regulation of business: An information sourcebook.* Phoenix, AZ: Oryx.

Gottfredson, M.R., & Hirschi, T. (1990). *A general theory of crime.* Stanford, CA: Stanford University Press.

Green, G.S. (1990). *Occupational crime.* Chicago: Nelson-Hall.

Hein, J. (1985). Will a few bad apples spoil the core of big business? *Business and Society Review, 55,* 4–13.

Hickson, D., Hinings, C.R., Lee, C.A., Schneck, R.E., & Pennings, J.M. (1971). A strategic contingencies theory of intraorganizational power. *Administrative Science Quarterly, 16,* 216–229.

Hirschi, T., & Gottfredson, M. (1987). Causes of white-collar crime. *Criminology, 25,* 949–974.

Katz, J. (1979). Legality and equality: Plea bargaining in the prosecution of white-collar and common crimes. *Law and Society Review, 13,* 431–459.

Katzman, R.A. (1980). *Regulatory bureaucracy: The Federal Trade Commission and antitrust policy.* Cambridge, MA: MIT Press.

Kitsuse, J.I., & Cicourel, A.V. (1963). A note on the uses of official statistics. *Social Problems, 11,* 131–139.

Levy, F. (1988). *Dollars and dreams: The changing American income distribution.* New York: W.W. Norton.

Mann, M. (1986). *The sources of social power* (Vol. 1). New York: Cambridge University Press.

New York State Organized Crime Taskforce. (1989). *Corruption and racketeering in the New York City construction industry.* New York: New York University Press.

O'Brien, R. (1985). *Crime and victimization data.* Beverly Hills, CA: Sage.

Parsons, T. (1960). The distribution of power in American society. In T. Parsons, (Ed.), *Structure and process in modern societies* (pp.199–225). Glencoe, IL: Free Press.

Paternoster, R., & Simpson, S.S. (in press). A rational choice theory of corporate crime. In R. Clarke & M. Felson, (Eds.), *Advances in criminological theory* (Vol. 5). New Brunswick, NJ: Transaction.

Perrow, Charles. (1972). *Complex organizations: A critical essay.* Glenview, IL: Scott, Foresman.

Reiss, A.J., Jr. (1987). White collar/institutional crime—its measurement and analysis. *Proceedings of Symposium 87* (pp.73–92). Sacramento, CA: Bureau of Criminal Statistics and Special Services.

Reiss, A.J., Jr., & Biderman, A. (1980). *Data sources on white-collar law-breaking.* Washington, DC: U.S. Government Printing Office.

Shapiro, S.P. (1984). *Wayward capitalists: Target of the Securities and Exchange Commission*. New Haven: Yale University Press.

Simon, R. (1975). *Women and crime*. Lexington, MA: Lexington.

Simpson, S.S. (1986). The decomposition of antitrust: Testing a multi-level, longitudinal model of profit-squeeze. *American Sociological Review, 51*, 859–875.

———. (1993). Strategy, structure, and corporate crime: The historical context of anti-competitive behavior. In W.F. Laufer & F. Adler, (Eds.), *Advances in criminological theory* (Vol. 4). New Brunswick, NJ: Transaction Press, 71–93.

———. (1992). Corporate crime deterrence and corporate control policies: Views from the inside. In K. Schlegel and D. Weisburd, (Eds.), *White collar crime reconsidered*. Boston: Northeastern University Press, 289–308.

Simpson, S.S., & Harris, A.R. (1987, November). The serial production of corporate crime. Paper presented at the annual meeting of the Society for the Study of Social Problems, Chicago, IL.

Simpson, S.S., & Koper, C.S. (1992). Deterring corporate crime. *Criminology, 30*, 347–375.

Steffensmeier, D.J. (1989). On the causes of "white-collar" crime: An assessment of Hirschi and Gottfredson's claims. *Criminology, 27*, 345–358.

Suits, D.B. (1977). Measures of tax progressivity. *American Economic Review, 77*, 747–752.

Sutherland, E.H. (1949). *White collar crime*. New York: Dryden.

Szasz, A. (1984). Industrial resistance to occupational safety and health legislation: 1971–1981. *Social Problems, 32*, 103–116.

United States Sentencing Commission. (1991). *United States Sentencing Commission guidelines manual*. Washington, DC: U.S. Government Printing Office.

Vaughan, D. (1983). *Controlling unlawful organizational behavior*. Chicago: University of Chicago Press.

Weber, M. (1968). *Economy and society*. New York: Bedminster.

Wellford, C., & Ingraham, B. (1990). *Toward a national uniform white-collar crime reporting system*. Washington, DC: National Institute of Justice.

Yeager, P. C., & Kram, K. E. (1990). Fielding hot topics in cool settings: The study of corporate ethics. *Qualitative Sociology, 13*, 127–148.

CHAPTER SIX

Theoretical Explanations of Corporate Crime

Neal Shover
Kevin M. Bryant

There is enormous variation in the frequency, duration, and types of criminal acts committed by corporations. Theories of corporate crime causation are developed, tested, and modified in order to explain and predict this variation. The majority of these efforts are meant to answer two questions. First, what factors account for variation in the *proportion* of corporations that commit at least one criminal act during a given period of time? Theories that address this type of variation explain temporal and spatial variation in the aggregate-level rate of corporate criminal participation by specifying conditions under which alternately few or many firms participate in crime. Aggregate-level theories typically focus on aspects of the broad political-economic, social, and legal environments in which firms operate. In a similar fashion, theoretical explanations of variation in rates of common crimes focus on aggregate-level differences in metropolitan areas or states. Explanations of variation in rape rates, for example, hypothesize as determinants state-level differences in gender inequality, the availability of cultural norms that legitimate interpersonal violence, and per capita consumption of pornographic materials (Baron & Straus, 1987).

The second question addressed by theories of corporate criminality is why some corporations commit at least one crime while others do not during any given period of time. Typically, theoretical answers to this question highlight the importance of intrafirm differences or variations in the nature of firm-environment transactions. Just as some explanations of criminal participation by individuals focus on variations in self-concept or internalized normative standards, these theories single out firm-level variables such as weak commitment to norms of honesty and law obeisance or the absence of internal compliance mechanisms to explain criminal participation. This chapter examines both aggregate-level explanations of corporate crime and firm-level theories of corporate criminal participation. We view corporate crime as a subtype of *organizational crime,* which encompasses crimes committed by individuals or groups of individuals on behalf of or in pursuit of organizational tasks or objectives (Clinard & Quinney, 1973; Shover, 1978).

Because theories of corporate crime have been constructed largely by borrowing directly, with only minor reshaping, from theories of street crime (Farrell & Swigert, 1985), they bear familiar names: strain, social disorganization, differential association, and control. A review of these theories could be organized and presented in the format common in criminology textbooks, by discussing each in turn. We employ an alternative, simpler, approach. We elected to strip from various theories of corporate crime the major explanatory concepts and to show, by using a common theoretical framework, how each contributes either to the level of corporate crime or to corporate criminal decision making. This approach obviates the need for potentially lengthy and detailed explication of the entire array of theories. The presentational framework we employ is constructed from criminal opportunity and crime-as-choice interpretations of crime. Both perspectives are built upon rational-choice assumptions about crime that have found favor among scholars and policy makers alike in recent years. The risk in using them as frameworks is unjustified interpretive license with variables wrenched from the theoretical contexts which give them meaning. The promise is their potential for highlighting commonalities of and possible omissions from theories otherwise thought to be logically or substantively incommensurable. Our approach has the added advantage of emphasizing again what Sutherland (1949) and his successors have argued, namely that the benefits of viewing street crime and corporate crime through a common theoretical lens may be substantial. While reviewing theories, we shall approach the meaning of corporate crime uncritically, ignoring the ambiguity that surrounds it. After the review is concluded, we note continuing controversy about the kinds of behavior appropriately labeled corporate crime and some implications of this controversy. This is followed by brief comments on research aimed at testing corporate crime theories and a review of empirical evidence bearing on the theoretical frameworks we employ and the variables we discuss. The chapter concludes by noting the continuing imbalance between the volume of corporate crime theories and the pace of theory-testing research.

Aggregate-Level Theory

Although a variety of aggregate-level measures of corporate criminal participation can be devised, the principal dependent variable employed here parallels the measure commonly used (Blumstein, Cohen, & Farrington, 1988) in studies of street crime: the number of firms (per 100,000 firms) in a given period of time that commit at least one criminal act. Beginning with Sutherland (1949), investigators have shown that this aggregate-level rate varies by industry and by geographic region, as well as historically. Research (Clinard et al., 1979) on federal enforcement actions taken against 477 large manufacturing firms by twenty-five federal agencies during 1975 and 1976 found that rates of violation were highest in the oil, pharmaceutical, and motor vehicle industries and lowest in the apparel and beverages industries. Analysis of data from different branches of Swedish industry (Barnett, 1986) found that high noncompliance branches generally are in nonmanufacturing, while low noncompliance branches are in manufacturing. Lane reported that "in some [New England] shoe-manufacturing communities none of the shoe firms violates, whereas in other shoe-manufacturing communities almost half of the firms get into trouble with the law" (Lane, 1953:95). Rates of noncompliance ranged from near zero percent of firms in Boston and Brockton, to 44 percent of firms in Auburn (Mass.). Shover et al. (1984) document regional variations in noncompliance with surface coal mining regulations; violations were more numerous in Appalachia than the far West. Simpson (1987) reports temporal variation in antitrust behavior by fifty-two large "survivor firms" during the period 1927 to 1981.

When applied to aggregate-level variation in corporate crime, criminal opportunity theory would have us focus on two fundamental determinants of the level of crime: the volume of criminal opportunities, and the size of the pool of offenders predisposed to take advantage of them. Criminal opportunity theory is compatible substantively and logically with interpretations and analyses of corporate crime that build on a conception of offenders as actors who assess opportunities and make choices, including criminal ones, although their calculus may not be apparent or rational when viewed by an external observer (e.g., Green, 1990; Vaughan, 1983). To understand what causes regional, industry-level, and historical variation in the proportion of firms whose officers, managers, or employees commit criminal acts, we must explore both the sources of criminal opportunities and the supply of offenders.

Supply of Criminal Opportunities

Criminal opportunities are objectively given situations or conditions encountered by corporate personnel that offer attractive potential for enriching corporate coffers or furthering other corporate objectives by criminal means. A major reason for their attractiveness is the absence of an immediate guardian or effective control procedure. In the realm of corporate crime analysis, criminal opportunities are the equivalent of homes filled with electronic equipment that are left unoccupied for much of the day, which have made household burglary increasingly attractive to property offenders in recent decades (Cohen & Felson, 1979). The principal axiomatic proposition linking criminal opportunities and corporate crime is straightforward: *The rate of corporate criminal participation varies directly with the supply of criminal opportunities* (Cook, 1986). This proposition is axiomatic in criminal opportunity theory. In geographic areas, at times, or in industries where there are abundant criminal opportunities, we expect correspondingly high rates of corporate crime. Where a paucity of criminal opportunities exists, the rate of corporate criminal participation will be lower.

Conditions that determine the supply of corporate criminal opportunities are poorly charted, but numerous and diverse. It is clear that legal, structural, economic, and technological forces may increase, redistribute, or decrease their numbers (e.g., Tonry & Reiss, in press; Vaughan, 1983). Among the most important sources of criminal opportunities are legislation and state-funded programs that provide access to state largesse.

Calavita (1990) has shown how the Immigration Reform and Control Act of 1986, ostensibly enacted to control employment of illegal aliens, created low-risk criminal opportunities for employers. The act's recordkeeping and validation requirements were evaded so easily that they appeared little more than symbolic. Calavita and Pontell (1990) point to presidential decisions and congressional legislation during the 1980s that produced new and increased criminal opportunities in the savings and loan industry. Under provisions of the Depository Institutions and Monetary Control Act of 1980, and the Garn-St. Germain Depository Institutions Act of 1982, S&Ls were permitted to invest funds in a wide array of projects with all investments underwritten by the federal government. This occurred even as changes in the regulatory environment of the thrift industry attenuated oversight and control.

The criminal opportunities produced by these twin changes set the stage for the massive fraud and "collective embezzlement" that plundered S&Ls and victimized taxpayers. Efforts to control environmental devastation also illustrate how legislation may shift criminal opportunities from one industry to another. Enacted by Congress in 1976, the Resource Conservation and Recovery Act permitted corporate generators of hazardous waste to contract with other firms to dispose of it properly while providing weak and easily evaded control procedures. These statutory provisions increased the supply of criminal opportunities available to firms in the waste disposal industry (Szasz, 1986).

The structure of relationships and the nature of transactions among firms is another source of criminal opportunities. As with variation in the rate of street crime, what may be of critical importance is the degree of inequality among firms operating in specific industries, markets, or geographic regions (e.g., Coleman, 1987; Yeager, 1986). Inequality in the market structure of industries can influence criminal opportunities by affecting the distribution of market power, which is "the relative ability of a firm to control market conditions" (Clinard & Yeager, 1980:131). Industries distinguished by a few, large dominant firms and numerous smaller and dependent ones may be prone to criminal conduct (Denzin, 1977).

In the automobile industry, for example, dealers are forced to engage in illegal practices, such as repair fraud, in order to meet performance quotas imposed on them by large, powerful manufacturers (Farberman, 1975; Leonard & Weber, 1970). The degree of economic concentration in an industry can be seen as a proxy for industrial inequality (e.g., Coleman, 1987; Yeager, 1986). Industries with relatively small numbers of firms and intermediate levels of economic concentration may present attractive opportunities for antitrust violations to firms because of intense competition and the relative ease of concealment (Yeager, 1986). Likewise, industries marked by high levels of economic concentration present opportunities for conspiracy because few firms are involved, thereby increasing their ability to conceal illicit activities (Coleman, 1987).

The level of inequality in industries affects the structure of relations among corporate firms. Competition in industries characterized by small numbers of firms during the early twentieth century created concentrated strata consisting of homogenous "organizational sets" (Gross, 1980). Numbers within any particular organizational set may be sufficiently small to create added opportunities for interaction that is illegal (Gross, 1980). For example, organizational sets often have a "price leader" which results in uniform pricing, thereby enhancing market control and stability. Similarly, organizational sets can provide conditions conducive to collusion and other illicit interfirm activities, as happened in the heavy electrical equipment (Geis, 1967) and folding box industries (Sonnenfeld & Lawrence, 1978).

Interfirm transactions also can create criminal opportunities (e.g., Vaughan, 1980). They may, for example, provide legitimate access to resources held by other firms, thus providing opportunities for illegal expropriation. The structure of interfirm transactions also may impede completion of the exchange, thus creating opportunities for illegal alternatives (Vaughan, 1982). Transactions between or among firms have four characteristics that create potential opportunities for illegal activity: formalization, advanced recording and processing techniques, relationships based on trust, and general monitoring techniques. The complexity and diversity of interfirm transactions is attended by highly technical recording and processing procedures. Computers are used to access large amounts of information and other resources, creating opportunities for illegal entry into a competitor's financial records or research and development projects. The frequency and complexity of interfirm transactions demands that trust and general rather than specific monitoring procedures be utilized on behalf of those involved.

Supply of Offenders

The second axiomatic proposition of criminal opportunity theory is that the rate of crime varies directly with the supply of motivated offenders. When applied to corporate crime: *The rate of corporate criminal participation varies directly with the proportion of corporations whose personnel are predisposed to exploit available criminal opportunities.* The supply of firms in which individuals and groups are predisposed to break the law is a product of three conditions: the level of uncertainty in critical corporate markets; cultures of noncompliance that acquire support and legitimacy in specific areas, industries, or historical periods; and the consistency and strength of the context of control in which firms operate. The first condition is created when personnel in an increasing number of firms are subjected to performance pressures and strain. The second condition for increased crime potential emerges when firms and their personnel are exposed to crime-facilitative attitudes, techniques, and shared linguistic constructions of criminal acts as ethically and legally justifiable conduct. The third condition occurs when prohibitions against law violations are ideologically and operationally inconsistent and weak, thus increasing the number of firms that are free to break the law.

To acquire financing, personnel, raw materials, and other resources that are needed to produce and sell their products, corporations must participate in a variety of markets. Conditions in any or a combination of these markets may range from financially depressed or unsettled to healthy and optimistic. When the former is the case, market uncertainty increases. This complicates planning, escalates anxiety, and increases the pool of potential offenders. The health of national, regional, or industry economies is one of the most important factors that may increase uncertainty in multiple corporate markets (Asch & Seneca, 1976; Lane, 1953).

Simpson (1987) argues that corporate crime, antitrust behavior specifically, is directly related to unemployment, and inversely related to stock prices and manufacturing output. Environments with scarce resources also exacerbate uncertainty, necessitating that firms expend more resources to secure needs, and thus are more likely to resort to criminal conduct (Baucus & Near, 1991; Pfeffer & Salancik, 1978; Staw & Szwajkowski, 1975). Competition, depending on whether it is weak or intense, may be another source of heightened uncertainty in product markets (Coleman, 1987). The criminogenic nature of relentless competition, in fact, is axiomatic for those who argue that the rate of corporate crime in capitalist societies exceeds the rate of crime committed by business units in countries with socialist or other systems of ownership and production (e.g., Barnett, 1982).

While uncertainty rooted in market fluctuations or pathogenic interfirm structures and relationships may increase the supply of corporate offenders, other conditions do so by presenting corporations with weak controls on their behavior. Weak or inconsistent controls enable personnel in some firms to commit crimes with minimal fear of adverse consequences.

Controls on corporate conduct acquire form in the structures and policies of professional associations and trade groups, in crime control ideologies promoted or endorsed by political leaders, and in state enforced strategies of crime control (Madden, 1977). This array of norms, organizations, ideologies, and practices is the *context of control*. Where contextual controls are inconsistent in focus and weak in application, the supply of potential offenders is large; where controls are consistent and strong, it is small (Braithwaite, 1989; Cressey, 1976; Shover & Link, 1986; Sutherland, 1949). In propositional form: *The supply of corporate offenders varies inversely with the consistency and strength of the context of control.*

It is possible hypothetically to distinguish alternative contextual *control styles* on the basis of their underlying crime control ideologies and the apparatus and strategies typically employed to control corporate conduct (e.g., Reiss, 1984; Kagan, 1989). Control ideologies are beliefs about the general nature of corporate officers and managers, the causes of corporate crime, and appropriate strategies for minimizing its occurrence. On the one hand, the *deterrence style* embodies an ideological conception of corporate actors as greedy, self-serving, and calculating actors who are indifferent to public welfare. Because they are believed to respond only to profit considerations and power, countervailing force, usually in the form of state coercion, is needed to restrain them. Strict and closely administered external controls are mandatory if corporations are to act responsibly. Proponents of the deterrence style advocate use of threats and punitive sanctions to promote compliance (Braithwaite & Geis, 1982).

On the other hand, the *compliance style* of corporate control assumes both the goodwill of industry and the power of market mechanisms to promote responsible corporate behavior (Bromiley & Marcus, 1989). Corporate pursuit of profit, coupled with the dynamics of free markets, will yield benefits for the collective good. By this conception of corporations, those caught committing criminal acts are dismissed as statistical and ethical aberrations. As corporate leaders generally are believed to be committed to operating ethically and responsibly, there is often a strong flavor of opposition to external control and regulation in this ideological conception of corporate crime. Characteristically, government regulation is derided as uninformed, heavy-handed, and harmful to productivity and competitiveness. In lieu of state regulation, proponents of the compliance style advocate the use of appeals to corporate conscience and goodwill, the provision of incentives for compliance, and the implementation of programs based on cooperative models or corporate self-regulation.

Historically, there has been substantial ideological and political conflict over appropriate and effective approaches to control of corporate behavior. The 1970s saw support for and the hegemony of the deterrence style reach a two-decade peak in the American political arena. Congress enacted additional statutory controls on corporate conduct and created new federal regulatory programs with enhanced enforcement powers (e.g., Barnett, 1990; Calavita, 1983; Scott, 1989; Shover et al., 1986; Yeager, 1991). The official favor enjoyed by the deterrence style waned rapidly in the 1980s, however. The Reagan administration rejected the deterrence ideology and sharply reduced the number of enforcement personnel in many regulatory programs. The diminished federal role was coupled with an abrupt shift of regulatory responsibility to state-level agencies and by increasing reliance on corporate self-regulation.

The effectiveness of the context of control in minimizing the supply of potential offenders is affected by geographic, temporal, or industrial-sector variation in corporate cultural support for or opposition to control. The contention that industries with high aggregate rates of noncompliance are distinguished by cultures of noncompliance has been argued, for example, by Barnett (1986). A culture of noncompliance is defined as a "set of commonly shared attitudes, techniques, and rationalizations which condition the likelihood that owners, managers, and employees with the typical . . . enterprise will use illegal means to pursue corporate goals" (Barnett, 1986:555).

Whenever or wherever a culture of noncompliance gains credibility and strength, it increases the supply of offenders by making available to firms shared understandings and ways of conducting business that excuse or even encourage criminal conduct as normal business practice. Where, by contrast, a culture of compliance is dominant, there is greater emphasis on

Figure 1

Summary Model of Determinants of the Rate of Corporate Criminal Participation

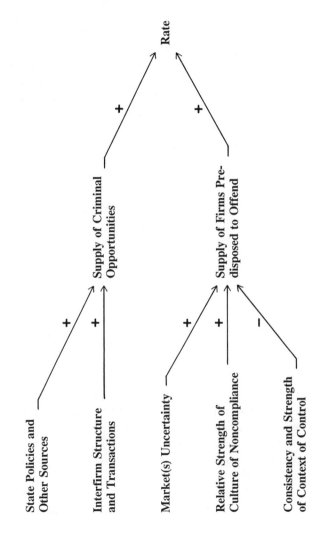

the priority of honest and lawful conduct as paramount and autonomous corporate objectives. By affirming both the priority of these norms and corporate obligation to operate in socially responsible and ethical fashion, a culture of compliance reduces the proportion of firms predisposed to lawbreaking. In propositional form: *The supply of corporate offenders varies directly with the strength of cultures of noncompliance.*

Our comments on aggregate-level theories of corporate criminal participation are depicted and summarized graphically in Figure 1. It shows that the supply of criminal opportunities is fed by state policies and qualities of intercorporate structures and transactions. Figure 1 shows also that the supply of firms predisposed to violate the law is constructed disproportionately by firms operating in competitively intense or uncertain markets, firms insufficiently restrained by the context of control, and firms operating in a cultural environment of support for noncompliance. We omitted from Figure 1 variables that reflect the nature and quality of interfirm conditions and their predicted effect on the supply of offenders. Current theoretical constructions of this relationship suggest that we have yet to unravel it clearly or satisfactorily.

Firm-Level Theory

Regardless of whether the rate of corporate criminal participation is high or low, some firms maintain exemplary records of compliance with the criminal law. Whether the supply of criminal opportunities is plentiful or scarce, all corporations and their personnel do not appreciate or exploit them equally. As with aggregate-level variation in corporate crime, there is ample evidence of variation in criminal participation by individual corporate firms (e.g., Baucus & Near, 1991; Simpson, 1986; Sutherland, 1949). Analysis of federal price control violations during World War II showed that many firms violated rules regulating prices but others did not (Clinard, 1946). A study (Ross, 1980) of 1,043 major corporations shows that only 117 firms were involved in any of five major types of crime during the 1970s. Clinard and Yeager (1980) found that approximately 40 percent of the firms they studied were not charged by twenty-five federal agencies with any violations during 1975 and 1976. Braithwaite (1984) found that some large pharmaceutical firms have much better records of compliance with federal law than others. Kagan and Scholz (1984:89) note "[t]here are major petroleum refineries in the same county in California each inspected for air pollution violations virtually every day [that] have sharply different [compliance records] according to enforcement officials." Analysis of data on 3,800 violations of the British Factory Act by 200 firms over a five-year period likewise show great variation in noncompliance (Carson, 1970).

The principal causal concepts in firm-level theories of criminal participation can be recast in the framework of the crime-as-choice approach that has found widespread adoption in studies of criminal participation by street offenders (e.g., Cornish & Clarke, 1986; Wilson & Herrnstein, 1985). The fundamental assumption underpinning this approach is that criminal behavior results from a comprehensible decision-making process in which actors seek to achieve valued objectives at a satisfactory level of performance. To conceive of crime as choice does not require that one assume their choices are rational in any a priori meaning of the term. It does assume, however, that the decision to commit a criminal act is based on an assessment, however crude or incomplete, of options and the potential risks and payoffs of each. Firm-level theories of corporate crime generally point to factors that increase the willingness of corporate decision-makers to weigh criminal opportunities as acceptable options, thereby increasing the probability of criminal participation.

Structural and Procedural Complexity

Belief that the structural and procedural complexities of firms are important sources of propensities toward criminal participation is fundamental to investigations of corporate crime. In propositional form: *The probability of corporate criminal participation varies directly with firms' structural and procedural complexity.* The rationale behind this argument is that complexity may distort decision-making processes and thereby increase the attractiveness of criminal options. The most common proxy for organizational complexity is firm size (Baucus & Near, 1991; Blau & Schoenherr, 1971). Large firms experience a disproportionate amount of uncertainty because of specialized organizational activities and decentralized decision-making, thus increasing the chances of illegal behavior. Increasing size may lead to increased internal diversity and greater structural complexity, both of which may exacerbate problems of maintaining effective internal controls on behavior. Also, the larger and more complex a firm is, the greater the chances that subcultures of neutralization or restraint may develop and persist in subunits of the firm.

Performance Pressure

No interpretation of the causes of corporate criminal participation has been asserted as often or with as much confidence as the belief that pressures and strain produced by the need to maintain or exceed acceptable levels of firm performance increases the probability of crime by corporate personnel (e.g., Gross, 1980; Passas, 1990; Shover, 1976). Firms that have difficulty acquiring the resources needed to produce and market their products, that fail to plan adequately, or firms that must struggle to compete successfully, are those in which officers and managers are more likely to engage in criminal behavior. In propositional form: *The probability of corporate criminal participation varies directly with performance pressures on firm personnel.*

There are several potential sources of performance pressure experienced by firms, but in a free-market economy the need to maintain profitability is paramount. In general, declining profitability increases the attractiveness of criminal opportunities and the probability of criminal participation (Coleman, 1987; Finney & Lesieur, 1982). Falling profits are a source of internal pressure for higher performance and output. Managers, for example, may demand higher output from workers during economic downturns thereby increasing pressure on them to maintain or increase production. Responding to this added pressure, employees may resort to criminal practices.

Estimated Aversive Consequences

Along with firm-level theories that point to the causal importance of strain caused by performance pressures, another common explanation of firm-level criminal participation points to variation in the perceived risks of choosing specific criminal options. The underlying proposition is: *The probability of criminal participation varies inversely with the estimated certainty and severity of the threatened aversive consequences of doing so.* The principal challenge posed by this explanation is to identify conditions that cause corporate personnel to believe that the risks of engaging in criminal behavior would exceed any benefits it might produce.

Risk is the potential for aversive consequences (e.g., sanctions) of varying types and degrees. Some are based outside of the firm while others are part of its internal world. Thus, corporate personnel may comply with the law because they fear the penalties the state may impose if they are caught violating the law, because they fear censure by professional peers, because they fear the effects of adverse publicity on the firm, because noncompliance would produce feelings of guilt and self-rejection, or because it would harm career prospects (Braithwaite & Makkai, 1991; Coleman, 1987; Fisse & Braithwaite, 1983; Scott, 1989).

The relationships among these various controls are largely unexplored (Reichman, 1990), but we assume that perceptions of and beliefs about the certainty and severity of sanctions threatened by external agents are influenced strongly by conditions and controls within the firm. In other words, estimates of the risks posed by the police, courts, and regulatory personnel are shaped and filtered by firm-level priorities and perspectives. The stance toward ethical conduct and compliance with the law taken by top management is critically important here (Goodpaster, 1985; Hambrick & Mason, 1984). Top management function as moral exemplars for middle management and employees by influencing their perceptions of the legitimacy, the credibility, and the risk (personal and financial) of control structures and procedures (Baumhart, 1961; Brenner & Molander, 1977; Clinard, 1983; Sonnenfeld & Lawrence, 1978).

Top management's signalling behavior is important also. As occupants of positions of power and authority in the corporation, they possess discretion to invest organizational resources in policies, structures, and procedures to minimize unethical and criminal conduct. These include management directives for handling many situations, codes of ethics, and internal compliance programs. When management establishes appropriate and effective control measures, and also communicates unequivocally the message that compliance is a principal corporate objective, their example and signals are not lost on employees.

When top management fails to take such measures, or supports them half-heartedly, this signals to employees that ethical behavior and compliance are not priorities within the firm and that noncompliance would not meet with severe or enduring aversive consequences. Firms with unambiguous policies that define obeisance to law as a priority should have fewer violations than firms whose policies are nonexistent or silent on these matters. To borrow Reckless' (1961) terminology, such policies and controls function potentially to "insulate" the firm from noncompliance while their absence constitute "organizational defects" which increase the probability of criminal participation (Braithwaite, 1985; Finney & Lesieur, 1982). Where top management supports internal compliance programs and personnel only grudgingly, awareness of this eventually will spread throughout the firm.

Crime-Facilitative Culture

The concept of culture as an explanation for differential corporate criminal participation has a long history. As compared with firms that do not commit crimes, those that do may be distinguished by cultures that facilitate illicit conduct (Needleman & Needleman, 1979). In propositional form: *The probability of corporate criminal participation varies directly with the strength of crime-facilitative components of corporate culture.*

To be useful as a theoretical and empirical guide, many have found it necessary to define the concept of *culture* narrowly and precisely. Several specific components or indicators of corporate culture that may facilitate, covary with, and predict criminal participation have been identified. One approach hypothesizes fundamental orientations toward state-imposed controls on corporations that are broadly shared by management and vary at the firm level (Kagan & Scholz, 1984). The culture of some firms elevates profit-seeking to paramount and unrivalled importance as an organizational objective. Personnel in these firms carefully assess options and risks, and they disobey the law when the risk and anticipated profits make it worthwhile to do so. The culture of these firms is distinguished by qualities of *amoral calculation*. Compare this culture with one that emphasizes *political citizenship*. These firms comply with the law out of respect or obligation, although this is limited by the belief that they are justified in resisting public policies they regard as arbitrary or unreasonable. Last, the culture of some firms is distinguished by *organizational incompetence*. Management in these firms often fail to supervise subordinates effectively, to estimate risks intelligently, or to create organizational mechanisms that promote compliance as a matter of routine.

Another approach to key aspects of firms' cultural worlds is to identify varieties of *ethical climate*. By one definition, ethical climates are "shared perceptions of what is ethically correct behavior and how ethical issues should be handled" (Victor & Cullen, 1987:51–52). Investigators have suggested dimensions of variation for industry and firm ethical climates, and also have demonstrated corresponding empirical variation (Victor & Cullen, 1988).

Perhaps the most widely accepted approach to identifying cultural facilitators of crime looks to the number and comparative strength of techniques of restraint and techniques of neutralization. Both are linguistic constructions of prospective behavior that affect the perceived options and preferences of decision makers and, therefore, the probability of criminal participation. *Techniques of restraint* function to reduce the probability that corporate personnel will select criminal options in their daily work. They do so by affirming and strengthening the perceived relationships among personal conduct and moral, and ethical principles, legal precepts, the expectations of legitimate significant others, and conscience.

Consider, for example, the guide to conduct expressed in admonitions such as "virtue is its own reward" and "honesty is the best policy." Balancing and diminishing the effectiveness of techniques of restraint, *techniques of neutralization* (Sykes & Matza, 1957) are linguistic devices that, when invoked by corporate managers or employees, blunt the moral force of the law, and neutralize the guilt of criminal participation (Hills, 1987). *Denial of responsibility* is the belief that individual offenders are blameless because responsibility for their criminal conduct lies elsewhere or with higher ranking employees of the corporation. *Denial of injury* finds expression in the claim that no one is harmed by specific acts of corporate crime, and those who commit them therefore have not acted improperly. *Denial of the victim* is the belief that victims of corporate crime are responsible for the harm and suffering they sustain. *Condemnation of the condemners* finds expression in the belief that those who would condemn the individual or the firm for engaging in criminal conduct are morally or legally unworthy to do so. *Appeal to higher loyalties* is the contention that those who transgress should not be held responsible for their behavior because they are acting in pursuit of broader or more important objectives, or they are blameless because their employer expects them to do whatever is necessary to achieve corporate goals. *Appeal to necessity* is the belief that the conditions of employment and competition require a willingness to engage in criminal conduct if one is to be successful and gain promotion within the firm (Coleman, 1987).

Techniques of neutralization function not only as post hoc rationalizations for involvement in criminal conduct, but they also may precede and thereby facilitate the commission of criminal behavior. The dominant culture of a firm, as determined by the proportionate mix of techniques of neutralization and techniques of restraint, is an important determinant of the likelihood of criminal participation (Braithwaite, 1989). An imbalance in the availability and approved use of these techniques alters the probability of criminal participation accordingly. Where a culture of neutralization or other crime-

Figure 2

Summary Model of Determinants of Corporate Criminal Participation

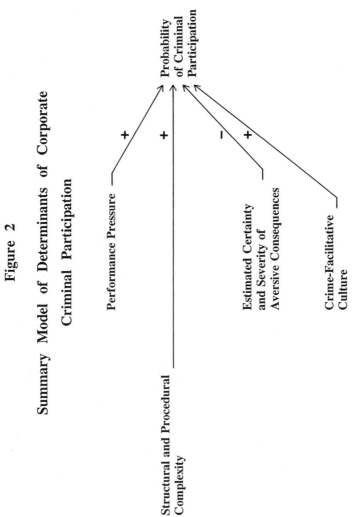

facilitative cultural components gain acceptance and use in decision making, the probability of criminal behavior is increased. Firms or subunits of firms in which a culture of neutralization is dominant will be more likely to commit criminal acts than firms or subunits dominated by a culture of restraint.

Figure 2 summarizes the presentation of materials on firm-level variation in criminal participation. It shows that structural and procedural complexity, performance pressure, estimates of the certainty and severity of potential aversive consequences, and the dominance of cultural components that facilitate lawbreaking are directly related to the probability of criminal participation.

Assessing Theories of Corporate Crime

How do we assess the merits of corporate crime theories? How do we distinguish those that are good or useful from those that hold little promise? A theory's value in part is based on how much it enhances our ability to think analytically and intelligently about a phenomenon. A good theory, by this measure, is one that sensitizes us to new or different aspects of our environment or ways of understanding it. Beyond this important way of judging the merit of theories social scientists generally ask how well they explain and predict the distribution of the subject phenomenon, in this case, corporate crime. *Explanation* is the extent to which patterns of corporate crime observed in the empirical world are consistent logically with propositions derived from the theory. *Prediction* is the extent to which testable propositions derived from a theory correctly specify what investigators find when they conduct appropriate research. The probative payoff from research that tests propositions derived from corporate crime theories is determined by how effectively it documents temporally asymmetric statistical covariation between appropriate measures of relevant independent and dependent variables, and refutes plausible rival interpretations of this variation.

Conceptual and Research Issues

Corporate crime investigators inevitably must contend with conceptual and data issues that plague efforts to arbitrate confidently theoretical disputes. While there is substantial agreement that corporate crime is *crime* committed on behalf of corporate employers or in pursuit of corporate objectives, there is continuing uncertainty and disagreement over the specific behaviors this encompasses. One issue is whether corporate crime should be defined broadly or narrowly. Should it, for example, be defined to include violations of international agreements which perhaps do not violate the criminal statutes of specific states or nations (Michalowski & Kramer, 1987)? Should violations of regulatory rules, no matter how unintentional or harmless they are, be counted as crimes together with violations of criminal statutes, or should they be treated as a category of less serious "illegalities," "violations," or "infractions" (Shapiro, 1980)? Following Sutherland's (1949) lead, Clinard and Yeager (1980:16) cast a wide net, defining crime as "any act committed by corporations that is punished by the state, regardless of whether it is punished under administrative, civil, or criminal law." Schrager and Short (1978:411–412), by contrast, limit the application of the label crime to "illegal acts of commission or commission of an individual or a group" of corporate officers or employees "which have a serious physical or economic impact on employees, consumers or the general public."

A second issue is whether substantively diverse forms of unethical or illegal corporate conduct have similar or dissimilar causes. To what extent are the antecedents of unethical corporate behavior and corporate crime the same? Are theoretical interpretations of and lessons learned from investigations of questionable foreign payments (Leitko & Kowalewski, 1985) applicable to violations of criminal laws? This issue also appears, with narrower focus, in continuing uncertainty about whether diverse forms of corporate behavior that do violate criminal statutes have similar causes. Are price fixing, violations of labor laws, and illicit disposal of toxic wastes, for example, sufficiently alike to justify an assumption that they have common causal origins or, like underage drinking and homicide, are they so dissimilar as to pursue the search for causes separately? Simpson (1986:860) contends that "[m]ost current theorizing about corporate crime is too broad to be testable. We cannot assume etiological invariance between and within corporate crime categories . . . Corporate illegality is as diverse as street crime and our conceptual imagery must account for this fact." While we await resolution of these issues, some have moved theoretically to identify antecedents of specific types of corporate crime. Asch and Seneca (1976) argue that depressed economic conditions generate increased levels of collusion and unfair trade practices. Others have suggested that the likelihood of false advertising, price-fixing, and industrial espionage increases in highly competitive industries (e.g., Clinard et al., 1979; Finney & Lesieur, 1982).

In addition to problems rooted in conceptual ambiguity and disagreement, investigations of corporate crime face challenges caused by data limitations. The process of calculating rates of corporate crime presents challenges that are not found in studies of street crime and street offenders (Simpson, Harris & Mattson, this volume). Should it reflect and take account of the fact that some corporate firms are extremely small, engage in relatively few transactions with individuals or other firms, and have few criminal opportunities while others are extremely large, engage in many transactions daily and, correspondingly, have many criminal opportunities (Hirschi & Gottfredson, 1987)? Should measures of the *intensity* of criminal participation, which have been developed and employed to analyze careers in street-crime participation, be developed for analyzing corporate crime (Blumstein, Cohen, & Farrington, 1988)? Further, although there are abundant sources of data on corporate criminal offending (Reiss & Biderman, 1980), data are not collected, collated, or disseminated by a designated federal-level agency or office, as is true of street crime. For corporate crime investigators there is no counterpart of the Federal Bureau of Investigation's Uniform Crime Reporting Program. Nor is there the same data variety and detail as are available to those who conduct research on street crime. The U. S. Department of Justice spends heavily to support the National Crime Victimization Survey, but displays no interest in systematic collection of comparable data on corporate crime and its victims (Moore & Mills, 1990).

Much of what is known about corporate crime and its causes is based on case studies (e.g., Block et al., 1981; Cullen et al., 1987; Ermann & Lundman, 1982; Geis, 1967; Sonnenfeld & Lawrence, 1978). Case study designs and methods, however, are poorly suited for theory testing. It is difficult if not impossible to demonstrate covariation, to control for the possible influence of extraneous variables and, therefore, to confidently refute rival interpretations. Even investigators who employ rigorous statistical techniques to overcome some of these challenges flounder on another shortcoming of case studies: limited external validity (e.g., Block et al., 1981). Other studies employ cross-sectional research designs, meaning that all relevant variables are measured at one time. This leaves the investigator unable to demonstrate that covariation of the independent and dependent variables occurs in the hypothesized temporal order. Because longitudinal designs permit investigators to measure exogenous variables at one time and the dependent variable at a later time, they can provide strong evidence of temporally asymmetric statistical covariation. To date, however, such studies have been rare.

Despite the overall shortcomings of previous investigations of corporate crime, there are indications of increasing use of more powerful research designs and statistical techniques. Clinard et al. (1979) used data on 575 large American corporations to examine the relationship between a variety of possible antecedents and corporate violations. Their broadly defined dependent variable was decomposed into specific categories of crimes and regulatory violations: administrative, environmental, financial, labor, manufacturing, and unfair trade practices.

Use of multiple regression analysis and a longitudinal research design enabled them to control for extraneous variation and establish proper causal order. Simpson (1986; 1987) collected data on antitrust behavior by fifty-two American firms over a fifty-five-year period. After documenting substantial historical variation in antitrust offenses, she used time series and regression analyses to examine economic and political factors related to violations. Her research illustrates the use of longitudinal data to test propositions about the, possibly delayed, effects on corporate crime of fluctuations in the broader economy. Baucus and Near (1991) examine firm-level antecedents of participation in "clearly illegal" behavior by eighty-eight *Fortune* 500 firms convicted of criminal conduct during the period 1974 to 1983. For a comparison group, they randomly selected a sample of 104 nonconvicted firms from the *Fortune* 500 list. The investigators use longitudinal, event history techniques to analyze their data. Studies such as these suggest increasing use of research designs and statistical procedures that permit more rigorous theory testing.

Empirical Record

How well do criminal opportunity and crime-as-choice theories of corporate crime, which we use as presentational frameworks, explain and predict its distribution? In a nutshell, we do not know. One reason is the sparsity of records of aggregate-level investigations in general. Another is the near-total absence of direct tests of criminal opportunity theory. Makkai and Braithwaite (1991) use interview data collected from 410 Australian nursing home chief executives to test the predictive merits of four theories of regulatory violations. Their results, after controlling for characteristics of the nursing home, nursing home residents, and the inspection team, show that performance pressure, as measured by the availability of legitimate opportunities, and the nature of illegitimate opportunities, both explain statistically significant portions of the variance in compliance. The findings support an interpretation of crime as choice. There are virtually no investigations of the relationship between state policies and the supply of criminal opportunities. The same is true of research into the effects of indicators of interfirm structure and transactions.

Empirical investigation of the relationship between uncertainty in critical corporate markets and the supply of firms predisposed to offend appears in several studies. Factors that affect profitability, such as competitive market structures, increase the supply of criminal opportunities (Albrecht, et al.

1980; Clinard et al., 1979; Conklin, 1977; Hay & Kelly, 1974; Leonard & Weber, 1970; Sonnenfeld & Lawrence, 1978; Staw & Szwajkowski, 1975). Depressed financial markets also enhance the supply of criminal opportunities (Albrecht et al., 1980; Clinard et al., 1979; Conklin, 1977; Simpson, 1986; 1987; Sonnenfeld & Lawrence, 1978).

The appeal of cultural explanations of corporate crime has not been matched by systematic empirical scrutiny. Aside from case studies (e.g., Geis, 1967), supporting evidence is largely indirect. Some investigators, who initially set out to test other theoretical variables, suggest post hoc that their findings affirm the potential importance of cultural variables (e.g., Baucus & Near, 1991). There are no studies "that develop systematic and independent measures of both business illegalities and corporate or industry cultures" (Yeager, 1986:100). Consequently, although the importance of cultural variation in escalating or dampening the rate of criminal participation is a matter of considerable consensus, compelling direct evidence has not appeared.

Studies of the impact of deterrence and compliance styles of control are rare. Historically, the compliance style has been preferred by Republican elected officials while the deterrence style has been advocated by their Democratic counterparts. Evidence shows inequivocally that the deterrence style in application is beset by a number of operational difficulties (e.g., Gallo, Craycraft, & Bush, 1985; Scott, 1989). Whether these difficulties also make it less effective than the compliance style in controlling corporate crime is unclear. Simpson (1986) found that corporate antitrust violations are more likely during Republican than Democratic administrations, suggesting that a compliance style may be less effective than the deterrence style. Her findings, however, are open to a variety of other interpretations as well. Generally, although evidence for a deterrent effect is weak, it does favor a proposition supporting deterrence more than it favors one asserting that deterrence is absent (e.g., Block et al., 1981; Gray & Jones, 1991).

As compared with significant gaps in empirical investigations of relationships depicted in Figure 1, there is a more extensive corpus of research bearing on the causal links summarized in Figure 2. Recalling that firm size is used as a measure of corporate complexity, most investigators find support for the hypothesized inverse relationship between size and criminal participation, but others do not (Clinard et al., 1979; Conklin, 1977; Yeager, 1991).

Support for the hypothesized direct relationship between firm financial performance and criminal participation has been reported by a host of investigators (Albrecht et al., 1980; Asch & Seneca, 1976; Bain, 1951; Clinard et al., 1979; Hay & Kelly, 1974; Lane, 1953; Perez, 1978; Staw & Szwajkowski, 1975). Simpson (1986; 1987) finds that poor economic performance results, specifically, in higher levels of antitrust activities. Yeager (1991), however, finds no relationship between firm profitability and water pollution offenses, while Baucus and Near (1991) find that firms are more likely to behave illegally at moderate and high levels of performance, although this relationship is not statistically significant. We interpret the preponderance of evidence, which shows that financially weak firms are more likely to commit violations than successful ones, as supportive of the relationship between performance pressures and criminal participation.

What about the link between estimates of the potential aversive consequences and criminal participation? Braithwaite & Makkai (1991) examine the relationship between management perceptions of the certainty and severity of sanctioning and organizational compliance with nursing home regulations. They find no evidence of a relationship between the variables. The dependent variable used by Briathwaite and Makkai (1991) is relatively minor forms of noncompliance with regulatory rules, which leaves unanswered the question of whether analysis of criminal violations would have yielded similar findings.

Concluding Comments

Theory development and empirical testing are complementary pursuits and progress in the former may hinge on progress in the latter as well. Whatever may be the shortcomings of contemporary corporate crime analysis, lack of theoretical interpretations is not among them. The greatest need is an accelerated pace of investigations utilizing research designs more sophisticated than in the past and a wider range of methodologies (Szwajkowski, 1985; 1986). Since the ranks of social scientists exploring corporate crime shows no signs of impending increase, we are unlikely to see a significant increase in the number of investigations. Prospects may be better for continued improvements in design and methods. We have noted the nascent movement toward increased use of longitudinal studies. Previous research on corporate crime has primarily focused on egregious and extremely harmful crimes, or industries in which criminal conduct flourished. The limits this imposes on the external validity of their findings suggest the need to devote more attention to crimes of varying seriousness committed in small as well as large corporations, and industries with little or a great deal of crime.

Although qualitative research techniques have found use in several studies of corporate crime (e.g., Braithwaite, 1985; Simpson, 1990; Yeager & Kram, 1990), increased use of ethnographic procedures may hold great promise for theory refinement. There is a need for procedures that enable the investigator to become immersed in the internal world of corporate firms. Reichman (1990:31) correctly notes that "we have not been very good at getting inside organizations to see how . . . controls actually operate." Studies of this process may be enormously valuable if we are to understand and document variation in the cultural worlds of corporate firms. Evidence does suggest that ethical climate and employee involvement in unethical behavior or misconduct other than corporate crime covary. Perceptions of "what my peers believe" and "what top management believes," for example, are significant predictors of individual involvement in crimes that victimize their employers (Zey-Ferrell et al., 1979; Zey-Ferrell & Ferrell, 1982). This lends support to what has been said about the potential importance of cultural beliefs and management signals as antecedents of misconduct. Whether the same is true of crimes is unknown.

Amid periodic and predictable corporate complaints, and sometimes acrimonious scholarly debate about over-zealous regulators (Bardach & Kagan, 1982; Hawkins, 1990; Pearce & Tombs, 1990; Snider, 1990), the absence of research on the comparative impact of deterrence and compliance control styles is remarkable. Post-Watergate America has seen distrust of corporations and the increasing strength of compliance styles of control prompt corporate development of codes of ethics and internal compliance programs. Yet research on the content and impact of codes of ethics raises doubt about their beneficial impact on decision makers (Cressey & Moore, 1983; Mathews, 1987; Robin et al., 1989). The jury is still out on the impact of compliance programs. Evidence eventually may show that they, like codes of ethics, have a significant impact on behavior only when they are backed by top management and operate autonomously.

REFERENCES

Albrecht, W.S., Romney, M.B., Chevington, D.J., Payne, I.R., & Roe, A.V. (1980). *Auditor involvement in the detection of managment fraud.* Englewood Cliffs, NJ: Prentice-Hall.

Aldrich, H.E. (1979). *Organizations and environments.* Englewood Cliffs, NJ: Prentice-Hall.

Asch, P., & Seneca, J.J. (1976). Is collusion profitable? *Review of Economics and Statistics, 58,* 1–12.

Bain, J.S. (1951). Relation of profit rate to industry concentration: American manufacturing, 1936–1940. *Quarterly Journal of Economics, 65,* 293–324.

Bardach, E., & Kagan, R.A. (1982). *Going by the book.* Philadelphia: Temple University Press.

Barnett, H.C. (1982). The production of corporate crime in corporate capitalism. In P. Wickman & T. Dailey (Eds.), *White-collar and economic crime* (pp. 157–170). Lexington, MA: D.C. Heath.

———. (1986). Industry culture and industry economy: Correlates of tax noncompliance in Sweden. *Criminology, 24,* 553–574.

———. (1990, May). Corporate liability for Superfund cleanup: An analysis of state funding and enforcement. Paper presented at the

Edwin Sutherland Conference on White-Collar Crime, Bloomington, Indiana.

Baron, L., & Straus, M.A. (1987). Four theories of rape: A macrosociological analysis. *Social Problems, 34*, 467–489.

Baucus, M.S., & Near, J.P. (1991). Can illegal corporate behavior be predicted? An event history analysis. *Academy of Management Journal, 34*, 9–36.

Baumhart, R.C. (1961). How ethical are businessmen? *Harvard Business Review, 39*, 6–9, 156–176.

Blau, P., & Schoenherr, R.A. (1971). *The structure of organizations*. New York: Basic Books.

Block, M.K., Nold, F.C., & Sidak, J.G. (1981). The deterrent effect of antitrust enforcement. *Journal of Political Economy, 89*, 429–445.

Blumstein, A., Cohen, J., & Farrington, D.P. (1988). Criminal career research: Its value for criminology. *Criminology, 26*, 1–36.

Braithwaite, J. (1982). Enforced self-regulation: A new strategy for corporate crime control. *Michigan Law Review, 80*, 1466–1507.

———. (1984). *Corporate crime in the pharmaceutical industry*. London: Routledge & Kegan Paul.

———. (1985). *To punish or persuade: Enforcement of coal mine safety*. Albany: State University of New York Press.

———. (1989). Criminological theory and organizational crime. *Justice Quarterly, 6*, 333–358.

Braithwaite, J., & Geis, G. (1982). On theory and action for corporate crime control. In G. Geis (Ed.), *On white-collar crime* (pp. 189–210). Lexington, MA: D.C. Heath.

Braithwaite, J., & Makkai, T. (1991). Testing an expected utility model of corporate deterrence. *Law & Society Review, 25*, 7–40.

Brenner, S.N., & Molander, E.A. (1977). Is the ethics of business changing? *Harvard Business Review, 55*, 57–71.

Bromiley, P., & Marcus, A. (1989). The deterrent to dubious corporate behavior: Profitability, probability and safety recalls. *Strategic Management Journal, 10*, 233–250.

Calavita, K. (1983). The demise of the Occupational Safety and Health Administration: A case study in symbolic action. *Social Problems, 30*, 437–448.

———. (1990). Employer sanctions violations: Toward a dialectical model of white collar crime. *Law & Society Review, 24*, 1041–1069.

Calavita, K., & Pontell, H.N. (1990). "Heads I win, tails you lose": Deregulation, crime, and crisis in the savings and loan industry. *Crime and Delinquency, 36,* 309–341.

Caplow, T. (1964). *Principles of organization.* New York: Harcourt Brace Jovanovich.

Carson, W.G. (1970). White-collar crime and the enforcement of factory legislation. *British Journal of Criminology, 10,* 383–398.

Clinard, M.B. (1946). Criminological theories of violations of wartime regulations. *American Sociological Review, 11,* 258–270.

———. (1983). *Corporate ethics and crime: The role of middle management.* Beverly Hills, CA: Sage.

Clinard, M.B., & Quinney, R. (1973). *Criminal behavior systems: A typology* (2nd ed.). New York: Holt, Rinehart and Winston.

Clinard, M.B., & Yeager, P.C. (1980). *Corporate crime.* New York: Free Press.

Clinard, M.B., Yeager, P.C., Brissette, J.M., Petrashek, D., & Harries, E. (1979). *Illegal corporate behavior.* Washington, DC: U.S. Government Printing Office.

Cochran, P.L., & Nigh, D. (1987). Illegal corporate behavior and the question of moral agency: An empirical examination. In W.C. Frederick (Ed.), *Research in corporate social performance and policy* (Vol. 9, pp. 73–91). Greenwich, CT: JAI.

Cohen, L.E., & Felson, M. (1979). Social change and crime rate trends: A routine activity approach. *American Sociological Review, 44,* 588–608.

Coleman, J.W. (1987). Toward an integrated theory of white-collar crime. *American Journal of Sociology, 93,* 406–439.

Conklin, J.E. (1977). *"Illegal but not criminal": Business crime in America.* Englewood Cliffs, NJ: Prentice-Hall.

Cook, P.J. (1986). The demand and supply of criminal opportunities. In M. Tonry & N. Morris (Eds.), *Crime and justice: An annual review of research* (Vol. 7, pp. 1–28). Chicago: University of Chicago Press.

Cornish, D.B., & Clarke, R.V. (Eds.). (1986). *The reasoning criminal.* New York: Springer-Verlag.

Cressey, D.R. (1976). Restraint of trade, recidivism and delinquent neighborhoods. In J.F. Short (Ed.), *Delinquency, crime and society* (pp. 209–238). Chicago: University of Chicago Press.

Cressey, D.R., & Moore, C.A. (1983). Managerial values and corporate codes of ethics. *California Management Review, 25,* 53–77.

Cullen, F.T., Maakestad, W.J., & Cavender, G. (1987). *Corporate crime under attack: The Ford Pinto case and beyond.* Cincinnati: Anderson.

Denzin, N. (1977). Notes on the criminogenic hypothesis: A case study of the American liquor industry. *American Sociological Review, 42,* 905–920.

Duncan, R.B. (1972). Characteristics of organizational environments and perceived environmental uncertainty. *Administrative Science Quarterly, 3,* 313–327.

Ermann, M.D., & Lundman, R.J. (1982). Corporate violations of the Corrupt Practices Act. In H. Edelhertz & T.D. Overcast (Eds.), *White-collar crime: An agenda for research.* Lexington, MA: D.C. Heath.

Farberman, H. (1975). A criminogenic market structure: The automobile industry. *Sociological Quarterly, 16,* 438–457.

Farrell, R.A., & Swigert, V.L. (1985). The corporation in criminology: New directions for research. *Journal of Research in Crime and Delinquency, 22,* 83–94.

Finney, H.C., & Lesieur, H.R. (1982). A contingency theory of organizational crime. In S.B. Bacharach (Ed.), *Research in the sociology of organizations* (Vol. 1, pp. 255–299). Greenwich, CT: JAI.

Fisse, B., & Braithwaite, J. (1984). *The impact of publicity on corporate offenders.* Albany: State University of New York Press.

Gallo, J.C., Craycraft, J.L., & Bush, S.C. (1985). Guess who came to dinner? An empirical study of federal antitrust enforcement for the period 1963–1984. *Review of Industrial Organization, 2,* 106–131.

Geis, G. (1967). The heavy electric equipment antitrust case of 1961. In M.B. Clinard & R. Quinney (Eds.), *Criminal behavior systems: A typology* (pp. 139–150). New York: Holt, Rinehart, and Winston.

Goodpaster, K.E. (1985). Ethical frameworks for management. In J.B. Matthews, K.E. Goodpaster & L.L. Nash (Eds.), *Policies and persons: A casebook in business ethics* (pp. 507–522). New York: McGraw-Hill.

Gray, W.B., & Jones, C.A. (1991). Longitudinal patterns of compliance with Occupational Safety and Health Administration health and safety regulations in the manufacturing sector. *Journal of Human Resources, 26,* 623–653.

Green, G.S. (1990). *Occupational crime.* Chicago: Nelson-Hall.

Gross, E. (1978). Organizational crime: A theoretical perspective. In N. Denzin (Ed.), *Studies in symbolic interaction* (Vol. 1, pp. 55–85). Greenwich, CT: JAI.

————. (1980). Organizational structure and organization crime. In G. Geis & E. Stotland (Eds.), *White-collar crime* (pp. 52–76). Beverly Hills, CA: Sage.

Hambrick, D.C., & Mason, P.A. (1984). Upper echelons: The organization as a reflection of its top managers. *Academy of Management Review, 9*, 193–206.

Hawkins, K. (1990). Compliance strategy, prosecution policy, and Aunt Sally: A comment on Pearce and Tombs. *British Journal of Criminology, 30*, 444–466.

Hay, G.A., & Kelly, D. (1974). An empirical survey of price fixing conspiracies. *Journal of Law and Economics, 19*, 13–39.

Hills, S.L. (1987). Epilogue: Corporate violence and the banality of evil. In S.L. Hills (Ed.), *Corporate violence: Injury and death for profit* (pp. 187–206). Totowa, NJ: Rowman & Littlefield.

Hirschi, T., & Gottfredson, M. (1987). Causes of white-collar crime. *Criminology, 25*, 949–974.

Kagan, R.A. (1989). Editor's introduction: Understanding regulatory enforcement. *Law & Policy, 11*, 89–119.

Kagan, R.A., & Scholz, J.T. (1984). The criminology of the corporation and regulatory enforcement strategies. In K. Hawkins & J.M. Thomas (Eds.), *Enforcing regulation* (pp. 67–96). Boston: Kluwer-Nijhoff.

Kram, K.E., Yeager, P.C., & Reed, G.E. (1989). Decisions and dilemmas: The ethical dimension in the corporate context. In J.E. Post (Ed.), *Research in corporate social performance and policy* (Vol. 11, pp. 21–54). Greenwich, CT: JAI.

Lane, R.E. (1953). Why businessmen violate the law. *Journal of Criminal Law, Criminology and Police Science, 44*, 151–165.

Leitko, T.A., & Kowalewski, D. (1985). Industry structure and organizational deviance: Multinational corporations and questionable foreign payments. *Contemporary Crises, 9*, 127–147.

Leonard, W.N., & Weber, M.G. (1970). Automakers and dealers: A study of criminogenic market forces. *Law & Society Review, 4*, 407–424.

Madden, C. (1977). Forces which influence ethical behavior. In C.C. Walton (Ed.), *The ethics of corporate conduct* (pp. 31–78). Englewood Cliffs, NJ: Prentice-Hall.

Makkai, T., & Braithwaite, J. (1991). Criminological theories and regulatory compliance. *Criminology, 29*, 191–220.

Mathews, M.C. (1987). Codes of ethics: Organizational behavior and misbehavior. In W.C. Frederick (Ed.), *Research in corporate social performance and policy* (Vol. 9, pp. 107–130). Greenwich, CT: JAI.

Michalowski, R.J., & Kramer, R.C. (1987). The space between laws: The problem of corporate crime in a transnational context. *Social Problems, 34*, 34–53.

Moore, E., & Mills, M. (1990). The neglected victims and unexamined costs of white collar crime. *Crime and Delinquency, 36*, 408–418.

Needleman, M.L., & Needleman, C. (1979). Organizational crime: Two models of criminogenesis. *Sociological Quarterly, 20*, 517–528.

Passas, N. (1990). Anomie and corporate deviance. *Contemporary Crises, 14*, 157–178.

Pearce, F., & Tombs, S. (1990). Ideology, hegemony, and empiricism: Compliance theories of regulation. *British Journal of Criminology, 30*, 423–443.

Perez, J. (1978). *Corporate criminality: A study of one thousand largest industrial corporations in the U.S.A.* Unpublished doctoral dissertation, University of Pennsylvania, Philadelphia.

Pfeffer, J., & Salancik, G.R. (1978). *The external control of organizations.* New York: Harper & Row.

Posner, R.A. (1970). A statistical study of antitrust enforcement. *Journal of Law and Economics, 13*, 365–419.

Reckless, W.C. (1961). A new theory of delinquency and crime. *Federal Probation, 25*, 42–46.

Reichman, N. (1990, May). Moving compliance backstage: Uncovering the role of compliance in regulating securities trading. Paper presented at the Edwin Sutherland Conference on White-Collar Crime, Bloomington, Indiana.

Reiss, A.J., Jr. (1984). Selecting strategies of social control over organizational life. In K. Hawkins & J.M. Thomas (Eds.), *Enforcing regulation* (pp. 23–36). Boston: Kluwer-Nijhoff.

Reiss, A.J., Jr., & Biderman, A.D. (1980). *Data sources on white-collar law-breaking.* Washington, DC: U.S. Government Printing Office.

Robin, D., Giallourakis, M., David, F.R., & Moritz, T.E. (1989). A different look at codes of ethics. *Business Horizons, 32*, 66–73.

Ross, I. (1980, October 1). How lawless are big companies? *Fortune, 102*, 56–62.

Schrager, L.S., & Short, J.F., Jr. (1978). Toward a sociology of organizational crime. *Social Problems, 25* (4), 407–419.

Scott, D.W. (1989). Policing corporate collusion. *Criminology, 27,* 559–587.

Shapiro, S. (1980). *Thinking about white collar crime.* Washington, DC: U.S. Government Printing Office.

Shover, N. (1976). *Organizations and interorganizational fields as criminogenic behavior settings: Notes on the concept organizational crime.* Unpublished manuscript, University of Tennessee, Department of Sociology, Knoxville.

———. (1978). Defining organizational crime. In M.D. Ermann & R.J. Lundman (Eds.), *Corporate and governmental deviance* (pp. 37–40). New York: Oxford University Press.

Shover, N., Clelland, D.A., & Lynxwiler, J.P. (1986). *Enforcement or negotiation: Constructing a regulatory agency.* Albany: State University of New York Press.

Shover, N., & Link, C.T. (1986). *Organizational determinants of corporate regulatory compliance.* (Available from University of Tennessee, Department of Sociology, Knoxville).

Shover, N., Lynxwiler, J., Groce, S., & Clelland, D.A. (1984). Regional variation in regulatory law enforcement. In K. Hawkins & J.M. Thomas (Eds.), *Enforcing regulation* (pp. 121–146). Boston: Kluwer-Nijhoff.

Simpson, S.S. (1986). The decomposition of antitrust: Testing a multi-level, longitudinal model of profit-squeeze. *American Sociological Review, 51,* 859–875.

———. (1987). Cycles of illegality: Antitrust violations in corporate America. *Social Forces, 65,* 943–963.

———. (1990, May). *Corporate crime deterrence and corporate control policies.* Paper presented at the Edwin Sutherland Conference on White-Collar Crime, Bloomington, Indiana.

Snider, L. (1990). Cooperative models and corporate crime: Panacea or cop-out? *Crime and Delinquency, 36,* 373–390.

Sonnenfeld, J., & Lawrence, P.R. (1978). Why do companies succumb to price fixing? *Harvard Business Review, 56,* 145–157.

Staw, B.M., & Szwajkowski, E. (1975). The scarcity-munificence component of organizational environments and the commission of illegal acts. *Administrative Science Quarterly, 20,* 345–354.

Sutherland, E.H. (1949). *White collar crime.* New York: Dryden.

Sykes, G.M., & Matza, D. (1957). Techniques of neutralization: A theory of delinquency. *American Sociological Review, 22,* 664–670.

Szasz, A. (1986). Corporations, organized crime, and the disposal of hazardous waste: An examination of the making of a criminogenic regulatory structure. *Criminology, 24,* 1–28.

Szwajkowski, E. (1985). Organizational illegality: Theoretical integration and illustration. *Academy of Management Review, 10,* 558–567.

———. (1986). The myths and realities of research on organizational misconduct. In J.E. Post (Ed.), *Research in corporate social performance and policy* (Vol. 8, pp. 121–147). Greenwich, CT: JAI.

Tonry, M., & Reiss, A.J., Jr. (Eds.). (in press). *Crime and justice: An annual review of research* (Vol. 17). Chicago: University of Chicago Press.

Vaughan, D. (1980). Crime between organizations: Implications for victimology. In G. Geis & E. Stotland (Eds.), *White collar crime:* Theory and research(pp. 77–97). Beverly Hills, CA: Sage.

———. (1982). Transaction systems and unlawful organizational behavior. *Social Problems, 29,* 373–380.

———. (1983). *Controlling unlawful organizational behavior.* Chicago: University of Chicago Press.

Victor, B., & Cullen, J.B. (1987). A theory and measure of ethical climate in organizations. In W.C. Frederick (Ed.), *Research in corporate social performance and policy* (Vol. 9, pp. 51–71). Greenwich, CT: JAI.

———. (1988). The organizational bases of ethical work climates. *Administrative Science Quarterly, 33,* 101–125.

Wilson, J.Q., & Herrnstein, R.J. (1985). *Crime and human nature.* New York: Simon & Schuster.

Yeager, P.C. (1986). Analyzing corporate offenses: Progress and prospects. In J.E. Post (Ed.), *Research in corporate social performance and policy* (Vol. 8, pp. 93–120). Greenwich, CT: JAI.

———. (1991). *The limits of law: Public regulation of private pollution.* New York: Cambridge University Press.

Yeager, P.C., & Kram, K.E. (1990). Fielding hot topics in cool settings: The study of corporate ethics. *Qualitative Sociology, 13,* 127–148.

Zey-Ferrell, M., & Ferrell, O.C. (1982). Role-set configuration and opportunity as predictors of unethical behavior in organizations. *Human Relations, 35,* 587–604.

Zey-Ferrell, M.K., Weaver, M., & Ferrell, O.C. (1979). Predicting unethical behavior among marketing practitioners. *Human Relations, 32,* 557–569.

CHAPTER SEVEN

Regulating Corporate Behavior

Laureen Snider

It is impossible to fully understand corporate criminality without an examination of the typical enforcement vehicle, the regulatory agency. Created by legislative fiat and empowered to enforce various administrative laws, these agencies, in concert with business and special interest groups, shape the enforcement process. Regulatory agencies are typically equipped by law with a wide array of powers to enforce legislative mandates. When an offense is first detected, regulatory officials may choose to invoke the formal regulatory process by filing charges or official complaints. The other regulatory alternative is an informal, educational role, which focuses on cooperation and mediation.

If agencies opt for the formal route, they can impose one or more civil or administrative remedies or seek to implement criminal procedures in certain circumstances. Once culpability is established, victims may collect double or treble damages. Regulatory agencies may also impose new operating standards on the offending company. Possible criminal remedies range from prison sentences and punitive fines to civil remedies such as cease and desist orders, injunctions, and consent agreements.

With the growing recognition of the frequency and seriousness of illegal corporate acts, attempts to control business by means of government regulation have been increasing in most countries in recent decades. However, it is not yet clear whether the deregulatory movement of the 1980s has reversed or merely slowed this trend toward regulating corporate behavior. The former seems unlikely because governments pass regulations for a variety of reasons, many of which are unrelated to the issues of deterrence and control.

Thus the heavy hand of political ideology also gives shape to the two basic functions of regulatory agencies: social control and service (Frank & Lombness, 1988). Which of these functions is preeminent and why is the focus of this chapter. In the ensuing sections, the workings of regulatory agencies are examined more closely in order to better understand the forces that shape the relationship between government and business.

Characteristics of Regulatory Agencies

The first modern corporation was the Dutch East India Company, founded in 1602 (Coleman, 1989:13). As the harmful potential of this newly invented organizational form became apparent, political authorities began to supplement existing common law doctrines with the concept of vicarious liability (Bernard, 1984). Direct statutory control through law was limited because existing police agencies had neither the expertise, interest, nor power to scrutinize the business sector. In time, quasi-police agencies evolved to fill the gap between legal doctrine and enforcement (Mitnick, 1980).

Thanks to a myriad of studies, much is now known about regulatory agencies and those who staff them. Like all organizations, the functions of regulatory agencies are shaped by the external environment, their organizational structure, and the goals and tasks that comprise their legislative edict. Kagan (1978) identified two categories of regulatory agencies based on their response to prescribed mandates.

Under the expert model, regulatory officials are encouraged to exercise maximum flexibility in deciding what action to take with target firms. Few fixed legal rules are used as *a priori* guides to behavior, although the legal structure determines the general boundaries of the regulatory tactics employed. On the other hand, those agencies that follow the legal model, as the name implies, emphasize strict observance of all pertinent laws and policies. Officials are directed to enforce regulatory legislation with paramount attention to the requirements of the legislation (Kagan, 1978). Because enabling legislation is typically worded ambiguously, agencies have to formulate "approved" versions of the "real" meaning of each law. The primary effect of the legal model, then, is to take discretionary power from inspectors located in the field and vest it with centralized administrators who directly influence the regulatory process.

The effects of the immediate external environment on regulatory agencies are also important. To maintain their existence, all federal, provincial/state, and local government agencies have certain maintenance needs they must meet. For example, agencies must secure resources, negotiate adequate (preferably increasing) budgets, weaken opposing forces, and line up political support for their continued existence (Thomas, 1989).

Many academics have, therefore, tried to specify attributes of "effective" agencies, defining effectiveness in terms of successful fulfillment of a given legislative mandate. However, such efforts have met with limited success. Much of the research suggests that long-term effectiveness may not be possible. Instead, many regulatory agencies seem to exhibit parasitic growth, historically displaying a pattern of expansion that, however irregular and cyclical, eventually outstrips the growth of the regulated industry (Meier & Plumlee, 1978; Noll, 1978; Stigler, 1975).

This expansion is most likely where the criteria and standards of regulation are imprecise, where the specific aim is to improve industry performance, and where regulators are free to correct unanticipated loopholes with additional regulations without the intervention of governing bodies (Wilson, 1980). Moreover, as regulatory agencies grow, they become more rigid in their decision making, with the result that the highly mobile, innovative, and ambitious officers who may have staffed them at their inception are replaced by (or turn into) conservative bureaucrats who seek only the comfort and safety of a long-term position (Downs, 1967).

Since evidence indicates that political bodies that establish regulatory agencies initially allocate little in the way of resources and staff, regulatory expansion may not be entirely negative.

However, from the standpoint of those who view regulation as anathema (a particularly powerful philosophy in certain academic and business circles in the U.S.), growth in regulatory agencies indicates government inefficiency, and mismanagement (while growth in private industry is a positive sign connoting superior management).

Theorists also posit that regulatory agencies have life cycles that extend from birth to immobility and paralysis rather than death. After an initial policy-creation stage, agencies typically enter a middle period marked by power consolidation and policy implementation, then proceed to a rigid and frequently captured old age where administrative procedures are emphasized at the expense of substance (Anderson, 1975; Bernstein, 1955; Cobb & Elder, 1972; Cobb, Ross, & Ross, 1976; Glaeser, 1957).

The process of agency capture, defined as the regulatory agency's adoption of the interests and perspective of the industry it is responsible for regulating, is an important one in the literature. Sabatier (1975, 1977) argues that rigidity and capture can be prevented, or at least postponed, if public groups actively intervene and monitor agency performance. These groups, by pressuring agencies to carry out their legislative mandates, can forestall capture by the industry.

Characteristics of Agency Personnel

While much is known about regulatory agencies, comparatively less is known about the people who staff them. As previously noted, regulators need a high level of education and a wide array of skills to do their jobs well. They also need some acquaintance with regulatory philosophies and issues. One study of appointments to two key American agencies, the Federal Commerce and Federal Trade Commissions (the FCC and FTC respectively), from 1949 to 1974, found only 10 of the total of 108 appointees had backgrounds with ties to pro-consumer or pro-regulatory groups. Sixty-four percent had legal backgrounds, often entering government service immediately after admission to the Bar. Thus while pro-consumer activists are rare, pro-business supporters are often found among the ranks of regulators.

One study found that more than half of those appointed to regulatory positions had prior experience in the industry they were now supposed to regulate (Parenti, 1983). Indeed, the Reagan Administration was notorious for the frequency with which it appointed former industry lobbyists to top positions in regulatory agencies—the appointment of Ann Gorsuch and Rita Lavell to the Environmental Protection Agency are cases in point (Messerschmidt, 1986).

This practice seems to have gained popularity in the 1980s, since an earlier study found that most regulators were not from the business sector at the time of appointment, although a full one-third entered it when they left, frequently taking jobs in the industry they had previously regulated (Graham & Kramer, 1976; Parenti, 1983). Since positions in business typically pay better and carry more prestige than those in government, especially in the United States where the tradition of disinterested, dedicated public service is weak, these "exit jobs" would appear to be important benefits for employees in the regulatory sector. Such career patterns are obviously not going to be open to regulators who take their jobs seriously and get labelled as "uncooperative" or "zealous" by industry.

Another study by the U.S. Senate Committee on Government Affairs (1977) reported that regulatory officials in federal agencies, on average, receive salaries that are lower than comparable ranks in the private sector. Salaries are higher at this level, however, than similar positions at state or municipal levels. Personnel who head such agencies (deemed commissioners and appointed by the party in power rather than the civil service) seldom serve out their terms, and reappointment for those who serve full terms is very unlikely. However, experienced regulators are found below this level in the civil service.

This combination of inexperienced political appointees and relatively experienced civil servants is the norm in democratic institutions. As early as 1936, law and public service were the primary former occupations of those going into regulatory agencies (Herring, 1936), although the percentage with law degrees had consistently increased (up to 59 percent by 1965) (Stanley, Mann, & Doig, 1967). Local and state agencies frequently serve as stepping-stones to the better paid, more prestigious federal agencies. Increasingly smaller percentages of appointees enter civil service positions after leaving the business sector. All of these factors illustrate the decreasing influence and prestige of government service as a career option and the increasing dominance of business both ideologically and pragmatically.

Characteristics of the Enforcement Process

Enforcing regulations is the official *raison d'être* of agencies. Regulatory vigor varies greatly over time and place, as one would expect. Nevertheless, a few generalizations are possible. We know, first of all, that nonenforcement is the most salient and frequently found characteristic of regulatory agencies. Summarizing his extensive survey of the American, British, and Australian literatures, Cranston concludes that "There is clear evidence of regulatory agencies failing to function in the manner expected" (Cranston, 1982:11). Faced with a choice between taking formal regulatory action as opposed to counseling, advising, educating, or even mollifying the offending organization, officials overwhelmingly choose the informal process.

The frequency with which nonenforcement occurs should not be surprising because regulatory agencies are creatures of government, and governments have good reasons to be lenient towards corporate criminality. Politicians require the money, power, approval, and confidence of the corporate sector to get elected and stay in power; as political appointees, those at the top of regulatory agencies must either have enormous political clout *or* the support of the industry they are regulating. Moreover, politicians and regulators frequently share the same viewpoint—that is, that businesses have to cut corners to survive, that profit maximization is the ultimate goal, and that to apply the law to corporations constitutes "government interference."

The belief in the magic power of market forces to correct all ills is now almost an article of religious faith for most regulators and many politicians. However, such philosophies do vary in strength (Vogel, 1986) and are most visible in countries where capitalist ideology is strongest, and where they have not been challenged historically by notions of social responsibility or the need for collectivity/community rights to take precedence over individual ones. Capitalist hegemony reinforces the belief that getting along with industry rather than taking formal enforcement actions against it is almost always the easiest and safest course of action for agencies to follow.

Thus we find that regulators tend to adopt a less confrontational and more educative attitude toward those industries they are regulating, often to the point of identifying with a particular industry. An American study found that the bosses of regulatory agencies typically believed the problem of corporate crime could be solved if the executive branch of government was more sympathetic toward the problems faced by business (Lane, 1953). Regulatory executives thought that deliberate infractions are committed only by the atypical business person, the proverbial "bad apple in the barrel." Since bad apples are more likely to be found at the bottom of the barrel, the second characteristic of enforcement activity, not surprisingly, is a tendency to focus on those organizations at the base of the business hierarchy.

Most intensive investigative efforts are directed toward smaller businesses, and the heaviest sanctions are meted out against them. The largest and most powerful organizations (typically multinational corporations) enjoy the best relations with regulatory officials. Not coincidentally, they are also the most likely to legally challenge any investigation or sanction. This discrimination by regulatory agencies against weak and peripheral organizations has been extensively documented for a wide range of corporate activity: combines, food and drug, and false advertising laws in Canada (Goff & Reasons, 1978; Snider, 1978); tax violations (Long, 1979); various mining operations (Gunningham, 1974, 1984, 1987; Lynxwiler et al., 1983); securities regulation (Shapiro, 1985); and a host of miscellaneous other regulatory sectors (Carson, 1970, 1980a; Ermann & Lundman, 1978; Olson, 1985; Thomas, 1982).

Such differential treatment can be understood by examining the advantages that small businesses hold for regulators. They are ideal political targets because they lack the power to block investigations and do not have the complexity and resources to conceal crimes well. They can be investigated and sanctioned in a relatively short time, and they are unlikely to have the clout to visit political repercussions back upon the regulatory agency or its staff. Each of these negative consequences can result from the prosecution of a powerful corporation. In an environment where the resources of business can dwarf those of regulatory agencies, litigation against puissant corporations can last for many expensive and draining years, only to be lost in court or abandoned due to lack of political conviction.

The power of big business is not apocryphal. The U.S. Federal Trade Commission, for example, devoted 12 to 14 percent of its annual budget, and an even heavier percentage of its staff complement, to an investigation of illegal combinations and price-fixing in the oil industry in the early 1970s. Regulators suspected that the great oil crisis, which culminated in the artificial oil "shortage" of 1973 and a doubling and tripling of the price of a gallon of gas, was created by the major oil companies restricting the oil supply. After more than eight years of investigation, the case was abandoned, but not because agency suspicions were without substance. The FTC, one of the strongest and best funded regulatory agencies in the world, was simply no match for the oil companies, with their extensive political clout and virtually limitless fiscal resources (Sampson, 1975).

Similar fates befell regulatory agencies after the election of Ronald Reagan in 1980, when dozens of hotly contested cases against powerful corporations in a wide range of spheres were dropped because of political intervention by the new regime on behalf of its friends and corporate allies (Calavita, 1983, 1986; Coleman, 1989). As one can imagine, this does not improve the morale of agency personnel; nor does it inspire them with regulatory vigor. Agency personnel may soon learn not to take regulation too seriously if they are interested in longevity.

The concentration of regulatory agency staff on small concerns in peripheral parts of the economy, then, is as understandable as it is ill-advised. Unfortunately, the extent and degree of corporate crime found today would not be possible if the only instigators were tiny, fly-by-night organizations or unethical and maladjusted individuals. As C. Wright Mills (1959) observed some years ago, if only one business person or company exhibits criminality, the cause may be an individual one, lodged in the particular pathology or circumstances of one person or company. But where many of the largest and most prestigious corporations turn up as habitual offenders (Clinard & Yeager, 1980; Sutherland, 1940), concentrating on the aberrant small business makes little sense in terms of impacting the frequency and severity of corporate offending.

Indeed, given the increasing dominance of mega-corporations, and the high profitability of corporate crime, the most logical inference is that larger and more successful organizations will be the most, rather than least, likely to offend. And even when the small and weak do break the law, concentrating on them, in an economy dominated by giants, means that one is, almost by definition, singling out those with the least chance of causing a major disaster and the smallest number of victims.

Moreover, there are certain offenses where the concentration associated with the creation of a small number of large successful firms is itself criminogenic. For example, four big companies that control 95 percent of the market are much better placed to engage in price-fixing or price-leadership conspiracies than 250 smaller concerns who must do battle with each other for their share of the market. Other things being equal, price-fixing could be better curbed by breaking up the oligopoly enjoyed by the four than by chasing after peripheral corporations (Green, 1972; Nader & Green, 1973).

Thus far we have examined two characteristics of regulatory agencies: the tendency to prefer nonenforcement or informal measures over official sanctions; and the focus of enforcement activity on the smallest and weakest operators and operations. The third characteristic of regulatory agencies is that the monetary sanctions they impose against corporations are rather insignificant sums compared to the financial assets of the offending organizations. Numerous examples reveal that the fines and assorted criminal and civil penalties typically handed out are minuscule, while the deterrent effect is questionable (Carson, 1982; Clinard & Yeager, 1980; Levi, 1981, 1984; Pearce, 1976; Tucker, 1987). The lack of deterrence should not be surprising; it has been calculated that average fines for the typical corporate crime represent, for large organizations, less than a fraction of company profits for a single hour of operation (Ermann & Lundman, 1978). The empirical evidence for this assertion is examined elsewhere in this book; for the moment, it is sufficient to observe that the typical penalties imposed or recommended are extremely light, both in terms of the profits made during the commission of a particular offense, and in light of overall company profits.

These characteristics can be illustrated by looking at the saga of the Beech-Nut Company and its production of adulterated apple juice. From 1977 to 1983, Beech-Nut, a major manufacturer of baby food in the United States, sold as "100% fruit juice, no sugar added," a liquid that was essentially apple-flavored water. When the U.S. Food and Drug Agency accidentally discovered substantial quantities of adulterated juice on the market, it immediately notified Beech-Nut and other manufacturers on the assumption that the major companies were innocent victims of some unscrupulous supplier. When Beech-Nut reacted in a hostile and uncooperative fashion, and no peripheral supplier could be found, the FDA slowly became suspicious.

While it prevaricated on FDA inquiries, Beech-Nut management launched a cover-up operation, ordering executives inside every plant to destroy incriminating evidence. Then, not wanting to lose one penny of potential profits, it sold the remaining stocks of "apple juice" to third-world countries. The company, which realized profits of $60 million or more from this operation, was eventually taken to court in 1987, convicted, and fined $2 million (Staff, 1989). Although the fine was considered a heavy penalty, the sanctioning process once again reveals the relative lenience accorded corporate criminals.

It is apparent that the regulatory process does not occur in a vacuum. The aforementioned characteristics of regulatory agencies and the people who staff them are not manifested by chance, but by design. The relationship between regulatory agencies and corporations is defined in a political context. The sections that follow describe this context in greater detail.

Politics and the Regulatory Process

In recent years the concept of agency capture has fallen into disrepute. For many researchers and policymakers, the term carries an implicit value judgment about the desirable balance of power between government and industry. Theorists on the political right, favoring a more thoroughgoing and intense relationship between agency and industry, prefer the term *cooperation*. Indeed, deregulation, the complete removal of government regulation over industry, is the epitome of the cooperative model. This position is founded on the belief that free markets are self-regulating. The political left, however, still views agency capture as sellout and pursues strategies that agencies can employ to avoid this fate. Wilson (1980) suggests agency capture will most likely occur where the regulatory issues at stake are crucial to the target industry, but not to opposing organized forces, or where such forces are absent.

Hopkins (1978), in his study of the origin and life cycle of several Australian agencies, points out that there are inter- and intra-national variations in the degree to which agency capture occurs, implying that the political economy of the nation-state is an important factor in the process of capture. Stigler (1975) and Peltzman (1976) take a different tack, arguing that capture is structurally inevitable. Regulation, they argue, is designed and operated for the benefit of the regulated industry, not in "the public interest" at all. Industries need the powers of the state to obtain subsidies, control market entry by rivals, regulate the market, and enhance public confidence in themselves and their products. The state, through the regulatory agency, needs the resources (votes, campaign donations, goodwill, and corporate legitimacy) that industry can provide. The shape regulation takes, then, is determined by the interaction of this symbiotic relationship (Bardach & Kagan, 1982; Cranston, 1982).

As this discussion illustrates, most of the controversies over regulating corporations rest on value judgments about the desirability of government regulation of business. It is not possible to assess the impact of regulation or the effectiveness of a particular agency unless the purpose of the legislation can unequivocally be enumerated. Multifarious purposes exist in relation to the number of interest groups promoting or opposing enabling legislation.

If the original purpose of legislation was to symbolically demonstrate concern for the public or prevent electoral losses by appearing to "do something" about a problem, then regulatory agencies have fulfilled this purpose by merely existing. In this instance, agencies do not have to do anything to be effective. If agencies are captured by industry, so much the better, as long as the public does not know about it. Because regulatory activity is not easily monitored, the inefficiency of regulatory agencies (from a nonbusiness standpoint) usually goes unnoticed by the public.

The recent ascendance of the law and economics movement, with its belief in the corrective powers of the marketplace and the futility of regulation, has sharpened the debate. Adherents argue that workers who are willing to take risky jobs get high wages, which makes government restrictions on health and safety in the work place financially and structurally superfluous (Leigh, 1989). Other advocates produce sophisticated economic calculations that suggest that current laws protecting workers' health cost more to administer and enforce than an individual human life is worth according to its value in the labor market. Such laws, and the regulatory structure they require, are therefore wasteful and inefficient and should be repealed (Dewees & Daniels, 1986).

Other studies suggest that regulation is important and that properly constituted agencies have the obligation to safeguard the environment, to protect the public, and to save the lives of workers and consumers. A study on federal occupational health and safety laws in the United States, for example, found a statistically significant negative relationship between penalties and violations, but no relation between violations and injuries. This finding suggests that assessment of penalties by regulatory agencies may lead to fewer violations, even though an increase in the number of injuries registered does not necessarily mean that more violations are occurring (Bartel & Thomas, 1985).

Other studies show that rates of compliance with water quality standards showed marked environmental improvements in the 1980s when industry began to take the issue seriously, resulting in reduced levels of lead, cyanide, cadmium, arsenic, and PCB's being discharged into watercourses. A 40 percent drop in lead poisoning cases and a 50 percent decline in crib deaths resulting from strangulation were reported after regulations (with crises and attendant publicity) were enacted to control lead emissions and regulate the space between bars in infant cribs. Following the passage of clean water acts and stricter enforcement procedures, fish are gradually returning to rivers in the United States and the United Kingdom (Pearce, 1990a).

Tabb (1980) argues that the benefits of regulation in the United States in the areas of worker safety and environmental pollution are five times greater than the costs, while Ackerman et al. (1974), Kelman (1974), and Smith (1976) take an opposing position (see summaries in Braithwaite, 1985b; Coleman, 1989). Over the long term, fatalities in coal mining are less than 10 percent of the levels they were 100 years ago, in the United States, the United Kingdom, Australia, France, and Japan (Pearce, 1990a). And Paulus (1974) showed that the adulteration of food and drugs in Britain dropped dramatically after a regulatory agency with inspectors and public analysts developed vested interests in effective control.

Despite the evidence that regulation can and does yield positive social benefits, it is easy to find examples that illustrate the fate of regulatory agencies that become too zealous for the liking of the industries they regulate and/or pro-business politicians. Agencies are always prime targets for government cutbacks, whenever deficits look too high or pro-business regimes take power. Although agencies have always been understaffed and underfinanced by "normal" enforcement standards (if the level of enforcement provided against traditional crime was applied to corporate crime, there would be a hundred-fold increase in the number of inspectors and budgets would quadruple), regulatory agencies were among the first victims of the Reagan regime in the United States.

The Environmental Protection Agency lost 25 percent of its staff between 1980 and 1983 (Coleman, 1989); the Occupational Safety and Health Administration, which had 2,800 inspectors for 4 million work places in 1978, was cut by 18 percent in 1980–81, resulting in a 37 percent decline in the number of citations issued and a 65 percent reduction in fines assessed (Calavita, 1983). The Federal Trade Commission, which launched eight antitrust actions and negotiated twenty-five consent orders per year between 1977 and 1981 (not an impressive record in the first place), instigated only three antitrust actions and eleven consent orders after the Reagan Administration came to power, a drop of more than 50 percent from 1981 to 1983 (Coleman, 1989:163). It was also forced to drop all cases then under investigation against major industries.

The history of the Occupational Safety and Health Administration (OSHA) provides a similar example. This was an agency that had strong union support. OSHA was largely responsible for the 1972 ban on asbestos in the workplace, which prevented an estimated 630 to 2,300 deaths a year. In 1974, OSHA placed limits on the use of vinyl chloride, again saving approximately 2,000 lives per year (Calavita, 1983). However, because of these limited successes and because of the direct challenge to management's dominance over the workplace, OSHA was widely despised by powerful elites in the manufacturing and industrial sector.

Improvements in worker safety cost industry a great deal, both in money and in negative publicity. But OSHA's most egregious sin, from the industry's perspective, was its official encouragement to workers to form health and safety groups in the workplace. The agency's policy was to help workers become knowledgeable and informed about workplace dangers, simultaneously focusing media attention on worker health and safety problems. Eventually there were well-publicized protests against the policies of several major multinational corporations. Indeed, OSHA had American Cyanamid fined $10,000 for its response to the publicity on reproductive hazards faced by female employees working with hazardous substances when it forced employees it could not fire or remove to undergo sterilization. All of this activity by OSHA, as Calavita (1983) points out, sent an important symbolic message to workers that they had a right to know the dangers they were asked to confront, as well as a right to refuse dangerous work.

In retaliation, one of the first acts of the Reagan administration, through a new Secretary of Labor (Ray Donovan) and a newly appointed director of OSHA, was to withdraw and then to weaken seven regulatory standards that were due to be implemented or had already been imposed. The abandoned standards, none of them revolutionary, would have required the following: all hazardous chemicals would be labelled; substances found to pose a "significant risk" of being carcinogenic would be regulated; an annual list of suspected carcinogens would be published and made available to workers; and maximum legal exposure levels for lead would be established.

New standards of allowable cotton dust levels, aimed at reducing the number of workers contracting brown lung disease, which kills at least 21,000 a year, were rescinded, as were regulations to protect workers' hearing from excessive noise, as well as "walk-around pay," monies paid to workers for time spent monitoring workplace conditions. OSHA also withdrew at least 9 films, pamphlets, and slide shows on various workplace dangers from circulation, going so far as to actually burn 100,000 copies of a pamphlet on cotton dust and brown lung disease because it was "not neutral" (Calavita, 1983:442). The policy of responding to every worker-reported complaint was discontinued. A system of voluntary compliance that allowed 73 percent of the manufacturing firms in the United States to avoid regular inspections if their record of worker injuries was low was implemented. These policy changes produced predictable results at OSHA, where the number of inspections dropped dramatically in 1981—serious citations declined by 37 percent, fines by 65 percent, follow-up inspections by 73 percent, while the budget of OSHA was cut by 40 percent again in 1982 (Calavita, 1983).

One of the corporations that escaped regulatory scrutiny under the new policy was Imperial Food Products. On September 3, 1991, rescue workers were summoned to a fire at the Hamlet, North Carolina, plant only to find that most of the emergency doors were locked, thus preventing many of the employees from escaping to safety. Twenty-five people were killed and fifty-five were injured as a result of negligent company policy and the absence of *any* inspection by state or federal agencies. Emmett Roe, president and owner of the company, negotiated a guilty plea and was sentenced to twenty years for manslaughter. The incident ably, if tragically, illustrates the folly of assuming that the records compiled by companies reflect their "real" accident rates, and of believing that corporations just "naturally" want workers to have a safe workplace.

The backlash against regulation resulted from declining corporate profits, increased international competition for business, and a swing to the political right that was not restricted to the United States and Britain, although Reagan and Thatcher emerged as symbols of it. Canada, not atypically, entered this phase a little later than the United States and Britain, but with equal vigor. When the Conservatives under Brian Mulroney were elected in 1984, the Prime Minister's first statement was to declare that, henceforth, the country was "open for business." The federal government, which has responsibility for the most significant Canadian regulatory laws, began catching up with a vengeance. The government took steps to bring corporate leaders directly into the legislative process, while simultaneously cutting back on public sector spending, directly hitting the staff and budgets of regulatory agencies.

These actions were not extreme or atypical examples of the New Right flexing its political muscles against a particularly despised opponent. These and other examples illustrate the political vulnerability of regulatory agencies and helps partially explain the cavalier attitudes taken by agencies and politicians toward regulating corporations. Thus political ideology plays a significant role in the regulatory process. In the following sections, this role is examined in more detail.

Ideology and the Regulatory Process

A debate has developed over the "proper" role of the regulatory agency (Frank & Lombness, 1988; Schlegel, 1988). Given the limited use of criminal sanctions in controlling corporate crime, some critics have called upon regulatory agencies to employ such penalties more often. As we have seen, regulators have been reluctant to do so in the past, typically preferring persuasion and education to filing criminal or civil charges. Moreover, their legislative mandate has usually been phrased in terms that direct them to balance the benefits of enforcement against the drawbacks, assessing whether or not enforcement is in "the public interest." For example, will sanctions have negative consequences such as a loss of jobs in a community, or the loss of votes or campaign contributions for a particular incumbent or party?

Identifying this reluctance to "get tough" with corporate offenders as the problem, many critics have advocated the use of imprisonment and higher criminal fines as the remedy. They argue that the stigma of criminality is the heaviest moral sanction a society can employ, and the only one the corporate sector will take seriously (Fisse & Braithwaite, 1983; Hawkins, 1984; Levi, 1984; Pearce, 1990b).

Criminalization has political advantages as well. Enacting laws against corporate crime is a difficult task. Legislation is typically passed only after an environmental crisis or major disaster has aroused public outrage (Snider, 1987). In situations where politicians are pressured to take immediate remedial action, criminalizing techniques represent the perfect response. They are visible, they appear tough, and they symbolize moral opprobrium.

The fact that increasing the number and severity of criminal laws has not provided better control over corporate crime is explained by focusing on insufficient utilization. In order to be effective deterrents, criminal sanctions must be imposed consistently and the chances of escaping criminal conviction must be perceived as minimal by potential offenders. Fines must be commensurate with the size of the firm and the profitability of the crime, while the possibility of an active prison sentence must always loom large (Braithwaite, 1984, 1988; Coffee, 1984; Elkins, 1976; Watkins, 1977).

In recent years, however, with increasingly sophisticated studies of regulatory agencies, criminalization models have come under heavy attack. The first and most serious charge has been simply that criminal law does not work against corporate offenders. Regulatory law is different from traditional criminal law because its goal is not to punish, but to secure compliance and to educate recalcitrant corporations. Corporate offenders may lack the technical competence required for compliance, they may be ignorant of the law, or they may be led to offend by unintentional organizational (system) failures. Moreover, invoking the criminal process against wayward corporations and their executives creates antagonism that threatens cooperation and goodwill. A certain amount of goodwill is presupposed in all legal systems, but it is particularly crucial to regulatory law because so many areas of corporate misbehavior are either invisible or beyond the purview of law (McQueen, 1990; Stone, 1975).

A second charge is that criminalization actually increases the amount of harm corporate crime does. The strict evidentiary requirements of the criminal courts mean that a regulatory agency, rather than stepping in when it first learns of an offense, has to allow it to continue long enough to gather evidence. The high cost of utilizing criminal justice procedures is also an issue. Since there are, by all accounts, even more corporate crimes than traditional offenses, and their damage to the society in terms of lives taken and money lost is much higher (see summary in Braithwaite, 1985a:12–13), reliance on the criminal justice system to control corporate crime, if anything close to full enforcement were attempted, would be fiscally impossible. Instead of creating a safer, healthier environment, more criminalization would leave the poor more vulnerable by putting them "in more dangerous factories, marketplaces and environments" (Braithwaite,

1985a:11; Fisse & Braithwaite, 1983; Kagan & Scholz, 1984; Shapiro, 1985; Smith, 1976; Thomas, 1982, 1989).

Jamieson's (1985) study of British factory regulation identified four assumptions inspectors make which make them unlikely to use punitive measures: industry is powerful enough to resist those regulations it defines as overly restrictive; regulations that threaten economic viability will not be passed in the first place; society only wants the harmful side effects of industry restricted, as it approves of the corporate sector in general; and societal consent for the regulatory function would be withdrawn if policing were seen as overzealous.

For example, in her examination of the Securities and Exchange Commission in the United States, Shapiro (1985:199) argues that "Criminal prosecution is associated with regulatory failure. It is a response to offenses that are discovered too late to prevent substantial harm." Criminal sanctions are pursued only when the SEC has failed to discover an offense in its initial stages, when the damage has become significant, and when the administrative or civil remedies that would have contained the offense at an earlier stage are no longer practical.

Sanctions are also employed against individuals who cannot be punished any other way because they lack the corporate connections and ongoing relationships with the agency to make alternate sanctions effective (as with small "fly-by-night" outfits). Shapiro also points out that the SEC's success rate is much higher for civil and administrative actions, and that the fines assessed under criminal law are consistently lower than administrative or civil fines (Hopkins, 1978; King, 1985; Levi, 1984; Shapiro, 1985).

Rankin and Brown drew similar conclusions in their comparison of two agencies in the province of British Columbia, one of which used administrative penalties, the other criminal sanctions. The Waste Management Branch, using criminal law, filed an average of forty-four charges annually from 1984 to 1986 and convicted an average of sixteen companies per year. They were assessed an average fine of $565 each. Taking 1986 alone, the agency registered nine convictions with a mean fine of $500. The Workman's Compensation Board, in contrast, issued 300 administrative penalties with a mean fine of $5,000 in the first half of 1986 (Rankin & Brown, 1988:6).

Increasingly detailed studies on the nature of the regulatory agency weaken the case for criminalization. The more we learn about the regulatory process, the better we understand the limited ability of the typical regulatory agency to employ a criminalization strategy. Many regulators argue that criminalization and effectiveness are simply not compatible. If agencies hope to protect their constituencies in the most efficient way—that is, using the fewest resources to accomplish legislated goals in the speediest fashion—they cannot rely on criminal law. It is too slow, too expensive, and there are too many legal safeguards for powerful corporations to exploit that allow them to circumvent punishment.

Cooperation: An Alternative to Criminalization?

In light of the evidence against criminalization, scholars have begun to consider the ramifications of cooperative regulatory models; those that either renounce criminalization or invoke it only in the final analysis. Indeed, in the popular and business press, cooperative models (specifically models that eschew criminalization entirely) have been heralded as the solution to the vexing problem of government "fetters" on business. Two proposals typify the more scholarly versions of cooperative models. Braithwaite (1982), for example, suggests a scheme whereby organizations would be required to implement their own proposals for policing potentially troublesome areas of operation, such as pollution control or worker health and safety. Strict minimum standards for such plans would be provided by legislation. A corporation's suggested regulations would have to meet specific criteria in each industrial sector. After formulation, each plan would be approved prior to implementation and monitored periodically by a government agency.

Such a system, Braithwaite argues, would have several key advantages over reliance on criminal law as an effective mechanism of corporate social control. Those primarily responsible for enforcing each company's plan would be company employees, not agents of an outside regulatory body.

As employees, they would have access to all kinds of formal and informal sources of information denied to outsiders. They would also have the technical knowledge of plant and industry processes that effective regulation requires, and they would be less likely to be perceived as "the enemy" by fellow employees, since they would interact daily with staff and management.

Because firms would draw up their own regulations, they could ensure that the rules meshed with their particular organizational structure, something that universal criminal laws or even quasi-universal external regulatory standards cannot accomplish. Standards and procedures could be adjusted in accord with technological changes in methods of production. Moreover, because the regulated organization would pay most of the costs of the scheme, governments would realize financial savings.

Braithwaite is not unaware of the potential hazards of such schemes; he concedes that company inspectors would be even more subject to capture than the externally hired present-day inspectors are, and that getting companies to formulate rules that potentially sacrifice profitability to corporate responsibility would not be easy. However, he concludes that problems could be overcome by strict monitoring before the initial approval of company-generated plans, and through laws requiring the issuance of a public report whenever management in a particular company overruled inspectors' recommendations (Braithwaite, 1982).

Building on these ideas, Fisse and Braithwaite have developed a model to maximize "behavioral restraint by means other than those formally directed by a court or administrative agency" (1983:1). Informal social control of corporate crime would rely heavily on stigma and adverse publicity as disincentives to antisocial behavior. They argue that there should be mechanisms to increase public access to and knowledge of corporate crimes, because public criticism could then be a useful deterrent to potential corporate criminality.

To demonstrate the potential of public opprobrium to bring about corporate compliance, Fisse and Braithwaite (1983) cite the change of policy about the health issues related to asbestos exposure by James Hardie, a former major asbestos manufacturer in Australia. Under intense public pressure the company progressed from the official position that asbestos was benign, with no potential for causing disease if properly used, to publicly stated recognition that asbestos posed such a health hazard that the company was phasing out production.

However, there were technological and financial reasons for James Hardie's change of policy as markets for asbestos were gradually disappearing as substitutes for asbestos became available. Fisse and Braithwaite (1983:76) recognize that "Perhaps the real lesson . . . is that informal social control can work when structural realities make it possible."

Braithwaite (1985b, 1988) further advocates a pyramidal approach based on a hierarchy of penalties. If industrial self-regulation, Braithwaite's ideal starting point, is either absent or has failed, the regulatory agency would be required to pursue a specific course of action from that point on. When infractions occur, the first mechanism to be employed is persuasion—the agency would contact the offending organization and try to convince its officers to comply with the legislation. Should that fail, the agency would next issue an official warning. The third step requires the regulatory agency to assess compulsory civil charges leading to mandatory monetary penalties if investigations confirm the offense. If all of these lesser options fail, the agency would then (and only then) initiate criminal charges.

If found guilty, the organization and its executives would face sanctions ranging from prison sentences and fines to removal of operating licenses. To reduce interference from "captured" regulators or politicians, the agency would be unable to halt or change this chain of events; each step would automatically lead to the next one until the problem has been resolved. The system, as Braithwaite conceptualizes it, would overcome problems he attributes to excessive reliance on any one regulatory device, be it civil/administrative measures, criminal laws, or persuasion and education.

A variation of Braithwaite's plan, based on the "prisoner's dilemma" logic game, seeks to demonstrate that cooperative strategies offer maximum advantage to both regulators and regulated (Scholz, 1984a; 1984b). Scholz begins with the reasonable assumption that both sides have an interest in minimizing costs, but only one, the regulated corporation, has an interest in minimizing sanctions. Thus cooperative strategies, because they normally cost less to enforce and to comply with, offer maximum benefits to both sides.

Under this model it is possible to theoretically demonstrate that corporations will derive less benefit from cheating than from cooperating; and that regulatory agencies will also benefit, being "suckered" at most one time before they move to more punitive positions. Scholz argues that the criminal law/deterrence strategies now used by regulatory agencies make law evasion a rational strategy for corporations to adopt (Kagan & Scholz, 1984).

This particular scheme dramatically illustrates the appeal of what has come to be called the law and economics movement. The cooperative model's imperatives are dictated by free-market rationality rather than based on "soft" concepts such as the needs of consumers or the moral obligations of business, which are viewed as politicized and irrational and part of the conflict-ridden environment that has brought business so much grief. Cooperative models, then, try to get around the demonstrated pitfalls of criminalization by advocating economically rational schemes that purportedly are in the interests of both regulated and regulators. For many policymakers, cooperative models are the perfect embodiment of the philosophical and ideological changes that have transformed regulatory law and practice in the 1980s and 1990s.

Limitations of the Cooperative Model

Neither criminalization nor cooperative models capture the essence of the regulatory contradiction because they both fail to take into account the broader socioeconomic realities of capitalist systems (Gough, 1979); specifically the power of capital and its ramifications. Advocates of criminalization call for stricter enforcement, higher fines, and longer prison sentences, but existing criminal laws are already underutilized. Since regulators, courts, and judges choose not to enforce the considerable arsenal of sanctions they already possess, how can securing even more punitive laws, that may be ignored in a similar fashion, represent an improvement? The sources of the resistance to criminalization cannot be overcome by clarion calls from academics.

Advocates of cooperative models also refuse to deal with the implications of class-based power. While they recognize that the overwhelming opposition of the corporate sector has consistently stymied state or regulatory efforts to use criminal law effectively, they overlook the fact that it will have precisely the same effect, or a more severe one, on cooperative models.

The basic conflict of interest between industry's need for quick, high, stable profits, and society's need for safe work places and humane operating procedures (to choose a most obvious example) is overlooked. It is corporate power that makes regulatory agencies and remedial measures ineffective, not some mysterious defect in the measures themselves. The same measures do, after all, function quite adequately in equally complex spheres of social control.

It is corporate resistance to effective regulation, to any and all measures that increase business costs and give outside agents the right to intervene in corporate affairs, which will make cooperative models equally futile. Indeed, we must expect such approaches to be considerably less effective than criminalization, although the extreme modesty of the typical cooperative system's regulatory goals may hide this flaw because evaluations typically compare goals with results. Cooperative models offer business a considerable advantage, then, because they tilt the regulatory struggle strongly in its direction.

Indeed, this fatal defect is the secret of their instant popularity among corporate analysts, the business press, and allied politicians. The reception accorded the law and economics movement in the public arena must be understood in ideological terms. With the decline of liberalism and the dramatic renaissance of the New Right, conservative business forces that had been quiescent during the prosperous 1960s and 1970s came into their own. The capitalist class and its allies in the governments of major western democracies promoted an economic agenda that favors austerity, capitalism and monetarism. A key component of this agenda has been the establishment of belief systems that make it appear both legitimate and inevitable that the share of national wealth received by working and lower classes be decreased. Concomitantly, in the interests of global competition and national survival, a larger share must go to the corporate sector. To compete successfully in the global marketplace, it is argued, business must lower costs by jettisoning labor, destroying unions, decreasing the corporate tax rate, and getting rid of government regulations that, from this perspective, serve only to increase costs and decrease efficiency (Comack, 1988; Horton, 1981).

Corporate activity, therefore, must be de-regulated, and all government "fetters" must be removed from business. Government stimulation of business, however, and massive direct and indirect subsidies through tax-free loans, depletion allowances, tax holidays, and the like, may continue as before. Representatives of the New Right herald scholarly critiques of criminalization as confirming their ideologically based position. They see arguments such as those advanced by the law and economics groups (Lewis-Beck & Alford, 1980; Smith, 1976, 1979; Whiting, 1980) as conferring scholarly blessings on their attempts to represent the corporate sector as the beleaguered scapegoat of social democracy in the postwar period.

Regulation is too expensive, while the overwhelming importance of business to the development of the capitalist economy warrants overlooking minor "mistakes" it might commit in its legitimate pursuit of profit. The congruence between the goals of this movement and the arrival of academic critiques of criminalization explain much more about the popularity of cooperative models than any "objective" examination of the evidence can provide.

In fact, the emphasis the models place on cooperation is not new. Virtually every regulatory agency has attempted, in the first instance, to cooperate with the business it is regulating. When the regulatory target is large and powerful rather than small and isolated, cooperation is mandatory regardless of the directives of the enabling legislation. Indeed, as noted earlier, every law requires that regulatory agencies negotiate some minimal level of consent from their target group(s) (Braithwaite, 1989; Yeager, 1991).

The limits of this negotiation, its starting and ending points, are the crucial factors. Limits are shaped by a number of variables, including the wording of the legislation and precedents; the power of the targeted groups and the enforcement body; and various structural variables such as the interests that will be served by nonenforcement, or the relevant policies of the nation-state. Obviously, this process grants considerably more negotiating leverage to the multinational corporation than the conventional street criminal. But since cooperative regulation in lieu of criminal sanctions is the norm and not the exception, it is obvious that if there is evidence that criminalization does not work (which there is), there is equally compelling evidence that cooperation does not lead to effective enforcement in this sphere either.

Regulatory ineffectiveness, then, results from the structural constraints of regulatory agencies and the ideological, political, and economic consequences of these constraints. An instance of ideological power is seen in the fact that regulatory officials themselves frequently "buy into" dominant perspectives that view corporations and executives as essentially incapable of "real" criminality. Political and economic power are seen in the disparity in resources between regulatory agencies and the corporate sector; a disparity that makes it necessary for regulators to employ strategies that will not annoy the targets of regulation. The less powerful are particularly dependent upon the goodwill of the more powerful, since they lack the clout to be effective in its absence. Agencies must therefore negotiate their path very carefully. Regulators need evidence that they are fulfilling some meaningful social role to continue to operate; however, effectiveness must be held to a minimum or powerful enemies will emerge.

From the regulators' point of view, cooperative strategies make eminently good sense. Because they require less of the regulatory agency, they do not force agents to continually measure themselves and their performance against an impossibly high set of goals that are frequently set during a political crisis to save the constituency of a particular politician or party. However, from a social benefit perspective, it is essential that regulatory agents and agencies continue to struggle with competing and conflicting objectives and even unrealistic or utopian goals.

If, because of the political and structural realities of regulation, agents can typically enforce no more than 30 percent of their mandate, then it is essential that this represents 30 percent of a worthwhile, meaningful goal. To advance a third of the way towards a goal cooperatively negotiated with industry that would not deliver cleaner air or safer workplaces were it enforced at the 100 percent level is futile. At the risk of oversimplification, the entire agenda of regulation depends on a struggle between the forces opposing regulation (typically the corporate sector and its allies) and the much weaker forces supporting it.

The risk of cooperative models is that regulatory agencies allow the goals of regulation to be set too low. They treat the status quo, the existing balance of power between regulators and the corporate sector, as a basic social fact, a starting point, a reality that determines the ability of governments to regulate corporate crime once and for all (Pearce & Tombs, 1988). But if we are to approach the goal of regulatory effectiveness, the status quo ought to be viewed as a moving target. One of the goals of those who wish to obtain more effective control over corporate crime must be to force corporations and regulatory agencies, through ideological, political, and economic struggle, to move closer to this goal. Making the dominance of the corporate sector the starting point for regulators, rather than a barrier that must be challenged and overcome, sets very low limits for regulation.

Summary

In this chapter, we have examined the characteristics of the regulatory agency, its political fragility, and the debate over how best to regulate corporations. At this point we have much more knowledge about what does not work to control corporate crime, than about what is effective. However, we do know a great deal about various types of regulatory agencies, the difficulties regulators face, and the solutions they tend to prefer. Because there is intense pressure from the targets of regulation in addition to those from political bosses, citizens, and sometimes external interest groups as well, regulating corporate crime is very different from traditional policing.

Politicians are likely to intervene to protest against lenience when the target of enforcement is a traditional criminal suspected of low-level theft, fraud, or homicide; for corporate crime, politicians are more likely to intercede to secure lenience. The corporate offender's control over precious resources such as jobs, prestige, and power make regulation a continuing intellectual and political challenge. As this chapter has illustrated, the regulation of powerful corporations requires a balance among different and frequently conflicting needs of agencies, constituencies, and society. Resolutions will always be tentative unless and until one side gains total control over the other. But given the very high costs of corporate crime—the staggering numbers of human lives lost, injuries sustained, and mammoth economic costs—the struggle to achieve more effective regulation is a critically important one.

REFERENCES

Ackerman, B., Rose, S., Sawyer, J., & Henderson, D. (1974). *The uncertain search for environmental quality.* New York: Free Press.

Anderson, J.E. (1975). *Public policy-making.* New York: Praeger.

Bardach, E., & Kagan, R.A. (1982). *Going by the book: The problem of regulatory unreasonableness.* Philadelphia: Temple University Press.

Bartel, A.P., & Thomas, L.G. (1985). Direct and indirect effects of regulation: A new look at OSHA's impact. *Journal of Law and Economics, 28,* 1–25.

Bernard, T.J. (1984). The historical development of corporate criminal liability. *Criminology, 22,* 3–17.

Bernstein, M.H. (1955). *Regulating business by independent commission.* Princeton, NJ: Princeton University Press.

Braithwaite, J. (1982). Enforced self-regulation: A new strategy for corporate crime control. *Michigan Law Review, 80,* 1466–1507.

———. (1984). *Corporate crime in the pharmaceutical industry.* London: Routledge and Kegan Paul.

———. (1985a). White collar crime. *American Review of Sociology, 11,* 1–25.

———. (1985b). *To punish or persuade: Enforcement of coal mine safety.* Albany: State University of New York Press.

———. (1988). *Toward a benign big gun theory of regulatory power.* Unpublished manuscript, Australian National University, Canberra.

———. (1989). *Crime, shame, and reintegration.* New York: Cambridge University Press.

Calavita, K. (1983). The demise of the Occupational Safety and Health Administration: A case study in symbolic action. *Social Problems, 30,* 437–448.

———. (1986). Worker safety, law and social change: The Italian case. *Law and Society, 20,* 189–229.

Carson, W.G. (1970). White-collar crime and the enforcement of factory legislation. *British Journal of Criminology, 10,* 383–398.

———. (1980a). The institutionalization of ambiguity: Early British factory acts. In G. Geis and E. Stotland (Eds.), *White collar theory and research* (pp. 112–135). Beverly Hills: Sage.

———. (1980b). The other price of Britain's oil: Regulating safety on offshore oil installations in the British sector of the North Sea. *Contemporary Crises, 4,* 239–266.

———. (1982). Legal control of safety on British offshore oil installations. In P. Wickham and T. Dailey (Eds.), *White collar and economic crime* (pp. 173–196). Toronto: Lexington Books.

Clinard, M.B., & Yeager, P.C. (1980). *Corporate crime.* New York: Free Press.

Cobb, R.W., & Elder, C.D. (1972). *Participation in American politics: The dynamics of agenda building.* Boston: Allyn and Bacon.

Cobb, R.W., Ross, J., & Ross, M. (1976). Agenda building as a comparative political process. *American Political Science Review, 70,* 126–138.

Coffee, J.C. (1984). Corporate criminal responsibility. In S.H. Kadish (Ed.), *Encyclopedia of crime and justice* (Vol. 1, pp. 253–264). New York: Free Press.

Coleman, J.W. (1989). *The criminal elite: The sociology of white-collar crime* (2nd ed.). New York: St. Martin's.

Comack, E. (1988, November). *Law and order issues in the Canadian context*. Paper presented to the American Society of Criminology, Chicago, IL.

Cranston, R. (1982). Regulation and deregulation: General issues. *University of New South Wales Law Journal, 5,* 1–29.

Cullen, F.T., Maakestad, W.J., & Cavender, G. (1987). *Corporate crime under attack: The Ford Pinto case and beyond.* Cincinnati: Anderson.

Dewees, D.N., & Daniels, R.J. (1986). The cost of protecting occupational health: The asbestos case. *Journal of Human Resources, 21,* 381–396.

Diver, C. (1980). Modesty and immodesty in policy-oriented empirical research. *Administrative Law Review, 32,* 73–78.

Downs, A. (1967). *Inside bureaucracy.* Boston: Little, Brown.

Elkins, J.R. (1976). Decision making model and the control of corporate crime. *Hobarth Law Journal, 85,* 1091–1129.

Ermann, D.M., & Lundman, R.J. (1978). Deviant acts by complex organizations: deviance and social control at the organizational level of analysis. *The Sociological Quarterly, 19,* 55–67.

Fisse, B., & Braithwaite, J. (1984). *The impact of publicity on corporate offenders.* Albany: State University of New York Press.

Frank, N., & Lombness, M. (1988). *Controlling corporate illegality.* Cincinnati: Anderson.

Glaeser, M. (1957). *Public utilities in American capitalism.* New York: Macmillan.

Goff, C., & Reasons, C. (1978). *Corporate crime in Canada.* Toronto: Prentice-Hall.

Gough, I. (1979). *The political economy of the welfare state.* London: Macmillan.

Graham, J.M., & Kramer, V.H. (1976). *Appointments to the regulatory agencies: The Federal Commerce Commission and the Federal Trade Commission.* Washington, DC: U.S. Government Printing Office.

Green, M. (1972). *The closed enterprise system.* New York: Grossman.

Gunningham, N. (1974). *Pollution: Social interest and the law.* Oxford Centre for Socio-Legal Studies.

————. (1984). *Safeguarding the workers*. Sydney, Australia: Law Book.

————. (1987). Negotiated non-compliance: A case study of regulatory failure. *Law and Policy, 9*, 69–97.

Hawkins, K. (1984). *Environment and enforcement: Regulation and the social definition of pollution*. Oxford: Clarendon.

Herring, E.P. (1936). *Federal commissioners: A study of their careers and qualifications*. Cambridge, MA: Harvard University Press.

Hopkins, A. (1978). *Crime, law and business: The sociological sources of Australian monopoly law*. Canberra: Australian Institute of Criminology.

Horton, J. (1981). The rise of the right: A global view. *Crime and Social Justice, 15*, 7–17.

Jamieson, M. (1985). *Persuasion or punishment—The enforcement of health and safety at work legislation by the British factory inspectorate*. Unpublished master's thesis, Oxford University, Oxford, England.

Kagan, R. (1978). *Regulatory justice*. New York: Russell Sage.

Kagan, R., & Scholz, J.T. (1984). The criminology of the corporation and regulatory enforcement strategies. In K. Hawkins and J. Thomas (Eds.), *Enforcing regulation* (pp. 243–265). Boston: Kluwer-Nijhoff.

Kelman, S. (1974). Regulation by the numbers—A report on the Consumer Product Safety Commission. *The Public Interest, 36*, 83–102.

King, D.K. (1985, November). *The regulatory use of the criminal sanction in controlling corporate crime*. Paper presented at the meeting of the American Society of Criminology, San Diego, CA.

Lane, R.E. (1953). Why businessmen violate the law. *Journal of Criminal Law, Criminology, and Police Science, 44*, 151–165.

Leigh, P. (1989). Compensating wages for job-related death: The opposing argument. *Journal of Economic Issues, 23*, 823–842.

Levi, M. (1981). *The phantom capitalists: The organization and control of long-term fraud*. London: Heinemann.

————. (1984). Giving creditors the business: The criminal law in inaction. *International Journal of Sociology of Law, 12*, 321–333.

Lewis-Beck, M.S., & Alford, J.R. (1980). Can government regulate safety? The coal mine example. *American Political Science Review, 74*, 745–781.

Long, S. (1979, May). *The Internal Revenue Service: Examining the exercise of discretion in tax enforcement*. Paper presented at the meeting of the Law and Society Association, Chicago, IL.

Lynxwiler, J., Shover, N., & Clelland, D. (1983, March). *Corporate size and international contexts: Determinants of sanctioning severity in a regulatory bureaucracy*. Paper presented at the meeting of the American Criminal Justice Society, San Antonio, TX.

McQueen, R. (1989). The new companies and securities schemes: A fundamental departure? *The Australian Quarterly, 26*, 481–97.

———. (1990). *Why company law is important to Left Realists*. Paper presented at Left Realist Conference, Vancouver, BC.

Meier, R., & Plumlee, J.P. (1978). Regulatory administration and organizational rigidity. *Western Political Quarterly, 31*, 80–95.

Messerschmidt, J. (1986). *Capitalism, patriarchy, and crime: Toward a socialist-feminist criminology*. Totowa, NJ: Rowman and Littlefield.

Mills, C.W. (1959). *The sociological imagination*. New York: Oxford University Press.

Mitnick, B.M. (1980). *The political economy of regulation*. New York: Columbia University Press.

Nader, R., & Green, M.J. (Eds.). (1973). *Corporate power in America*. New York: Viking.

Noll, R. (1978). *Reforming regulation: An evaluation of the Ash Council proposals*. Washington, DC: Brookings Institute.

Olson, S. (1985). Comparing Justice and Labor Department lawyers: Ten years of occupational safety and health litigation. *Law and Policy, 7*, 286–313.

Parenti, M. (1983). *Democracy for the few*. New York: St. Martin's.

Paulus, I. (1974). *The search for pure food: A sociology of legislation in Britain*. London: Martin Robertson.

Pearce, F. (1976). *Crimes of the powerful, Marxism, crime and deviance*. London: Pluto.

———. (1990a). *Commercial and conventional crime in Islington*. (Second Islington Crime Survey). Economic and Social Research Council, United Kingdom.

———. (1990b). "Responsible corporations" and regulatory agencies. *Political Quarterly, 61*, 415–430.

Pearce, F., & Tombs, S. (1988, November). *Regulating corporate crime: The case of health and safety*. Paper presented at the meeting of the American Society of Criminology, Chicago, IL.

————. (1989). Union Carbide, Bhopal, and the hubris of a capitalist technocracy. *Social Justice*, June, 116–145.

Peltzman, J. (1976). Toward a more general theory of regulation. *Journal of Law and Economics*, 19, 211–240.

Rankin, R, & Brown, R. (1988, June). *The treatment of repeat offenders under B.C.'s occupational health and safety and pollution control legislation.* Paper presented at the meeting of the Canadian Law and Society Association, Windsor, Ontario.

Regush, N. (1991, April). Health and Welfare's National Disgrace. *Saturday Night*, pp. 9, 53.

Reiman, J. (1990). *The rich get richer and the poor get prison* (3rd ed.). New York: Macmillan.

Sabatier, P. (1975). Social movements and regulatory agencies: Toward a more adequate—and less pessimistic—theory of "Clientele capture." *Policy Sciences*, 6, 301–341.

————. (1977). Regulatory policy-making: Toward a framework of analysis. *Natural Resources Journal*, 17, 415–460.

Sampson, A. (1975). *The seven sisters: The great oil companies and the world they shaped.* New York: Viking.

Schlegel, K. (1988). Desert retribution and corporate criminality. *Justice Quarterly*, 5, 615–634.

Scholz, J. (1984a). Deterrence, cooperation and the ecology of regulatory enforcement. *Law and Society Review*, 18, 179–224.

————. (1984b). Voluntary compliance and regulatory enforcement. *Law and Policy*, 6, 385–404.

Shapiro, S. (1985). The road not taken: The elusive path to criminal prosecution for white collar offenders. *Law and Society Review*, 19 (2), 179–217.

Smith, R. (1976). *The Occupational Health and Safety Act.* Washington, DC: American Enterprise Institute.

Smith, R.J. (1979). The impact of OSHA inspections on manufacturing injury rates. *Journal of Human Resources*, 14, 145–154.

Snider, L. (1978). Corporate crime in Canada: A preliminary report. *Canadian Journal of Criminology*, 20, 142–168.

————. (1987). Towards a political economy of reform, regulation and corporate crime. *Law and Policy*, 9, 37–68.

Staff. (1989, May). *Consumer Reports*, 29, 294–296.

Stanley, D.T., Mann, D.E., & Doig, J.W. (1967). *Men who govern.* Washington, DC: Brookings Institute.

Stigler, G. (1975). *The citizen and the state: Essays on regulation.* Chicago: University of Chicago Press.

Stone, C.D. (1975). *Where the law ends: The social control of corporate behavior.* New York: Harper and Row.

———. (1980). The place of enterprise liability in the control of corporate conduct. *Yale Law Journal, 90,* 1–77.

Sutherland, E.H. (1940). White-collar criminality. *American Sociological Review, 5,* 1–12.

Tabb, N. (1980). Government regulations: Two sides to the story. *Challenge, 23,* 40–48.

Thomas, J. (1982). The regulatory role in the containment of corporate illegality. In H. Edelhertz & T. Overcast (Eds.), *White-collar crime: An agenda for research* (pp. 88–112). Toronto: D.C. Heath.

———. (1989). *Making regulatory policy.* Pittsburgh: University of Pittsburgh Press.

Tucker, E. (1987, June). *Making the workplace "safe" in capitalism: The enforcement of factory legislation in nineteenth-century Ontario.* Paper presented at the meeting of the Canadian Law and Society Association, Hamilton, Ontario.

Vogel, D. (1986). *National styles of regulation: Environmental policy in Great Britain and United States.* Ithaca: Cornell University Press.

Watkins, J.C. (1977). White collar crimes: Legal sanctions and social control. *Crime and Delinquency, 23,* 290–303.

Whiting, B.J. (1980). OSHA's enforcement policy. *Labor Law Journal, 31,* 259–272.

Wilson, J.Q. (1980). *The politics of regulation.* New York: Basic Books.

Yeager, P.C. (1991). *The limits of law: Public regulation of private pollution.* New York: Cambridge University Press.

CHAPTER EIGHT

Corporate Criminal Liability

Barbara A. Belbot

Corporate crime is a relatively new topic for criminologists, but legal theorists have travailed over the concept for centuries. Terms such as "organizational deviance" appear frequently in discussions of criminological theory about corporate misbehavior, while the term "corporate offense" appears most frequently in legal discussions. Both sets of terminology refer to conceptually different approaches to the same phenomena.

Criminal law is concerned with whether, in a specific case, there is proof beyond a reasonable doubt that a *person* (juristic as opposed to natural) intentionally violated a penal statute or intended to commit an act that resulted in a legal violation (with the exception of strict liability offenses where intent is irrelevant). Criminology is concerned with "the process of making laws, of breaking laws, and of reacting toward the breaking of laws" (Sutherland & Cressey, 1978:3).

This chapter focuses on legal theories of corporate criminality, emphasizing criminal law and criminal sanctions. In order to better understand corporate criminality, it is important to appreciate the corporate form of business organization and how the structure of a corporate entity can facilitate illegal behavior. To complete the picture, corporations must also be understood as historical creatures, with corporate criminal liability developing slowly as commercial businesses grow in size and influence.

It may seem problematic to study the criminality of organizations while ignoring the individuals who comprise those organizations. Organizations, however, are collections of "jobs or social positions, each with its own skill, power, rules, and rewards" (Ermann & Lundman, 1987:4). Rather than viewing a corporation as a collection of people, it should be viewed as a collection of jobs occupied by individuals who frequently are replaced. These replaceable individuals have limited knowledge about the corporation as they perform their assigned tasks. Those in high-level positions are also replaceable and have been socialized by years of working in corporations (Whyte, 1956).

Organizational structure and policy can encourage corporate deviance (Ermann & Lundman, 1987; Stone, 1975; Vaughan, 1982). In large corporations, individuals can perform well in their positions; however, because they have limited information and responsibility, no single person reviews and analyzes every operation. Illegal actions can occur unintentionally and can escape internal detection (Ermann & Lundman, 1987). High-level officials within the organization develop goals and delegate responsibility for their implementation to middle management. The goals are accompanied by reward and punishment systems. While attempting to meet the goals, middle managers may unintentionally resort to actions that result in crimes. The Ford Pinto case is an example. Then CEO Lee Iacocca committed the company to producing an inexpensive, light-weight automobile. The result was the creation of a dangerous automobile that eventually led to a criminal indictment. Although Ford officials intended to build an inexpensive car, they never intended to build a car that would kill people (Cullen, Maakestad, & Cavender, 1987).

Not all corporate crime is unintentional, of course. Organizational elites may knowingly and intentionally undertake illegal actions to achieve goals on behalf of the organization. For two decades, bribery of foreign government officials was common in the aerospace industry. A special review committee of seven Lockheed outside directors determined that the policy was not confined to junior executives, but was instigated and supported by the company's chairman of the board and its president (Clinard & Yeager, 1980). In like manner, senior management in most of the twenty-three corporations involved in price-fixing in the folding carton industry were aware of the antitrust violations (Clinard & Yeager, 1980).

Organizations create their own internal moral and intellectual worlds (Vaughan, 1982). Ermann and Lundman (1987) describe the "institutionalization of deviance" in which deviant solutions to organizational problems become a routine part of a company's ethos. A short step separates accepted, although unethical, business practices from violations of the law (Clinard & Yeager, 1978; Conklin, 1977).

An example is the 1961 prosecution of several companies and corporate executives in the heavy electrical equipment industry for violations of the antitrust laws. The participants, including General Electric and Westinghouse, had been involved for several years in a highly secretive conspiracy to fix prices. Many executives took the position that although their behavior was technically illegal, they had helped stabilize prices and did no harm to the public. Many defendants testified that when they arrived on the job, they discovered that price-fixing was an established way of life. Participation in the conspiracy was expected, and they entered into the conspiracy just as they did other aspects of their jobs (Geis, 1967).

What Is a Corporation?

The corporate structure has several major advantages that explain why it has become the dominant form of business organization in this country. Although the number of corporations in the United States is far fewer than the number of sole proprietorships and partnerships, corporations account for significantly higher revenues than other types of businesses. Business enterprises that reach a certain scale almost exclusively adopt the corporate structure (Choper, Coffee, & Morris, 1989). There are four main reasons why a business would decide to incorporate: (1) the owners of a corporation, its shareholders, have limited financial liability; (2) a corporation has a perpetual existence; (3) ownership of a corporation is easily transferable; and (4) management of a corporation is centralized.

A corporation's primary advantage is that the organization insulates the shareholders from individual liability. When a business is incorporated it becomes a new legal entity that is distinct from its employees and its shareholders. The corporate entity has the power to enter into contracts, to take, hold, and convey property, and to sue and be sued in its name. Unlike other forms of business organizations, the owners of a corporation risk only the amount of their investment in the company, which is the purchase price they paid for their stock. Their personal assets are not available to creditors or anyone else who has claims against the business. A judgment against a corporation can be executed only against the property of the corporation. In contrast, a general partner in a partnership or a sole proprietor has unlimited personal liability for the debts of a business entity.

The second advantage of the corporate form is its perpetual existence. A corporation survives the deaths of its shareholders and employees because it exists separately from them. In a solo proprietorship or a partnership, the death, withdrawal, or insolvency of an owner terminates the business, unless a partnership agreement provides otherwise. Corporations are referred to as legal or juristic *persons* because they are artificial persons created by law (Henn & Alexander, 1983). A juristic person is a creation of legal fiction that allows the law to confer rights and obligations to nonhuman, as opposed to natural, persons (Bernard, 1984).

The third major advantage of the corporate structure is that shareholders can easily sell or otherwise transfer all or portions of their stock in a corporation. Free transferability is important because it is possible to sell stock on a regular and continuing basis, making it easy for corporations to raise capital and for investors to liquidate their assets. Partnership interests usually cannot be transferred without the consent of the other partners.

The fourth advantage of corporations is centralized management. In large, publicly held corporations, shareholders have few management responsibilities. Their role is to elect a board of directors, to adopt, amend, and repeal bylaws, and to ratify certain actions by the board of directors. Shareholders also vote on extraordinary corporate matters, such as amending the articles of incorporation, the sale or lease of corporate assets not in the regular course of business, merger, consolidation, and dissolution. Modern corporations are characterized by the separation of ownership, which is in the hands of the shareholders, and control, which is exercised by the board of directors and their agents (Choper et al., 1989). In contrast, unless the partnership agreement provides differently, each partner has an equal right to manage the business and enter into binding relationships on behalf of the partnership.

The board of directors of a corporation is responsible for determining and executing corporate policy with regard to products, services, prices, wages, labor relations, selection and supervision of officers, executive compensation, determination of dividends, financing, and supervision of the general welfare of the entire enterprise (Henn & Alexander, 1983). It is authorized to delegate many of these management responsibilities to officers. State incorporation laws usually provide that a corporation must have certain specified officers, generally a president, one or more vice-presidents, a treasurer, and a secretary. The officers have their functions delegated to them by the board, the articles of incorporation, the bylaws, and statutes of the state in which the corporation resides (Henn & Alexander, 1983). Below the officers in the hierarchical corporate structure are managers and supervisors, who are hired by the officers and are responsible for the daily operations of the business.

A closely held corporation is one whose ownership shares are held by one shareholder or a closely knit group of shareholders. They are usually smaller businesses with no public investors. The shareholders are more active in the conduct and management of the company and are involved in developing policies and practices (Parisi, 1984).

The life of a corporation begins with a corporate charter granted by the state in which the corporation is formed. Incorporation laws vary from state to state. There are no federal statutory provisions providing for incorporation. All states require that a business wanting to incorporate must apply for a charter and submit a set of articles of incorporation that elaborate, among other things, the name of the corporation, its period of duration, which is typically perpetual, the purpose or purposes for which the corporation is organized, the aggregate number of shares of stock that the corporation has authority to issue, the address of its registered office, and the number and names of the directors serving on the board. Modern statutes permit incorporation for any lawful business purpose with various exceptions related to certain types of businesses, such as banks, trust companies, loan and insurance companies, public utilities, and railroads. With few exceptions, corporations can pursue any and all lawful business ventures. (Henn & Alexander, 1983).

Development of the Corporate Business Structure

The corporate structure originated sometime during the Middle Ages in Europe and was well established in England by the end of the fourteenth century (Brickey, 1984; Cullen et al., 1987). The earliest corporations involved ecclesiastical bodies that owned and managed church property. Feudal lords had constructed churches on their lands and with the decline of feudalism it was necessary to decide who owned the church and its related properties. Eventually, the church itself was recognized as a juristic person who owned itself and its income. For legal purposes, the church's congregation was considered a single person (Bernard, 1984).

During the thirteenth and fourteenth centuries, the concept of a juristic person was extended to English boroughs and townships that owed rents and fines to the Crown and had the right to levy tolls and sell franchises. Boroughs and townships were granted the authority to conduct business as juristic persons through royal charters granted by the Crown (Cullen et al., 1987).

The corporate organizational form became more common during the sixteenth and seventeenth centuries as hospitals, universities, and similar associations evolved (Brickey, 1984).

Most important to the development of the corporation, however, was the growth of joint-stock companies that were formed in response to the need to raise greater sums of capital to conduct more costly business enterprises. A joint-stock company was typically formed for a single business venture. After the venture was completed, the company was disbanded and its assets and profits distributed to the stockholders. New stock was issued for each venture.

By the late sixteenth century, the English Crown was chartering joint-stock companies to develop foreign trade and colonies. Unchartered joint-stock companies risked prosecution for criminal conspiracy against the national interests. The royal charter legitimized the activities in which the trading companies engaged, including installing local governments and exercising police powers (Hurst, 1970).

By the eighteenth century, English law provided that only the king could create a corporation. The reason for such a policy was not economic interests but to secure the power of the Crown (Hurst, 1970). By the eighteenth century, however, the common law of partnership and trust had developed to such a degree that a large number of unincorporated businesses were competing with corporations. In 1719, the English Parliament passed the Bubble Act that declared the operation of unchartered joint stock companies illegal. The act was passed as the result of a national scandal created by unincorporated companies indulging in wild and risky speculations (Silets & Brenner, 1986). Lawyers then devised methods to circumvent the act's vague restrictions so that unchartered companies could once more do business as trusts. Indeed, unchartered joint-stock companies became even more popular than before the passage of the act (Cullen et al., 1987). In 1844 and 1855, The English Companies Acts, which replaced the Bubble Act, made incorporation more generally available. The focus had shifted from securing power in the Crown to fostering economic growth (Hurst, 1970).

Corporations grew slowly in the United States. Initially, the English Parliament refused to allow colonial legislatures to grant corporate charters for business purposes (Elkins, 1976). Before 1800, most of the corporations that did exist were churches, charities, cities, and boroughs. Only 335 businesses were issued corporate charters during the entire eighteenth century in the United States, most of which were quasi-governmental in nature. They included banks, insurance companies, water companies, and companies created to build and operate canals, roads, and bridges (Brickey, 1984; Friedman, 1985).

Early state incorporation laws granted charters to businesses on an individual basis. Each charter was designed for the particular business entity requesting it, and corporations were chartered to perform specific, limited tasks. In this way, states were able to exercise control over the power and influence of business (Elkins, 1976). The charters usually provided for limited corporate life spans. It was common for states to issue charters for five, twenty, or thirty years. Perpetual duration charters were rare until after the Civil War (Friedman, 1985). Some charters provided for terms other than one share, one vote; other charters restricted the number of shares one individual could own. It is unclear whether limited shareholder liability was universal until the early part of the nineteenth century (Campbell, 1975). The typical American was suspicious of corporations and the political and economic influence that could be concentrated into the hands of a few (Friedman, 1985).

Gradually, as the corporate form became the most popular and practical form of business organization, state legislatures were overwhelmed with special charter requests and moved in the direction of passing general incorporation statutes that provided few restrictions on the entry, duration, or management of a company (Friedman, 1985). By the turn of the eighteenth century, more and more charters were being issued to business enterprises. By the middle and late 1800s, the corporation was firmly established and was contributing to the development of American cities and westward expansion. Corporations began to grow rapidly in size and numbers. By the turn of the nineteenth century, they were the dominant form of business organization in this country (Cullen et al., 1987).

While corporations grew in number and in influence, the corporate structure itself was undergoing significant growth and change. At the beginning of the twentieth century, professional corporate managers often shared management decisions with members of the family holding the majority of stock, or with the financial institutions that provided the outside capital necessary for the corporation's growth.

Technological advances, however, tremendously increased both the number of tasks that needed coordination and the level of expertise required to coordinate. Large firms, especially in the railroad and telegraph industries, moved toward vertical integration whereby they bought the companies that were their sources of supply and their retail distributors, assuring access to raw materials and protecting markets. Managers were addressing an expanded range of decisions. By 1917, professional managers were making management decisions. Members of entrepreneurial families and financial institutions were no longer involved in the process except occasionally to exercise a negative vote over an important management matter. The control of the corporation was in the hands of trained managers. For the stockholder and the investor, the corporation became a source of income. The United States economy had moved through entrepreneurial and financial capitalism to managerial capitalism (Chandler, 1977).

Development of Corporate Criminal Liability

Although corporations gradually took on many of the characteristics of natural persons, such as the authority to own property and enter into contracts, a coherent theory of corporate criminal liability developed much more slowly. Initially, the corporation was considered an abstract entity without a mind and without the ability to form the intent necessary to establish criminal liability (Brickey, 1984). Lord Holt, the Chief Justice of the King's Bench during the early eighteenth century, is reputed to have stated that "[a] corporation is not indictable, but the particular members of it are" (Elkins, 1976).

An exception to the general rule, however, involved the criminal liability of incorporated English municipalities, counties, and boroughs for the failure to abide by their common law duty to repair and maintain the roads and bridges they erected. As early as 1635, courts held that the responsibility for the upkeep of public thoroughfares fell to the incorporated entity rather than its individual office-holders, even though the office-holders and the inhabitants of the city or town who constructed the thoroughfares were no longer members of the community (Brickey, 1984; Elkins, 1976). By the middle of the eighteenth century, it was firmly established in English common law that a governmental corporate entity could be held criminally responsible for a public nuisance resulting from nonfeasance (Brickey, 1984).

Not until 1842 did the English courts decide that a strictly commercial corporation could be held criminally liable for failure to perform a legal duty. In *Queen v. Birmingham and Glouchester Railway Co.* (1842), the court held that the corporation had a duty to carry out certain acts, specifically the removal of a bridge it had erected over a road. The corporation was held criminally liable for its nonfeasance.

Eventually, the issue arose as to whether a corporation could be held criminally liable for its affirmative acts, and the debate surrounding nonfeasance versus misfeasance ensued. The argument against corporate liability for misfeasance emphasized that a corporation is a noncorporeal being, and, therefore unable to commit any affirmative actions, limiting liability to sins of omission (Silets & Brenner, 1986). Corporate criminal liability for affirmative actions was not imposed until the tort theory of vicarious liability was applied to corporations.

Under the vicarious liability doctrine, a person can be held liable for the acts of another person. Even in ancient times, the vicarious liability doctrine imposed civil sanctions in the form of monetary damages on employers for the tortious conduct of their employees. As corporations began to form, it was a natural step to hold them civilly liable for their employees' torts (Bernard, 1984). As early as 1682, a court ordered the forfeiture of an incorporated city's charter, holding the city corporation civilly liable for the actions of its officials (Brickey, 1984).

In the 1846 case, *The Queen v. Great North of England Railway Co.*, a corporation was indicted for cutting through an existing highway with a railway line and leaving behind dangerous debris. In answer to the company's argument that it could not be held criminally liable for the failure to perform an affirmative act, the prosecutor noted developments in tort law that imposed civil liability on corporations for torts committed by their employees, such as trespass. He urged expanding corporate vicarious liability to include criminal acts. Lord Denman, who delivered the court's opinion, held that the affirmative acts of employees could be imputed to a corporation in a criminal case. He cautioned, however, that because a corporation lacked the capacity to form the corrupted mind necessary to commit certain types of crimes, his ruling did not extend to acts of immorality such as perjury or offenses against a person (Brickey, 1984).

As in England, the first cases in the United States to uphold criminal indictments against corporations involved towns and municipalities resulting from the neglect of their legal duties (Elkins, 1976). Not until the 1820s and 1830s did American courts consider the criminal liability of strictly commercial corporations. Because most of the early business corporations in the United States were involved in public transportation and other quasi-governmental activities, it was relatively easy for courts to impose criminal liability for nonfeasance of duties, even though English law concerning the criminal liability of business corporations was not yet firmly established (Elkins, 1976).

American courts, however, did not abide very long with the nonfeasance-misfeasance dichotomy that had so troubled English judges. In the case *State v. Morris and Essex Railroad Co.* (1852), the court considered a criminal indictment against a corporation for constructing a building on a public highway and obstructing the road with its railroad cars. The court rejected the argument that a corporation could not be held criminally liable for an affirmative act, by citing the civil liability that a corporation has under the vicarious liability doctrine for the torts committed by its employees and agents. Furthermore, the court rejected the *ultra vires* defense that a corporation cannot commit a crime because legally it cannot perform any act beyond the scope of its charter and the laws governing incorporation. The court reasoned that a successful *ultra vires* defense in a criminal action should logically be extended to lawsuits involving tort liability, and that such an extension would oppose already established tort law (Brickey, 1984). Two years later in

Commonwealth v. Proprietors of New Bedford Bridge (1854), another American court ruled that a corporation responsible for building a bridge across a river in a way that obstructed navigation could be held criminally liable for its affirmative actions. The court characterized the distinction between nonfeasance and misfeasance as absurd (Brickey, 1984; Elkins, 1976).

At the same time that courts were expanding corporate criminal liability to encompass affirmative acts resulting in public nuisances, both England and America were legislating public welfare offenses that imposed strict criminal liability on both individuals and corporations. Strict liability implies that there is no concern for the actor's state of mind at the time of the offense, or whether he or she was even aware that the act was criminal. All that is needed for a criminal conviction is proof that the person performed the act that violated the statute. Various statutes enacted in the United States prior to 1900 created standards of care for railroad operators as well as for the sale of food and liquor (Cullen et al., 1987; Elkins, 1976), and imposed punishments for violations.

Both courts in *State v. Morris and Essex Railroad Co.* (1852) and *Commonwealth v. Proprietors of New Bedford Bridge* (1854) noted *in dicta* that their decisions did not hold that a corporation was liable for an offense requiring criminal intent, since a corporation does not have a soul or a mind and is incapable of forming the requisite *mens rea* for many crimes. Other scholars and jurists argued against corporate liability for intent crimes because such acts go beyond the purpose of a corporation and what is authorized under a corporate charter. Because death or dismemberment was a frequent punishment for crimes requiring intent, until other sanctions evolved, it was impossible to punish a corporate criminal for an intent offense (Brickey, 1984).

With the law developing on many different fronts, however, United States courts gradually lost their reluctance to recognize corporate *mens rea*. In 1909, in *New York Central & Hudson River Railroad Co. v. United States*, the United States Supreme Court upheld the Elkins Act that declared the acts of officers, agents, and employees of a common carrier could be imputed to a carrier itself. In that case, a railroad had been convicted of illegally granting rebates to sugar refineries in violation of the act. The court conceded that there are some crimes that cannot be committed by corporations, but held that the statute involved a type of general intent offense that consisted of purposively doing something prohibited by law. For such general intent crimes, the court ruled that logic and policy considerations mandated the imposition of corporate liability for the wrongdoing of the company's agents. The Supreme Court emphasized that if corporations were immunized from criminal prosecution because of a theory that corporations cannot commit crimes, Congress would lose its ability to effectively control corporate misconduct.

Not long after the 1909 Supreme Court decision, lower federal and state courts began to rule that corporations could also be held liable for crimes requiring specific intent. Unlike general intent crimes where it must be shown that the accused committed the offense knowing it was illegal, specific intent offenses require additional proof that the accused desired the prohibited result. Relying on the fact that corporations could be held vicariously liable in civil court for the intentional torts of their agents, and flatly rejecting the position that corporations lacked the ability to form specific intent, by the early twentieth century courts had removed the remaining barriers to establishing corporate criminal liability, making corporations subject to prosecution for the same offenses applicable to natural persons (Brickey, 1984). The distinction between the natural and juristic person had proved unworkable (Silets & Brenner, 1986).

Current Status of Corporate Criminal Liability

Since a corporation acts only through its employees, once it was decided that a corporation can commit specific intent crimes, the legal issues shifted to: for what acts, performed by which agents could a corporation be held liable. The theory of imputing an employee's criminal intent to a corporate employer is built on the doctrine of vicarious liability (Parisi, 1984). The general theory of imputation and the rule adopted by the federal courts, is that a corporation is liable for all acts performed by an employee within the scope of their employment and intended to benefit the corporation (Brickey, 1984; Tigar, 1990).

The requirement that an employee be acting within the scope of employment has been interpreted liberally to include actions that are not authorized by the company. Illegal acts in direct disobedience to corporate instructions or policy are also considered acts within an employee's scope of employment, even if the corporation has made good faith efforts to prevent employees from engaging in them. As interpreted by the courts, the requirement means little more than that the act was somehow connected to an employee's performance of a job-related activity (Brickey, 1984).

An intent to benefit the corporation is also a requirement of the general rule. If an employee is seeking only his or her personal gain, a corporation is not criminally liable (Tigar, 1990). If the scheme is unsuccessful and a corporation does not reap the intended benefits, or actually suffers a loss as a result of the illegality, a corporation is still liable. If a corporation reaps unintended benefits from an employee's wrongdoing, the corporation is not liable *(Standard Oil Co. v. United States, 1962; Tigar, 1990).*

By far the most troubling aspect of the imputation doctrine is determining which employees' actions should provide the basis for vicarious corporate liability. The acts of members of the board of directors and corporate officers are most clearly imputable to the corporation. Board members and officers are responsible for directing the affairs of the corporation and, theoretically, have the most control over the business. Some scholars argue that high-level officials in many publicly held companies and officials of closely held corporations are actually a corporation's *alter ego,* and their actions should result in direct, not vicarious, liability (Elkins, 1976; Parisi, 1984).

It is more difficult to assess a corporation's accountability for the actions of managers, supervisors, and subordinate employees. Federal case law has developed an expansive approach in which corporate liability is not limited based on the offender's position within the corporate hierarchy (Brickey, 1984). In *C.I.T. Corporation v. United States* (1945), the Ninth Circuit Court of Appeals rejected the argument that an area manager's false credit applications should not be imputed to the corporation because the manager was low in the corporate structure, and the officers and directors were unaware of his actions. The appeals court ruled that position and title are irrelevant considerations. It is the function delegated to an officer or employee that determines his or her power to involve a company in an illegal activity.

Federal courts have overwhelmingly ruled that a corporation is criminally liable for the acts of even subordinate or menial employees. It is not necessary that higher-level officials be aware of the action or in some way acquiesced in its commission. It is also not necessary that a supervisor or officer ratify the action after it has been committed (Elkins, 1976; Parisi, 1984).

The collective knowledge doctrine has been adopted by several federal courts. It imposes criminal liability on a corporation in situations where there is no single employee who has complete knowledge concerning an illegal transaction. A corporation acquires the collective knowledge of several of its employees. Courts have emphasized that corporations compartmentalize their operations and duties such that it is irrelevant whether one individual employee had complete overall knowledge of an illegal action. Judges have upheld convictions that involved aggregating the knowledge of several employees to equal specific intent (Tigar, 1990).

Criticisms of the Current Federal Law

The lack of restrictions on corporate criminal liability under federal law is not without its critics. The Model Penal Code, drafted by the American Law Institute, and some state statutes have adopted the position that a corporation is liable for the unlawful acts of its agents under only four circumstances: (1) the offense is a minor infraction; (2) the offense is defined by a statute that expresses a legislative intent to hold corporations liable for the acts of their employees; (3) the offense involves nonfeasance; and (4) the offense is performed, authorized, or recklessly tolerated by the board of directors or a high managerial agent acting on behalf of the corporation and within the scope of his or her employment. High managerial officials include only those employees whose corporate position support a reasonable inference that their conduct reflects corporate policy (American Law Institute, 1962; Brickey, 1984, 1988; Tigar, 1990).

The rationale behind the Model Penal Code recognizes that management in a modern corporation cannot possibly know about or supervise all the activities of its employees. It is essential that tasks be delegated on many hierarchical levels. It is probable that lower-level employees exercise more responsibility for the day-to-day operations of a corporation than do its directors or officers. A legal standard that holds a corporation liable in circumstances where a higher-level employee has not performed, authorized, or tolerated the activity has limited deterrent effect (Tigar, 1990). The Model Penal Code also provides that a corporation is not liable for illegal conduct if a high managerial employee who had supervisory responsibility over the subject matter of the offense exercised due diligence to prevent its commission. The drafters of the code believed that if a crime was committed despite due diligence, there is no deterrent effect in holding the corporation responsible (American Law Institute, 1962; Brickey, 1984, 1988).

A further rationale for the Model Penal Code is the externality problem. The economic burden of a criminal fine falls on the innocent shareholders because the value of their stock may be reduced. Just as likely, the cost of the fine may be passed onto employees in terms of reduced wages and potential work reductions, or to consumers as higher prices (Brickey, 1988; Coffee, 1981). For these reasons the corporation should be held criminally liable under very restricted circumstances. The apprehension rate for corporate crimes is very low, encouraging corporations to take risks. A meaningful criminal fine is limited by the wealth of the corporation, but it should also include a factor for the risk of getting caught. The monetary amount of a corporate criminal sanction that would successfully serve as a deterrent, given the low risk of punishment, would too often exceed a company's resources and further exacerbate the externality problem (Coffee, 1981).

Despite the limits it places on corporate criminal liability, the code affirms that there exist some situations where such liability is just and serves a useful purpose. There are a significant number of legal scholars, however, who do not endorse the doctrine of corporate criminal liability in even the restricted form provided in the Model Penal Code. They question the advisability of applying the criminal law to an artificial person that "has no soul to be damned, and no body to be kicked" (Coffee, 1981).

Deterrence has long been recognized as the primary rationale for imposing criminal sanctions for the types of criminal activities engaged in by businesses, many of which do not involve morally culpable behavior. More so than individuals, corporations choose their actions based on a rational evaluation of projected costs and benefits. Deterrence, not retribution, is the goal of punishing corporate crime (Corporate Crime, 1979). The major argument against corporate criminal liability is that a corporation can only act through its employees. Punishing a business entity does not serve to deter the individuals who are actually committing the crimes. Deterrence is only accomplished by penalizing the natural person who made the decision to engage in crime, a fact recognized by civil law countries that impose the criminal law only against the truly guilty individual and not the noncorporeal entity (Mueller, 1957). Especially in those situations involving morally culpable behavior, punishing a corporation is inappropriate and fails to deter, because only human beings can form criminal intent.

Response to the Criticisms

As vociferous as those who object to the notion of holding corporations criminally liable for their acts are its defenders. Shareholders in a corporation are investing in a risk that may or may not be profitable. The possibility that the value of a corporation's assets may be diminished by a criminal fine is no different than if they are diminished by a civil law tort suit for the same type of behavior, or through poor business decisions that failed to maximize profits. Furthermore, shareholders should not be allowed to profit from benefits reaped by illegal behavior. To date, corporate criminal fines have not been significantly high, making it unlikely that either stockholders or consumers have been adversely affected (Brickey, 1988; Coffee, 1981). In competitive industries, consumers can chose not to be affected by purchasing lower-priced products.

Advocates of imposing criminal sanctions against corporate wrongdoers refute the argument that relying solely on personal liability is a sufficient deterrent to corporate crime. Many state indemnification statutes permit corporations to indemnify officers and directors for individual criminal liability incurred while serving in their corporate capacities, if they acted in good faith on behalf of the company (Brickey, 1988).

Corporations are more than the sum of their parts. Federal courts have long recognized that corporations can be held criminally liable in addition to, or even apart from, their corporate agents. In many cases, a corporation has been found guilty of a crime, although the individual agents whose acts led to the commission of the crime and who were also prosecuted were acquitted (Brickey, 1984; Silets & Brenner, 1986).

Decision making in corporate entities is necessarily decentralized. Directors and officers delegate large amounts of authority. As a result of delegation, it may be difficult or even impossible to determine specific individuals who are responsible for an offense. Sanctions against corporations are also essential because by delegating authority, higher-level company officials are often able to insulate themselves from legal responsibility (Coleman, 1975; Silets & Brenner, 1986). In addition, as recognized by the collective knowledge doctrine, there are circumstances where it is appropriate to impute to a corporation the aggregate or collective knowledge of a number of its employees. When no one employee has sufficient knowledge of a criminal scheme to be held individually liable, the corporation can be held accountable.

Finally, adherents of the doctrine of imposing criminal liablity against corporations take issue with the assertion that corporations are not stigmatized by the imposition of criminal sanctions (Corporate Crime, 1979). Fisse (1983) and Fisse and Braithwaite (1983) argue that corporations are concerned about their public image and are adversely affected by the impact of bad publicity. The process of investigation, accusation, and adjudication produces a stigma that can have a significant deterrent effect and encourage companies to repair their images so as to regain the public's confidence.

Evidentiary Problems in Prosecuting Corporations

The prosecution of corporate crime is complicated by some of the same problems that face the social science researcher investigating corporate deviance. Because corporations are made up of replaceable people who function with limited knowledge and responsibilities, it is often impossible to determine where and when in the corporate structure a decision to violate the law was made. Sometimes the effects of corporate criminal activities are not readily apparent because they are diffuse. A price-fixing scheme may cost an individual consumer only several cents on the dollar, although it results in several million dollars worth of total damages. Even if the effects are not diffuse, victims are often unaware that they have been victimized.

Criminal prosecutions of corporations rely heavily on the introduction of documentary evidence that memorialize the activities and motives of corporate officers, directors, and employees such as letters, internal memoranda, and financial records. Corporations are complex, as are their books and records with which prosecutors must often establish a case. Corporations have talented legal staffs to help them make the task of prosecution more complicated. The complexity of science is itself an impediment to criminal prosecution (Braithwaite & Geis, 1982). Because it is based on probabilities, scientific evidence concerning such matters as pollution, product safety, and occupational safety violations is often uncertain. Proving that a particular action caused a specific result beyond a reasonable doubt is frequently impossible. Because of these difficulties, particularly important evidentiary issues arise concerning the Fourth and Fifth Amendments and the attorney-client privilege.

The Fourth Amendment

The Fourth Amendment protects corporations from unreasonable searches and seizures just as it protects individual persons. Investigators must secure a warrant based on probable cause to search for and seize a company's records in order to meet the requirements of the amendment, with the exception of certain highly regulated businesses where the public's interests allow for warrantless searches. Such industries include liquor (*Colonnade Catering Corp. v. United States*, 1970), guns (*United States v. Biswell*, 1972), and strip-mining (*Donovan v. Dewey*, 1931). An alternative to the warrant is a grand jury subpoena that requests the turnover of documents without the necessity of establishing probable cause that a crime has been committed. In investigations of corporations, probable cause may be difficult to establish because a major issue is whether a crime has been committed, making the grand jury subpoena power very important (Corporate Crime, 1979). In addition, an administrative agency responsible for regulating a specific aspect of corporate activities can issue a summons or civil investigative demand forcing the turnover of records that can later be used in a criminal investigation.

The Fifth Amendment

The Fifth Amendment's privilege against self-incrimination does not extend to corporations because they are not natural persons who need protection from overbearing governmental coercion (*Wilson v. United States*, 1911; *Bellis v. United States*, 1974). A corporation, however, can only act through its officers and employees who may avail themselves of the privilege in their personal capacities. In *Bellis v. United States* (1974), the Supreme Court warned that an organization should not be allowed to undermine the rule that it is not permitted to claim the privilege against self-incrimination, by allowing an officer or employee to assert it on his or her own behalf with respect to company records that they are called upon to produce. As a result, an officer or employee may not assert the privilege to justify refusing to produce records of a company that are in his or her possession in a representative capacity, even if the records might also incriminate him or her personally (*Wilson v. United States,* 1911).

Attorney-Client Privilege

It is the attorney-client privilege that proves most troublesome in the prosecution of corporate entities. The privilege pertains to those documents that constitute or contain communications between a corporate client and its attorney concerning legal advice. The purpose of the attorney-client privilege is to encourage a client to seek legal counsel, free from the worry that communications with an attorney will be subject to disclosure. In this way, a client can speak openly and completely about the facts. Courts have long recognized that the privilege is applicable to corporations; however, the difficulty has been where to draw the line between privileged and unprivileged communications in a way that will not chill the attorney-client relationship and still produce guidelines that are sufficiently clear (Corporate Crime, 1979).

The major issue is who in the corporate structure can represent the client for the purposes of the attorney-client privilege. If any employee can represent the client, a great deal of evidence would be undiscoverable. Under the "control group test," in order for the privilege to apply, the employee who is communicating with the attorney must have authority to control or play a major role in making the decision regarding the action to be taken on the attorney's advice, or be an authorized member of a group that has that power (*Natta v. Hogan,* 1968). This test has been criticized because in order to secure the privilege, a higher-level employee must use his or her time to confer with an attorney, even in those instances when a lower-level employee possesses the information and could more efficiently and effectively handle the communication and implement the advice (Corporate Crime, 1979). In 1981, the United States Supreme Court suggested that it was rejecting the control group test in *Upjohn Co. v. United States* (1981). Since 1981, several lower federal courts have ruled that they would sustain the attorney-client privilege whenever the subject matter of a corporate employee's communication involved the performance of his or her employment duties, substituting the control group test with a much broader test. Difficult questions remain, however, especially when counsel is advising his or her corporate client about both business and legal matters, a situation likely to arise when the attorney is also a director or officer of the corporation.

Summary and Conclusion

Modern law has never addressed how best to deal with institutions. Throughout the nineteenth century, the focus of law was individuals as opposed to groups. Shaped by the social and political philosophy of liberalism, law was concerned with the rights and responsibilities of individual persons. With few changes, this model of law has been transferred to corporations (Stone, 1975). The common law gradually recognized corporations as juristic persons that exist separately and apart from owners and employees. As business and commercial establishments grew larger and more complex, the corporate form of organization, which offered limited investor liability with long-term, and eventually, perpetual existence, was a critical component in the economic growth of both England and America. Corporations became persons that can own and transfer property, arrange business transactions, and sue and be sued in their own names.

Although the common law recognized corporations as artificial persons, the concept of corporate criminality evolved much more slowly. Courts were reluctant to accept corporate criminality, and judges were slow to agree that institutions can commit crimes for which they should be punished. In 1909, the Supreme Court noted in *New York Central & Hudson River Railroad Co. v. United States* that imposing criminal liability was the only way to effectively enforce the provisions of the Elkins Act. Since the turn of this century, legal theorists and jurists in the United States have increasingly adopted the opinion that corporations are capable of committing not only general intent crimes but also crimes with specific *mens rea* requirements. A model of law designed for individuals has now been almost fully tailored to suit institutions as well. The practicalities of modern commercial business practice has encouraged the demise of the protection afforded corporations from criminal prosecution.

The legal issues surrounding corporate criminality, however, are complicated and controversial. Should corporations be punished for all of the illegal acts performed by their employees? Do high-level corporate officials have to be aware of or somehow sanction an employee's illegal activities before the corporation can be held responsible for them? Must the employee have performed the acts on the corporation's behalf? The federal courts have fashioned an expansive approach to corporate criminal liability. Corporations are held liable for all of their employees' unlawful actions that are undertaken for the benefit of the corporation, regardless of the employees' positions in the corporate hierarchy. Federal law is not without its critics, who argue that imposing criminal liability on a corporation serves as little or no deterrent, and often unfairly sanctions organizations that are working to discourage the illegal behavior of their employees.

Prosecuting the corporate criminal is made more complicated because corporations are comprised of people who function with limited knowledge and responsibilities. It can be very difficult to prove where and when in the corporate structure a decision to violate the law was made. Often the victims of corporate criminal activities are not even aware that they are victims because the effects of corporate illegalities can be extremely diffuse. Prosecuting attorneys are faced with massive amounts of documentary evidence, corporate books, and records that must be examined carefully for their probative value, a time consuming and expensive task.

Sanctioning a convicted corporate criminal is also complicated and controversial. Only very recently has there been a concerted effort to fashion a body of sentencing law informed by an understanding of the unique characteristics of organizational deviance. With the passage of The Sentencing Reform Act of 1984, there have been a number of important developments on the federal level in the area of corporate probation and more severe monetary criminal fines.

Although there is heated debate about how best to punish "crime in the suites," there is little question that corporations, either as institutions or through their employees, are involved in a troublesome amount of illegal activity. Clinard and Yeager (1980) conducted the first large-scale investigation of law violations of major business firms since Edwin Sutherland's work in 1949. They systematically analyzed federal administrative, civil, and criminal actions either initiated or completed by twenty-five federal agencies against the 477 largest publicly owned manufacturing corporations in the United States, during the years 1975 and 1976. Among their many findings, Clinard and Yeager found that large firms are most likely to commit violations. They further concluded that economic pressures and the business characteristics of particular firms do not solely account for the violations. Corporations that violate the law and those that do not are distinguished by different corporate cultures, defined as the degree to which a corporation has decided to be or not to be unethical. Certain industries, such as the oil, pharmaceutical, and motor vehicle industries, have an industry culture that is favorable to unethical and illegal behavior.

Whether to use the criminal law against errant corporations is more than an interesting philosophical question. How it is answered has serious repercussions for public policy. During the Reagan administration, the Justice Department criticized then President Carter's preoccupation with white-collar crime, and shifted its resources away from the investigation and prosecution of economic crime (Braithwaite & Geis, 1982). In the wake of the crises among financial institutions, oil spills, and major industrial plant explosions, questions arise regarding the efficacy of reliance on civil sanctions to regulate corporate misconduct. The debate over whether to criminalize certain types of corporate behavior is one of the most important social and legal issues facing the United States during the 1990s.

REFERENCES

American Law Institute. (1962). *Model penal code, final draft*. Philadelphia: Author.

Bernard, T.J. (1984). The historical development of corporate criminal liability. *Criminology, 22*, 3–17.

Braithwaite, J., & Geis, G. (1982). On theory and action for corporate crime control. *Crime & Delinquency, 28*, 292–314.

Brickey, K.F. (1984). *Corporate criminal liability*. Chicago: Callaghan.

———. (1988). Rethinking corporate liability under the Model Penal Code. *Rutgers Law Journal, 19*, 593–634.

Campbell, R.B. (1975). Limited liability for corporate shareholders: Myth or matter-of-fact. *Kentucky Law Journal, 63*, 23–41.

Chandler, A.D. (1977). *The visible hand: The managerial revolution in American business*. Cambridge, MA: Belknap.

Choper, J.H., Coffee, J.C., & Morris, C.R. (1989). *Cases and materials on corporations* (3rd. ed.). Boston: Little, Brown.

Clinard, M., & Yeager, P. (1978). Corporate crime—issues in research. *Criminology, 16*, 255–272.

———. (1980). *Corporate crime*. New York: Free Press.

Coffee, J.C. (1981). No soul to damn: no body to kick: an unscandalized inquiry into the problem of corporate punishment. *Michigan Law Review, 79*, 386–459.

Coleman, B. (1975). Is corporate criminal liability necessary? *Southwestern Law Journal, 29*, 908–927.

Conklin, J. (1977). *"Illegal but not criminal": Business crime in America*. Englewood Cliffs, NJ: Prentice-Hall.

Corporate crime: Regulating corporate behavior through criminal sanctions. (1979). *Harvard Law Review, 92*, 1227–1375.

Cullen, F.T., Maakestad, W.J., & Cavender, G. (1987). *Corporate crime under attack: The Ford Pinto case and beyond*. Cincinnati: Anderson.

Elkins, J.R. (1976). Corporations and the criminal law: An uneasy alliance. *Kentucky Law Review, 65*, 73–129.

Ermann, M.D., & Lundman, R. (Eds.). (1987). *Corporate and governmental deviance* (3rd ed.). New York: Oxford University Press.

Fisse, B. (1983). Reconstructing corporate criminal law: Deterrence, retribution, fault, and sanctions. *Southern California Law Review, 56*, 114–1225.

Fisse, B., & Braithwaite, J. (1984). *The impact of publicity on corporate offenders*. Albany: State University of New York Press.

Friedman, L. (1985). *A history of American law*. New York: Simon & Schuster.

Geis, G. (1967). The heavy electric equipment antitrust case of 1961. In M.B. Clinard & R. Quinney (Eds.), *Criminal behavior systems: A typology* (pp. 139–150). New York: Holt, Rinehart & Winston.

Henn, H.G., & Alexander, J.R. (1983). *Laws of corporations and other business enterprises*. St. Paul: West.

Hurst, J.W. (1970). *The legitimacy of the business corporation in the law of the United States, 1780–1970*. Charlottesville: University Press of Virginia.

Mueller, G.O.W. (1957). *Mens rea* and the corporation: a study of the Model Penal Code position on corporate criminal liability. *University of Pittsburgh Law Review, 19*, 21–43.

Parisi, N. (1984). Theories of corporate criminal liability (or corporations don't commit crimes, people commit crimes). In E. Hochstedler (Ed.), *Corporations as criminals* (pp. 41–68). Beverly Hills: Sage.

Silets, H.M., & Brenner, S.W. (1986). The demise of rehabilitation: sentencing reform and the sanctioning of organizational crime. *American Journal of Criminal Law, 13*, 329–380.

Stone, C. (1975). *Where the law ends: The social control of corporate behavior*. New York: Harper and Row.

———. (1977). Controlling corporate misconduct. *Public Interest, 48*, 55–71.

Sutherland, E.H., & Cressey, D.R. (1978). *Principles of criminology* (10th ed.). Philadelphia: Lippincott.

Tigar, M.E. (1990). It does the crime but not the time: Corporate criminal liability in federal law. *American Journal of Criminal Law, 17*, 211–234.

Vaughan, D. (1982). Toward understanding unlawful organizational behavior. *Michigan Law Review, 80*, 1377–1402.

Whyte, W.H. (1956). *The organization man*. New York: Simon & Schuster.

CASES CITED

Bellis v. United States, 417 U.S. 85 (1974).

C.I.T. Corporation v. United States, 150 F.2d 85 (9th Cir. 1945).

Colonnade Catering Corp. v. United States, 397 U.S. 72 (1970).

Commonwealth v. Proprietors of New Bedford Bridge, 68 Mass. (2 Gray) 339 (1854).

Donovan v. Dewey, 452 U.S. 594 (1931).

Queen v. Birmingham & Glouchester Railway Co., 114 Eng. Rep. 492 (Q.B. 1842).

Queen v. Great North of England Railway Co., 15 Eng. Rep. 1294 (Q.B. 1846).

Natta v. Hogan, 392 F.2d 686 (10th Cir. 1968).

New York Central & Hudson River Railroad Co. v. United States, 212 U.S. 481 (1909).

Standard Oil Co. v. United States, 307 F.2d 120 (5th Cir. 1962).

State v. Morris & Essex Railroad Co., 23 N.J.L. 360 (1852).

United States v. Biswell, 406 U.S. 311 (1972).

Upjohn Co. v. United States, 449 U.S. 383 (1981).

Wilson v. United States, 221 U.S. 361 (1911).

CHAPTER NINE

Sanctioning Corporate Criminals

Colin Goff

On February 10, 1983, Stefan Golab, a fifty-nine-year-old illegal immigrant, became ill while at work. He began to retch, then staggered outside and died as a result of overexposure to cyanide fumes, a by-product of the process used at Film Recovery Systems, a silver reclamation plant where Golab worked. Investigators were informed by other plant workers that the fumes were so bad that they often had to run outside to escape the noxious smell. Most of the workers were illegal aliens who were afraid to report their employer to the authorities for fear of deportation.

In addition, the workers often were not proficient in English and were unable to read the warning labels on the chemical products they used, nor were they capable of understanding that the law required the company to ensure that they wear protective clothing and breathing apparatus at all times. The investigators also discovered that the president, vice-president, and plant supervisor were at the plant the day Golab died and should have been aware of the conditions that led to his death.

Both Film Recovery and its sister corporation, Metallic Marketing, were charged with involuntary manslaughter while two company officials and two management employees were charged with murder. The prosecution argued that Film Recovery and Metallic Marketing

> unintentionally killed Stefan Golab by authorizing, requesting, commanding and performing certain acts of

commission and acts of omission by their officers, board of directors and high managerial agents . . . who were acting within the scope of their employment . . . performed the said acts recklessly in such manner as was likely to cause death and great bodily harm to some individual and . . . caused the death of Stefan Golab. (*Criminal Law Reporter*, 1990:1423)

The defense argued that plant officials had never been told by federal and state regulatory authorities that there was anything wrong. The presiding judge dismissed the charges against a vice-president on the grounds that the prosecution failed to prove he knew that the plant conditions were likely to cause injury or death. As for the others, the judge stated that the mere fact that corporate executives have never before stood trial for murder would not prevent criminal prosecution in this case. The two corporate defendants were ultimately convicted of involuntary manslaughter, while the three individual defendants were convicted of murdering Golab. In addition, all five defendants were convicted of fourteen counts of reckless conduct involving fourteen other Film Recovery employees and were sentenced to twenty-five years in prison. On January 19, 1990, however, the Illinois Appellate Court overturned the convictions on the ground that the criminal charges against the executives and the corporation were inconsistent with each other.

Murder and involuntary manslaughter require distinctly different mental states (*mens rea*), yet both sets of homicide convictions were apparently based on the fact that Film Recovery's managers failed to disclose to employees that cyanide was present in the workplace and failed to take reasonable steps to abate the attendant health risk. The court combed the trial record for evidence to distinguish the verdicts between the corporations and the executives, but finding none, concluded that they must be set aside. Similar reasoning led the court to hold that verdicts against the individual defendants for reckless conduct are inconsistent with their murder convictions.

While the trial verdict was overturned on appeal, the *Film Recovery* case raises some fundamental questions about the nature of sentencing in the area of corporate crime. First, does corporate crime refer to the corporation itself, to corporate officials, or can it be applicable to both? In the *Film Recovery* case, both individual officials as well as two corporations were charged. Are both considered to be corporate criminals? Or is it best to refer to the individuals as white-collar criminals? Part of the difficulty of answering these questions is the fact that Sutherland's original works confused this issue by describing the criminal records of the seventy largest corporations in the United States, but then attempted to explain their crimes in the context of the actions of individuals he referred to as white-collar criminals. Since the earliest writings, there has been a fundamental, and as yet, unresolved question as to the precise meaning of "corporate crime."

What is clear, however, is that Sutherland (1949) was upset about the disparities in sentencing that enabled corporate and white-collar criminals consistently to receive lighter penalties than those given to conventional criminals. Furthermore, he argued that corporations and white-collar criminals were also accorded lenient treatment by regulatory agencies. According to Sutherland (1949), this leniency resulted in large part from lawmakers who developed alternatives to the criminal law, such as civil or administrative penalties, in order to benefit offending corporations and white-collar criminals. As a result, corporations were most commonly charged with civil and regulatory infractions and subsequently received penalties and suffered stigma much less severe than those dealt out by the criminal courts.

Since Sutherland's pioneering efforts, criminologists have tested his arguments concerning the differential treatment of corporations. In general, these efforts have discovered that corporations and their officials regularly violate the law, but rarely are tried for their actions. Instead they receive warnings or are punished civilly or administratively. As a result, criticisms are directed toward judges for their failure to inflict appropriate criminal penalties on corporations; in addition, the public has come to question the fairness, integrity, and equality of the justice system (Geis, 1972).

A variety of explanations have been offered to explain this disparity, which can be classified into two general categories.

The first includes political and ideological factors, such as: (a) the common cultural backgrounds shared by judges, regulatory officials, legislators, and corporate officials (Conklin, 1977; Sutherland, 1949); (b) laws designed to control illegal corporate activity that are rarely used or actually thwart the enforcement process (Coleman, 1989); (c) minimal penalties for white-collar offenders caught and convicted (Clinard & Yeager, 1980); (d) the paucity of resources to pursue possible corporate offenders (Yeager, 1991); and (e) the fact that many of the laws governing corporate activity are noncriminal, reflecting the ability of corporate officials to influence the creation and application of law (Sutherland, 1949).

The second category focuses upon legal impediments that make it difficult to control corporate activity. Factors associated with this explanation include: (a) the difficulties of developing and administering laws to control the complexities of corporate activity (Lynxwiler, Shover, & Clelland, 1983); (b) the ability of corporations to obstruct the investigations of regulatory agencies (Shover, Clelland, & Lynxwiler, 1986); (c) the paucity of resources given to investigatory agencies (Clinard & Yeager, 1980); (d) the exemplary prior record of the offenders (Wheeler, Weisburd, & Bode, 1982); and (e) the procedural and evidentiary problems related to establishing corporate culpability (Yeager, 1991).

Whatever the explanation, there is a common belief that corporations and their executives receive penalties much lighter than those received by conventional criminals who commit similar crimes. Research efforts, however, have varied in their approaches to the measurement of sentencing disparity, and produced a degree of confusion about the issue.

This chapter is divided into three major subjects: (1) studies that focus on the sanctions received by individual corporate officials or white-collar criminals in the United States Federal District courts for violating certain criminal offenses; (2) studies that focus on the role of regulatory agencies in the sanctioning process; and (3) studies that analyze the penalties assessed against the corporation itself, including criminal, civil, and regulatory actions.

Sentencing Disparity

A central issue involving the sentencing of corporations and their officials has been the complexity of determining the exact meaning of equality before the law (Hagan, Nagel & Albonetti, 1982). Nettler (1979), for example, has identified numerical, proportional, and subjective meanings of the phrase. Subjective equality is the most difficult of the three to define; corporate criminals, for example, undergo the impact of sanctions differently than common criminals because of the stigma associated with the criminal justice process (Fisse & Braithwaite, 1983).

The precise nature of sentencing disparity varies according to the individual defining the term. Disparity has most commonly been examined with emphasis on trial outcomes. That is, "when 'like cases' with respect to case attributes—regardless of their legitimacy—are sentenced" (Blumstein, Cohen, Martin, & Tonry, 1983:8). Another definition focuses upon the variations of sentences within a particular jurisdiction or across jurisdictions. Becker (1968), for example, views disparity as the imposition of the exact same penalty (e.g., a fine) regardless of the size of a corporation or of differences among individuals. An alternative viewpoint suggests that penalties should be assessed "according to the nature of the violation and in proportion to the assets or annual sales of the corporation" (Clinard & Yeager, 1980:317). Yet another definition centers upon the relationship between social harms and sanctions, in particular "whether or not equal harms are treated equally . . . " (Cohen, 1989:628).

In contrast to disparity, discretion is defined as "the latitude of decision provided by law by someone in imposing sentence" (Hagan & Bumiller, 1983:8). Of particular interest are the principles used by judges to govern their sentencing decisions. Lovegrove (1989:4) states that these principles

> cover the purposes of punishment, the case factors relevant to the determination of sentence, and the rules prescribing the way in which this information should be selected, classified, and aggregated to determine the appropriate goals of the sentence and to give effect to these goals.

In the area of corporate crime, there are many sentencing principles. A nonexhaustive list would include the extent of the potential and actual harm, intent, savings, or gain derived from the offense, ability to pay, the size, and wealth of the corporation, cooperation, and anthropomorphic factors such as the corporate character and remorse (Swaigen & Bunt, 1985). In addition, Cohen (1989) points out that judges often focus on whether there are collateral punishments. That is, if the judge has determined that a corporation is guilty of a criminal offense, the final sentence may reflect successful civil and/or administrative action taken against the offending corporation (Cohen, 1989).

This situation may highlight a major explanation of illegal activities by corporations and their officials: since they are rarely charged or punished for violating criminal law, it stands to reason there is little or no incentive to obey the law. Adverse civil and administrative rulings are not considered to be successful deterrents since there is little stigma attached to them. The bulk of the criticism directed toward judicial discretion and sentencing disparity in the literature on corporate crime underlines the low number of criminal charges. As Schlegel (1990:19) points out, a review of the literature on corporate punishment

> reveals a virtual consensus calling for the increased use of criminal sanctions, as well as ongoing theoretical debate as to the kind of criminal punishment that would be most effective in deterring corporate crime.

White-Collar and Corporate Offenders

Initially, studies concerned with the issue of sentencing disparity with regard to corporations utilized data from United States' state courts. Such cases, however, are relatively rare at this level, because local prosecutors usually refer possible corporate misconduct allegations to United States District Attorneys for prosecution since the behavior in question typically violates federal regulations. Ayers and Frank (1987:435) point out that local prosecutors use criminal sanctions only in specific case contexts.

> [They] generally used criminal sanctions in incidents where fraudulent behavior was actionable and where embezzlement and theft were present. These forms of conduct are conventional, individual-oriented crimes, lacking the problems of culpability that exist in corporate behavior.

Studies utilizing offense data, specifically law-breaking offenses committed by individual white-collar offenders, employ data from U.S. Federal District Courts since "the vast majority of white-collar cases [are] prosecuted and brought to [this] sentencing level . . . " (Nagel & Hagan, 1982:1427).

Hagan, Nagel, and Albonetti (1980) studied sentences received by offenders in ten U.S. Federal District Courts between 1974 and 1977. Their analysis included 6,518 offenders sentenced for white-collar and traditional crimes, and they sought to determine whether college-educated persons were sentenced more leniently for white-collar offenses than less-educated persons for traditional crimes. Their roster of white-collar offenses initially was devised intuitively from all statutes that could plausibly fit the category. U.S. Attorneys and Assistant U.S. Attorneys in the ten districts were also asked for their views about thirty-one offenses. The final list included such white-collar offenses as failure to file a tax return, embezzlement or theft by bank employees, and mail fraud swindles. The results of their study showed that individuals who were convicted of white-collar crimes received less severe sentences than individuals convicted of traditional crimes. Hagan et al. also discovered that college-educated white-collar criminals received the most lenient sentences. The mean sentence for "high-income white-collar crimes" was 4.98 years, but was 6.18 years for "high-income common crimes." For "low-income white-collar crimes" the mean sentence was 4.38 years, while it was 7.31 years for "low-income common crimes." Nine of the ten federal districts studied were found to employ reactive policies in their white-collar crime enforcement. The tenth district, however, used proactive enforcement strategies, producing the highest numbers of convicted white-collar offenders. Yet it was also the district that imposed the most lenient average sentences on white-collar offenders. Hagan et al. (1980:802) suggested that "there may be an inverse relationship between the volume of white-collar prosecutions and the severity with which they are sentenced."

In another study, Hagan, Nagel and Albonetti (1982) replicated their previous inquiry but substituted income for education to assess its effect on sentencing disparity. They again discovered sentencing differences, with higher-income, white-collar criminals receiving more lenient sentences than the other offenders.

Mann, Wheeler, and Sarat (1980) investigated the process by which federal district court judges conceptualize the sentencing process in white-collar crime cases. After interviewing fifty-one federal judges in seven federal districts, it was clear

> that factors intimately related to the defendant's social status do receive weight in the judges' thinking. Sometimes, as in the violation of public trust, the weight goes against the white-collar defendant. But often, . . . they cut in the opposite direction. Questions are also raised by the predisposition to use economic sanctions when the defendant can clearly pay for them—sanctions that are unavailable to the defendant who is poor. These matters raise questions of fundamental fairness in the sentencing process . . .

Mann, Wheeler, and Sarat (1980:497) commented that despite questions of fairness and disparity, the judges interviewed believed the punishments handed out to white-collar offenders were severe punishments.

> Most judges have a widespread belief that the suffering experienced by a white-collar person as a result of apprehension, public indictment and conviction, and the collateral disabilities incident to conviction—loss of job, professional licenses, and the status in the community—completely satisfies the need to punish.

In the next major federal district court sentencing study, Wheeler et al. (1982) employed eight broad, nonviolent categories for their representation of white-collar crime—antitrust violations, securities fraud, bribery, tax violations, bank embezzlement, postal and wire fraud, false claims and statements, and credit and lending institution fraud—suggested by federal district court judges. Drawing data from presentence investigation reports, they examined the severity of sentences handed out in 1,094 cases in order to assess whether persons with higher social status were sentenced more leniently than those with lower social status.

To determine if such disparity existed, Wheeler et al. developed an "impeccability index" that measured the moral and social propriety of a white-collar defendant's criminal conduct. It was argued that defendants, in most cases, had contributed to the well-being of their communities. They found that white-collar offenders with higher scores on the impeccability index received more lenient sentences than those with lower scores. Rarely were antitrust violators sent to prison, whereas convictions for tax evasion or securities fraud were more likely to result in incarceration. There was a positive relationship between the socioeconomic status of the offender and the severity of the sentence: white-collar defendants who were found guilty and were considered to have low impeccability received tougher sentences.

The Wheeler et al. study was replicated in a different federal court district by Benson and Walker (1988). Another offense—embezzlement or theft of public monies by a public employee—was added to the list of white-collar crimes. The data, collected for a ten-year period, did not include bribery, antitrust, or securities and exchange offences. Benson and Walker (1988:299) report that high-status offenders "faced no greater risk of being sent to prison than low-status offenders." However, they found offenders with higher scores on the impeccability index devised by Wheeler et al. got longer sentences than those with low scores. They attributed their results largely to differences between the districts included in the two studies. Wheeler et al. studied major urban federal court districts while Benson and Walker analyzed data from a less urban district located in a midwestern state.

Hagan and Nagel (1982) investigated sentences handed out by federal judges in the Southern District of New York between 1963 and 1976. In the initial phase of their study, they treated white-collar crime as an aggregated category differentiated on the basis of whether white-collar offenders had received a college education. This analysis indicated "that college-educated persons convicted of white-collar crimes received sentences that on the average were more than a year shorter than those received by non-college-educated persons convicted of common crimes" (Hagan & Nagel, 1982:279). Furthermore, when all convicted offenders (including those not sentenced to prison) were included in the analysis, the difference of two years was reduced to four months. Important differences were found, however, when the particular white-collar crimes were compared in terms of sentences.

Individuals convicted of white-collar crimes (e.g., mail fraud, fraudulent claims against government agencies, and tax fraud) similar to conventional thefts received comparable sentence lengths, while most of the other white-collar crimes (e.g., price-fixing) received more lenient sentences. Judges, aware of these differential penalties accorded to convicted white-collar offenders, attempted to compensate for the shorter prison sentences for white-collar offenders by adding probation or fines (Hagan & Nagel, 1982:271–272). Despite these sentence combinations, white-collar criminals continued to enjoy advantages not available to conventional criminals with regard to the legal sanctions imposed on them.

The conclusions from the foregoing studies have been disputed on the ground that they fail to look at "persons who might reasonably be regarded as white-collar criminals" (Geis 1991:19). Since the studies use an offense-based criterion, there is a strong possibility that many individuals convicted of such offenses did not hold positions of occupational prestige and power, which are the qualities of white-collar criminals that received the attention of Sutherland. This criticism has also been made by Daly (1989) in her study of gender and varieties of white-collar crime.

Daly reanalyzed the Wheeler et al. data to evaluate the sentences of women who committed white-collar crimes and came to the conclusion that it was "occupational marginality" that best explained such offenses. Indeed, Daly discovered that all the bank embezzlers in the sample were clerical workers and that as many as one-third of the women in some of the other offense categories were unemployed. The labelling of such offenders as "white-collar" led Daly (1989:790) to comment that "women's socio-economic profile, coupled with the nature of their crimes, makes one wonder if 'white-collar' aptly describes them or their illegalities." It is also worth noting that only slightly more than half the male offenders were managerial or professional workers.

Responding in part to the criticisms of Geis (1985) that he had corrupted the essential nature of white-collar crime in his sentencing study, Hagan, along with Parker (1985), studied securities violations in Ontario, Canada, between 1966 and 1983. They employed "relational indicators" such as ownership and authority as determinants of white-collar power. These criteria located individuals in class positions directly relevant to the perpetuation of their offenses.

Hagan and Parker (1985) also turned their attention from the criminal courts to study regulatory enforcement under the Ontario Securities Act, arguing that the majority of the offenses they were interested in were not tried in the Ontario criminal courts. Their research contradicted the previous conclusion that white-collar offenders are treated more harshly. Instead, they found that employers generally escaped both criminal and regulatory punishments, but that lower-level supervisors and rank-and-file employees received the harshest sentences. This led Hagan and Parker to endorse substituting class for status measures of white-collar criminality.

Shapiro (1985) attempted to develop a clearer picture of white-collar sanctions by pointing out that studies on the sanctioning of white-collar offenders suffered from sample selection bias. In her opinion, this bias marked the work of many contemporary white-collar crime researchers because they used cases that were highly selective, involving offenders "whose wrongs are so egregious, whose positions so marginal, or whose tactics so inept that they were unable to take advantage of the rich array of opportunities to escape from the criminal justice system" (Shapiro, 1990:362).

Shapiro argued that the lenient sentences given to offenders are mistakenly explained as class bias; such an interpretation, she insists, misrepresents the structural sources of leniency. She proposed that white-collar crime researchers should attend to violations of trust by examining settings of trust, how trust norms are defined and enforced, structural opportunities for the abuse of trust, the types of misconduct that results from violations of trust, and the impact of the ensuing social control. This work would be accomplished, according to Shapiro, by detailing the process through which white-collar offenders pass, and it would determine the reasons why certain cases are dropped.

In her study of the U.S. Securities and Exchange Commission (SEC), Shapiro was able to follow the process of enforcement for 499 randomly selected investigations of 2,101 suspects initiated between 1948 and 1972. She discovered that in 88 percent of the cases, criminal charges were not pursued against an offender. But this does not mean the person escaped prosecution altogether. The SEC also has civil and administrative penalties available, and those who avoid the criminal justice system oftentimes face such charges.

In her analysis, Shapiro chose location within the organizational hierarchy as her indicator of social standing. Defendants were divided into upper-status employees (e.g., officers, directors, partners) and those of lower status (e.g., managers, employees, consultants, salespersons). She found enforcement varies according to the status of the offenders within the organization. Lower-status offenders are usually charged with criminal offenses, whereas upper-status offenders are diverted in many cases to the civil or administrative courts.

Hypotheses concerning class bias therefore explain little about the exercise of prosecutorial discretion at the SEC (though they may account somewhat for the post-conviction experience). Upper-status offenders are less vulnerable to criminal prosecution, but must defend themselves frequently in civil and administrative proceedings. Lower-status wrongdoers who collaborate with their bosses are treated more like their bosses than like lower-status perpetrators acting alone. The data suggest that any apparent discrimination against lower-status offenders in prosecutorial discretion is more readily explained by greater access to legal options than by social standing.

Regulatory Offenses

Some of the best evidence for sentencing disparity has come from studies analyzing the enforcement record of regulatory agencies. This literature has consistently revealed the reluctance of regulatory agencies to use their powers in a manner that ensures penalties are invoked against the most powerful and largest corporate offenders, despite "the enormous damage to persons and property caused by their offending" (Braithwaite, 1985:13). When charges are filed, they usually are applied to offending corporations that are small in size. Generally speaking, studies on the sentencing of corporations that have violated regulatory statutes have shown an inverse relationship: the harshest and most punitive punishments are directed toward the smallest corporations, while the lightest sanctions are applied to the largest and most powerful offenders.

This outcome also extends to the sentencing of corporate officials. In their study of corporate crime, Clinard and Yeager (1980) found sixteen executives had been sentenced to a total of 594 days of actual imprisonment. Two executives accounted for 360 (61 percent) of the total number of days. Excluding these two cases, the sentences averaged nine days each. Clinard and Yeager also reported that of the 231 cases between 1955 and 1975 with individual defendants, prison sentences were given in only nineteen. In addition, of the total 1,027 individual defendants, only forty-nine were sentenced to prison. They also found large corporations to be the worst violators in terms of both the number of violations, as well as the most serious offenses.

On the basis of their data, Clinard and Yeager (1980:119) concluded that the largest corporations "accounted for 72.1 percent of the serious and 62.8 percent of the moderately serious violations." However, when they studied the penalties assessed to the worst violators, they learned that the amount of the fine bore no systematic relation to the size of the firm.

> In fact, of all fines imposed in 1975 and 1976, the median fine ... for large corporations ($1,000) was smaller than that for medium-size corporations ($1,690), although larger than fines for smaller firms ($750). In addition, smaller fines were used in proportionately more cases

involving the largest corporations: for these firms, 86 percent of all fines were $5,000 or less, while only 6.5 percent were over $45,000. The corresponding percentages for medium-size corporations were 68 percent and 18 percent respectively, and for smaller firms 54 and 38.5 percent respectively.

McCormick (1977), in his historical study of antitrust enforcement in the United States from 1890 to 1969, obtained similar results. His data revealed that regulatory authorities investigated 1,551 cases, but that only 45 percent were prosecuted as criminal complaints. It remains unclear what factors determined if a case should be handled civilly or criminally. Furthermore, when monetary fines were imposed on convicted corporate offenders, the amounts were significant.

When fines are compared with the amount gained through the illegal conduct, disparity is hard to conceal. Ermann and Lundman (1982:148) noted that the $437,000 fine assessed General Electric in 1961 for its part in a conspiracy to rig bids was approximately the equivalent of fining a person making $15,000 a year $12.30. Geis (1972), commenting on the same case, pointed out that the fine was about the equivalent to a parking fine for many citizens.

Similar results in regard to fines have been found by others. Carson (1970), in his study of the British Factory Inspectorate, reported that it was only on a rare occasion that a corporation was found guilty. And when a fine was assessed, the average amount was less than $100 (U.S. currency). Shapiro (1985) found the median fine assessed against individuals convicted of violating U.S. Securities and Exchange Commission regulations was $2,700, although their median profit per offense was $300,000. And Shover et al. (1986) reported that the mean fine in their study of sanctions against coal mining companies was $1,027, while the maximum fine imposed was $4,500.

Recent studies have continued to discover sentencing disparity in the enforcement records of regulatory agencies. In their detailed investigations of the U.S. Federal Office of Surface Mining Reclamation and Enforcement, Shover et al. (1986) sampled approximately equal numbers of large, medium, and small mining companies which received notices of violations. By focusing on fines they were able to support the inverse relationship thesis.

However, in their analysis of the enforcement decision-making processes, Shover et al. (1986) also examined the tactics used by the inspectors to enforce the regulations and the impact of their decisions. They discovered agency inspectors operated on the basis of two key criteria: (1) larger mining companies were more responsive to and cooperative with regulatory demands than smaller firms; and (2) that these larger companies were more likely to challenge various legal notices of violation through formal legal hearings.

Smaller mining companies were viewed by inspectors as less cooperative and less able to comply with the technical—and expensive—demands placed upon them. This led inspectors to conclude that violations by smaller companies were more serious, quite apart from the objective measures of harm involved. As a result, smaller companies were assessed larger fines due to "the structural arrangements of the regulated industry as they exist regardless of any particular sanctionable activity" (Shover et al., 1986:162).

Yeager (1987, 1991) studied the U.S. Environmental Protection Agency's (EPA) enforcement of the Federal Water Pollution Control Act between 1972 and 1979. He sampled 214 manufacturing plants found to be discharging wastes into waterways, subsampling three types of pollution control violations: effluent discharge violations, reporting violations, and the failure to keep to the EPA-mandated schedule for installing pollution abatement equipment. For all violations, Yeager (1991:282) found that

> large companies are twice as likely to receive no-action determinations, and conversely half as likely to receive warning letters for infractions, as the small firms. Moreover, the small firms were more than twice as likely to receive administrative orders as the large, and the former received all of the civil or criminal referrals in these data while the large companies experienced none. . . .

Yeager (1991:283) discovered this pattern of differential sanctioning to hold true for each type of violation as well.

Taken together, these results begin to suggest that sanctioning decisions favor the largest corporations as compared to smaller firms. They suggest that the agency is reluctant to issue formal sanctions, particularly the more serious orders and referrals, to very large companies.

Organizational Offenders

The majority of the studies reviewed above deal with individuals convicted of white-collar crimes. Rarely has there been an interest in the punishment meted out to the corporation itself. The two studies that have come closest to a systematic analysis of corporate crime are those done by Sutherland (1949) and Clinard and Yeager (1980). Sutherland studied the records of the seventy largest manufacturing, mining, and mercantile corporations in the United States, selecting these corporations on the basis of their appearance on two lists of the two hundred largest nonfinancial corporations in the United States in 1929 and 1938. His data indicated that these seventy corporations committed crimes resulting in 779 adverse decisions. Sutherland also studied the records of fifteen utility corporations.

Clinard and Yeager focused on the records of 582 American corporations for the years 1975 and 1976. These corporations included 477 of the largest publicly owned manufacturing corporations as well as 105 of the largest wholesale, retail, and service corporations. The study was restricted to actions initiated against corporations for the actions completed against them (Clinard & Yeager, 1980:111). Data on enforcement actions taken against these corporations were drawn from a variety of federal agencies, law service reports, reports to the Security and Exchange Commission, and newspaper articles. A total of 1,553 federal cases were initiated against the corporations during the two years studied, or an average of just under three cases for each company.

The two studies, conducted some forty years apart, were not able to include all the relevant data in their analyses. Neither study was able to locate and report all the offenses registered against each corporation; Clinard and Yeager (1980:111), for example, admit that the figures of corporate criminal activity included in their study "are minimal figures of government actions against major corporations: the undercount may be as high as one-fourth to one-third."

The most systematic data on crimes committed by corporations is now being collected by the U.S. Sentencing Commission. In 1988, they began gathering information in order to construct a comprehensive database regarding corporate defendants appearing in the federal courts between 1984 and 1990. In order to assess corporate sentencing practices, the commission has collected information on more than eighty relevant variables from 774 organizations and related individual defendants sentenced between 1988 and 1990. The purpose of the data set was to enable the commission to explore the relationship between estimates of loss caused by the offenses and sanctions imposed by the courts (U.S. Sentencing Commission, 1991:1). For the years 1984 to 1987, the commission assembled data on the sentencing of 1,226 organizations for non-antitrust offenses. It charted the types of organizational offenses and offenders, the sentences imposed, and the factors that may have influenced the fine levels.

In a preliminary analysis of the prosecutions, convictions, and sanctions of organizations as defendants in the federal courts for 1984 through 1987, Cohen (1988) found that of the 1,659 organizational defendants, 1,283 (77 percent) were convicted. In addition, multiple defendants were found in 51 percent of the cases. Fines were the most typically used sanction, with 90 percent of the defendants ordered to pay a fine. Approximately 48 percent of the defendants were fined less than $5,000, and just under 80 percent were fined $25,000 or under. Less than two percent received fines totaling more than $500,000. The average fine imposed was $85,536, although the defendants may have received additional fines as a result of penalties handed out in civil trials. While they were not able to arrive at an exact dollar amount of these noncriminal fines, Cohen estimated them to total an average of $55,085. In comparison, nonmonetary sanctions were rarely imposed on organizational defendants—10 percent were ordered to make restitution and 2 percent were ordered to pay enforcement costs or to participate in community service. Nonmonetary sanctions alone were used in less than 10 percent of the convictions.

Presentence investigation reports were analyzed to obtain data on both the offender and the offense. Cohen found, however, that such reports were prepared for only about 30 percent of the defendants and, as a result, they were able to systematically study only 288 of the convicted defendants. According to the investigators, this sample, "while not totally representative of the entire population of corporate offenders, it is large enough so that it encompasses virtually all types of offenses that normally appear in the federal system" (Cohen, 1988:108). They did point out, however, that presentence investigation reports were not likely to be prepared for cases involving fines of less than $1,000 or greater than $500,000.

In terms of sentencing patterns, Cohen discovered that, *generally* speaking, the higher the loss, the higher the sanction. But they also commented that "the most obvious pattern is the large amount of disparity in the system. There are many instances where virtually identical crimes and losses result in different sanctions . . . " (Cohen, 1988:111).

While his first article presented summary data on the sentencing of corporate offenders in the federal court system, Cohen's (1989) second report offers a systematic analysis of the sentencing practices for corporate criminal offenders. Its central component is the recognition that in order to develop a rational test for determining the source(s) of sentencing disparity, factors beyond the final disposition need to be included in the analysis. These might include the detection of the offense, the level of cooperation, the existence of collateral civil actions, the number of codefendants, and the solvency of the firm. After including such items in his analysis, Cohen (1989:605) determined that they led to significant amounts of sentencing disparity.

> Thus, any comprehensive analysis of disparity should control for these other factors before asking the question of whether equal harms are treated equally. In fact, . . . numerous attempts at estimating the relationship between the sanction and relevant factors have shown the difficulty in determining any rational structure to the current

sentencing system. This itself indicates that there is substantial disparity between offenders.

Cohen also analyzed the relationship between the social harm done and the sanctions imposed on corporate offenders. Social harm was defined as "the harm to direct victims of an offense." The study was of various types of fraud (e.g., consumer, government, procurement) tax offenses, property offenses such as property theft and destruction, environmental offenses, food, drug, and agricultural offenses, as well as regulatory reporting violations. Cohen was able to explain between 35 and 65 percent of the variance found in sentencing on the basis of his calculation of harm.

Cohen also advocated the need for research in two areas that could contribute significantly to a greater understanding of the process of sentencing corporate offenders. Researchers, he insisted, need to move beyond collecting data from only one source of the legal system, i.e., the criminal courts. Fines assessed by the criminal courts are, in Cohen's opinion, only one aspect of the overall sanction imposed on corporations. And it is this overall perspective that judges consider in their judgments about the final sentences.

> Once other sanctions such as voluntary or civil restitution, debarment, civil penalties, private tort suits and lost business/reputation are factored in, the impact of a criminal case on a corporate violator is likely to be considerably larger than the criminal penalties (Cohen, 1989:658).

Cohen's second suggestion is to examine more closely court cases when both individuals and corporations are on trial for the same event(s). He pointed out that 70 percent of the 288 cases he analyzed included individual codefendants.

Conclusion

The research reviewed above testifies to the ever-increasing roster of studies in corporate crime during the past decade. More diversified data sources, a wider scope, and the application of sophisticated measuring instruments have produced an impressive accumulation of results. Each article discussed has its special merit. However, certain problems continue to exist.

The first issue is the development of an adequate definition of corporate crime. Sutherland clearly intended to broaden the defintion of crime to include the illegal behavior of people of high social status. This broader definition of *crime* involves the abuse of power by persons who are situated in relatively high places where they are given the opportunity to commit such acts. The failure to include the illegal activities of corporations has led to a definition of white-collar crime that is "so broad and indefinite as to fall into inevitable desuetude" (Geis, 1962). Sutherland was quite adamant about who was to be investigated, and his agenda seems to have merit. As Braithwaite (1985:19) suggests, "[P]robably the most sensible way to proceed . . . is to stick with Sutherland's definition." The work by Hagan and Parker is probably the best piece of research to date that attempts to follow through on the original intention of Sutherland.

Another issue concerns the research conducted by Wheeler and his colleagues. While the results of their interviews with judges and their views on how they sentence white-collar offenders are rich in detail, their analysis misses the spirit so essential to Sutherland's definition. Missing is an understanding of why there is so much discretion and variation among the judiciary. Their argument that sentencing disparity is the result of judges' own discretionary views about the relative weights of case factors is not surprising. What is needed, instead, is further empirical analyses that question the judiciary's justification for more lenient treatment of corporate criminals.

The ever-increasing focus on the illegal acts of corporations will no doubt bring about a better understanding of the nature of corporate crime. But this focus, too, suffers from a serious shortcoming when compared to Sutherland's original directive, because of the legalistic emphasis that ignores the issues of power and persuasion so fundamental to this area of study. Therefore, questions basic to this area remain unresolved: Why are certain offenders processed through the legal system when others are not? And what factors provoke initiation of the criminal process?

The fundamental issues raised by Sutherland remain, at best, only partially answered. And while the optimist will state that this is good for the field as a whole, the tendency to date has been to drift away from the type of analyses required to bring this line of inquiry into sharper perspective. Perhaps the goals laid out by Sutherland will never be reached, but it is essential to realize that his work remains a criminological classic, not only due to its scope and insight, but also because of the impact on how future generations of criminologists construct the social reality of crime.

REFERENCES

Ayers, K.A., & Frank, J. (1987). Deciding to prosecute white-collar crime: A national survey of state attorneys general. *Justice Quarterly, 4,* 425–439.

Becker, G. (1968). Crime and punishment: An economic approach. *Journal of Political Economy, 76,* 169–217.

Benson, M.L. & Walker, E. (1988). Sentencing the white-collar offender. *American Sociological Review, 53,* 294–302.

Blumstein, A., Cohen, J., Martin, S.E., & Tonry, M.H. (Eds.). (1983). *Research on sentencing: The research for reform* (Vol. I). Washington, DC: National Academy Press.

Braithwaite, J. (1985). White collar crime. *Annual Review of Sociology, 11,* 1–25.

Carson, W.G. (1970). White-collar crime and the enforcement of factory legislation. *British Journal of Criminology, 10,* 383–398.

Clinard, M.B., & Yeager, P.C. (1980). *Corporate crime.* New York: Free Press.

Cohen, M.A. (1988). Organizations as defendants in federal court: A preliminary analysis of prosecutions, convictions, and sanctions, 1984–1987. *Whittier Law Review, 10,* 103–124.

————. (1989). Corporate crime and punishment: A study of social harm and sentencing practice in the federal courts, 1984–1987. *American Criminal Law Review, 26*, 605–660.

Coleman, J.W. (1989). *The criminal elite: The sociology of white collar crime* (2nd ed.). New York: St. Martin's.

Conklin, J.E. (1977). *"Illegal but not criminal": Business crime in America.* Englewood Cliffs, NJ: Prentice-Hall.

Criminal Law Reporter, 46 (February 21, 1990):1423.

Daly, K. (1989). Gender and varieties of white-collar crime. *Criminology, 27*, 769–794.

Ermann, M.D., & Lundman, R.J. (1982). *Corporate and governmental deviance* (2nd ed.). New York: Oxford University Press.

Fisse, B., & Braithwaite, J. (1984). *The impact of publicity on corporate offenders.* Albany: State University of New York Press.

Geis, G. (1962). Toward a delineation of white-collar offenses. *Sociological Inquiry, 32*, 160–171.

————. (1972). Criminal penalties for corporate offenders. *Criminal Law Bulletin, 8*, 377–392.

————. (1985). Criminological perspectives on corporate regulation: A review of recent research. In B. Fisse and P.A. French (Eds.), *Corrigible corporations and unruly law* (pp. 63–84). San Antonio: Trinity University Press.

————. (1991). White-collar crime: What is it? *Current Issues in Criminal Justice, 3*, 9– 24.

Hagan, J.L., & Bumiller, K. (1983). Making sense of sentencing: A review and critique of sentencing research. In A. Blumstein, J. Cohen, S. Martin, & M.H. Tonry (Eds.), *Research on sentencing: The search for reform* (Vol. II, pp. 1–55). Washington, DC: National Academy Press.

Hagan, J.L., & Nagel, I. (1982). White-collar crime: The sentencing of white-collar offenders in the Southern District of New York. *American Criminal Law Review, 20*, 259–289.

Hagan, J.L., Nagel, I., & Alboneti, C. (1980). Differential sentencing of white-collar offenders in ten federal district courts. *American Sociological Review, 45*, 802–820.

Hagan, J.L., Nagel, I., & Albonetti, C. (1982). The social organization of white-collar sanctions: A study of prosecution and punishment. In P. Wickman and T. Dailey (Eds.), *White-collar and economic crimes* (pp. 259–275). Lexington, MA, Lexington.

Hagan, J.L., & Parker, P. (1985). White-collar crime and punishment: The class structure and legal sanctioning of securities violations. *American Sociological Review, 50,* 302–316.

Lovegrove, A. (1989). *Judicial decision making, sentencing policy, and numerical guidelines.* New York: Springer-Verlag.

Lynxwiler, J., Shover, N., & Clelland, D.A. (1983). The organization and impact of inspector discretion in a regulatory bureaucracy. *Social Problems, 30,* 425–436.

McCormick, A.E. (1977). Rule enforcement and moral indignation: Some observations on the effects of criminal anti-trust conviction upon societal reaction processes. *Social Problems, 25,* 30–39.

Mann, K., Wheeler, S., & Sarat, A. (1980). Sentencing the white-collar offender. *American Criminal Law Review, 17,* 479–500.

Nagel, I.H., & Hagan, J.L. (1982). The sentencing of white-collar criminals in federal courts: A socio-legal exploration of disparity. *Michigan Law Review, 80,* 1427–1465.

Nettler, G. (1979). Criminal justice. In A. Inkeles, J. Coleman & R.H. Turner (Eds.), *Annual review of sociology* (Vol. 5, pp. 27–52). Palo Alto: Annual Reviews.

Schlegel, K. (1990). *Just deserts for corporate criminals.* Boston: Northeastern University Press.

Shapiro, S.P. (1985). The road not taken: The elusive path to criminal prosecution for white-collar offenders. *Law and Society Review, 19* (2), 179–217.

———. (1990). Collaring the crime, not the criminal: Reconsidering "white-collar crime." *American Sociological Review, 55,* 346–365.

Shover, N., Clelland, D.A., & Lynxwiler, J. (1986). *Enforcement or negotiation: Constructing a regulatory bureaucracy.* Albany: State University of New York Press.

Sutherland, E.H. (1949). *White collar crime.* New York: Dryden.

Swaigen, J., & Bunt, G. (1985). *Sentencing in environmental cases.* Ottawa: Law Reform Commission of Canada.

United States Sentencing Commission. (1991). *United States Sentencing Commission guidelines manual.* Washington, DC: U.S. Government Printing Office.

Wheeler, S., Weisburd, D., & Bode, N. (1982). Sentencing the white-collar offender: Rhetoric and reality. *American Sociological Review, 47,* 641–659.

Yeager, P.C. (1987). Structural bias in regulatory law enforcement: The case of the U.S. Environmental Protection Agency. *Social Problems*, 34, 330–344.

———. (1991). *The limits of law: The public regulation of private pollution.* New York: Cambridge University Press.

About the Authors

Barbara A. Belbot graduated from the University of Houston Law School in 1980. She is currently completing her doctoral degree at Sam Houston State University, while also a faculty member in the Criminal Justice Program at the University of Houston. Ms. Belbot practiced commercial business law for four years, and was a court-appointed monitor in the Texas prison reform lawsuit *Ruiz v. Estelle*.

Michael B. Blankenship is an assistant professor at East Tennessee State University. He received his doctorate from Sam Houston State University. He has published articles on policing, education, epistemology, and ideology. He is coauthor (with Gennaro Vito) of *Your Research: Data Analysis for Criminal Justice and Criminology* and is currently at work on a police text. He is a past president of the Southern Criminal Justice Association and is editor of the *American Journal of Criminal Justice*.

Stephen E. Brown is chair of the Department of Criminal Justice and Criminology at East Tennessee State University. He received his doctorate from the University of Maryland. His research interests include criminological theory, education, and white-collar crime. He is coauthor of *Criminology: Explaining Crime and Its Context* with Finn Esbensen and Gilbert Geis.

Kevin M. Bryant is a criminology research assistant in the Department of Sociology, University of Tennessee, Knoxville. His interests include the study of neighborhood-level correlates of crime, social network analysis, and testing social disorganization and opportunity theories of crime.

Chau-Pu Chiang is currently an assistant professor of criminal justice and criminology at East Tennessee State University. Her research interests include race and the criminal justice system, deviant behavior, and white-collar crime.

Francis T. Cullen is a professor in the Department of Criminal Justice at the University of Cincinnati, where he also holds a joint appointment in sociology. He is author of *Rethinking Crime and Deviance Theory*, and coauthor of *Reaffirming Rehabilitation, Corporate Crime Under Attack*, *Criminological Theory*, and *Criminology*. He is president-elect of the Academy of Criminal Justice Sciences and previously was editor of *Justice Quarterly* and the *Journal of Crime and Justice*.

Paula J. Dubeck is an associate professor in and Head of the Department of Sociology at the University of Cincinnati. She is coeditor of *Urban Professionals and the Future of the Metropolis* and the *Encyclopedia of Women and Work* (forthcoming). Her research interests are in the areas of work and occupations, complex organizations, and the status of women. Currently, she is coauthoring a book on the effects of a plant closing on automobile worker's economic and social well-being.

T. David Evans is an assistant professor in the Department of Sociology, University of North Carolina at Wilmington. He received his Ph.D. in sociology at the University of Cincinnati in 1992. His primary research interests include criminological theory, white-collar and corporate crime, religion and crime, and the history of crime and punishment in America.

Gilbert Geis (Ph.D., University of Wisconsin, 1953) is professor emeritus in the Criminology, Law and Society Program of the School of Social Ecology, University of California, Irvine. He is a former president of the American Society of Criminology and the recipient of that group's Edwin H. Sutherland Award for distinguished research, as well as the recipient of research awards for the Western Society of Criminology (Paul Tappan Award), the National Organization for Victim Assistance

(Stephen Schafer Award), and the American Justice Institute (Richard A. McGee Award).

David J. Giacopassi is a professor in the Department of Criminology and Criminal Justice at Memphis State University. He received his doctorate in sociology from the University of Notre Dame. He is the author of numerous journal articles with his major substantive interest lying in the area of the relationship between law and society.

Colin Goff is an associate professor in the Department of Sociology at the University of Winnipeg, Canada. His publications include *Corporate Crime in Canada* (with Chuck Reasons) and the preface to the uncut version of Sutherland's *White Collar Crime* (with Gil Geis). He is currently finishing an intellectual biography of Edwin Sutherland with Gil Geis to be published by Northeastern University Press.

Anthony R. Harris is professor of sociology at the University of Massachusetts at Amherst and holds a Ph.D. in sociology from Princeton University. He has been an invited fellow at the Netherlands Institute for Advanced Studies, and a visiting scholar at the Department of Psychology and Social Relations, Harvard University. He has devoted most of his research to the study of deviant self-concepts and to links between gender, race, and crime. His articles have appeared in *American Sociological Review*, *Social Science Quarterly*, and *Social Problems*.

Brian A. Mattson is a graduate student at the Institute of Criminal Justice and Criminology at the University of Maryland. His research interests are corporate crime, drugs and crime, and juvenile delinquency. In addition to his academic pursuits, Brian works for the Criminal Justice Coordinating Commission in Montgomery County, Maryland.

Neal Shover is Professor of Sociology at the University of Tennessee, Knoxville. He is coauthor (with Donald Clelland and John Lynxwiler) of *Constructing A Regulatory Bureaucracy*. In addition to his interest in corporate crime, Professor Shover has investigated criminal careers of ordinary property offenders and is author of *Aging Criminals*.

Sally S. Simpson is an assistant professor at the Institute of Criminal Justice and Criminology, University of Maryland. She holds a Ph.D. in sociology from the University of Massachusetts at Amherst. She has written several articles appearing in *American Sociological Review*, *Criminology*, and *Social Forces* that address corporate crime causation and deterrence. She is currently at work on a book that examines alternatives to criminal justice control of corporate crime. In addition to corporate crime, her research interests include criminological theory, and gender, race, and crime.

Laureen Snider is an associate professor of sociology and an associate dean of the Faculty of Arts and Sciences at Queen's University. She has been interested in issues of reform, regulation, and praxis since earning her doctorate from the University of Toronto in 1978. Her recent publications have appeared in the *International Journal of the Sociology of Law* and *Crime and Delinquency*. She has just completed a book on corporate crime to be released in the fall of 1992.

B. Grant Stitt received his doctorate from the University of Arizona and is an associate professor of criminal justice at the University of Nevada, Reno. His research interests include ethical dilemmas in criminal justice, as well as theoretical and etiological aspects of crime. His articles have appeared in *Law and Philosophy*, *Journal of Crime and Justice*, *Criminal Justice Review*, *International Journal of Comparative and Applied Criminal Justice*, and *Criminal Justice Policy Review*.